Augustine of Hippo

Ashmolean Museum, University of Oxford, UK/The Bridgeman Art Library International.

Thomas F. Martin, O.S.A

Villanova University

Allan D. Fitzgerald, O.S.A.

Director of The Augustinian Institute

Villanova University

Augustine of Hippo
Faithful Servant, Spiritual Leader

THE LIBRARY OF WORLD BIOGRAPHY

Series Editor: Peter N. Stearns

Prentice Hall

Boston   Columbus   Indianapolis   New York   San Francisco   Upper Saddle River
Amsterdam   Cape Town   Dubai   London   Madrid   Milan   Munich   Paris   Montreal   Toronto
Delhi   Mexico City   Sao Paulo   Sydney   Hong Kong   Seoul   Singapore   Taipei   Tokyo

Executive Editor: Jeff Lasser
Editorial Project Manager: Rob DeGeorge
Senior Marketing Manager: Maureen Prado Roberts
Production Manager: Fran Russello
Cover Art Director: Jayne Conte
Cover Designer: Karen Salzbach
Manager, Visual Research: Beth Brenzel

Image Cover Permission Coordinator: Karen Sanatar
Cover Art: Dagli Orti/Picture Desk Inc./Kobal Collection
Full-Service Project Management: Nitin Agarwal/Aptara®, Inc.
Printer/Binder: Courier Companies, Inc.
Text Font: Times New Roman

Credits and acknowledgments borrowed from other sources and reproduced, with permission, in this textbook appear on appropriate page within text.

Library of Congress Cataloging-in-Publication Data
Martin, Thomas F. (Thomas Frank)
 Augustine of Hippo: faithful servant, spiritual leader/Thomas F. Martin,
Allan D. Fitzgerald.
  p. cm.— (The library of world biography)
 Includes bibliographical references.
 ISBN-13: 978-0-205-56831-4
 ISBN-10: 0-205-56831-9
 1. Augustine, Saint, Bishop of Hippo. 2. Christian
saints—Algeria—Hippo (Extinct city)—Biography. I. Fitzgerald, Allan.
II. Title.
 BX395.B37A5 2011
 270.2092—dc22
 [B]

                                        2010034545

10 9 8 7 6 5 4 3 2 1

Prentice Hall
is an imprint of

www.pearsonhighered.com

ISBN-10:   0-205-56831-9
ISBN-13: 978-0-205-56831-4

*For Anna, of course, and for Thomas,
who cheered me on.*

Contents

Editor's Preface

"Biography is history seen through the prism of a person."

LOUIS FISCHER

It is often challenging to identify the roles and experiences of individuals in world history. Larger forces predominate. Yet biography provides important access to world history. It shows how individuals helped shape the society around them. Biography also offers concrete illustrations of larger patterns in political and intellectual life, in family life, and in the economy.

The Longman Library of World Biography series seeks to capture the individuality and drama that mark human character. It deals with individuals operating in one of the main periods of world history, while also reflecting issues in the particular society around them. Here, the individual illustrates larger themes of time and place. The interplay between the personal and general is always the key to using biography in history, and world history is no exception. Always, too, there is the question of personal agency: How much do individuals, even great ones, shape their own lives and environment, and how much are they shaped by the world around them?

PETER N. STEARNS

Author's Preface

Humans are a race curious to know of others' lives, but slothful to correct their own. Why should they wish to hear from me what I am, when they do not wish to hear from *You* what they are themselves. (*conf.* X.3.3)

Augustine wrote these words shortly after beginning Book X of his thirteen-book *Confessions*, a work that in its originality defies precise definition. In it Augustine offers us something of a life-narrative, but the vehicle he chose to do so is a far cry from modern autobiography. He tells us "his story" using the language and imagery of the Christian Bible. It is a kind of "self-portrait" which takes the form of an extended prayer to his God. We are invited both to listen and to be part of the conversation.

By the time he arrives at Book X of the work, he has, for all practical purposes, stopped talking about himself, addressing rather questions about memory, time, temptation, and the interpretation of the Bible—just to name central themes that will carry through to Book XIII. Calling this work an "autobiography that is not an autobiography" serves to highlight the many challenges involved in engaging this complex man of Late Antiquity who has become known as Augustine of Hippo. We have more writings from him than any other ancient figure: more than 5 million words. (Shakespeare, by comparison, has only left us 884,647 words.) If it is virtually impossible to separate someone from his writings—especially in this case—the challenge Augustine offers to anyone seeking to "make sense of the whole," is not only simply the enormous volume of his writings, but also the remarkable diversity of those writings: sermons to ordinary people, letters to the intellectual and political elite of his day, technical theological treatises, and tracts that can be called *adversarial*—those which argue *against* certain religious opponents. If Augustine left an enormous *written* legacy, the way that he has been interpreted—his *historical* legacy—is just as daunting and even more diverse. The commentary on him since his death nearly 1,600 years ago has been continuous, thus adding to the difficulty of engaging the man. Any treatment of Augustine of Hippo, therefore, must "proceed with caution." The many varied and diverse views about the man, about his impact on history, and about his thought can be daunting.

Since the publication of Peter Brown's landmark *Augustine of Hippo: A Biography* in 1967 (revised in 2000), there has been a virtual explosion of studies on Augustine. The recent publication, in English, of the distinguished French scholar Serge Lancel's (†2005) *Saint Augustine* in 2002 and James O'Donnell's revisionist *Augustine: A New Biography* (2005) ought to raise the question—why another biography? In many ways, the three biographies mentioned cover every possible issue and question concerning Augustine—each from its own perspective—and this present work in no way claims to be a substitute for them nor for the host of other excellent studies of Augustine. But those studies presuppose a certain familiarity, either with the man and his thought, or with his world and its concerns, or with the many controversies that continue to surround attempts to discover and present the "real Augustine." This work, on the other hand, is meant for someone with little familiarity with Augustine of Hippo and his world. It is meant to introduce the reader to Augustine and his thinking and to give the reader some "direct" contact with him by keeping the focus on his own words. Hence, some chapters will conclude with an excerpt from Augustine's writings and others will be heavily laden with Augustine's own words. (The word *direct* is placed in quotes because those readings are given in English translation rather than in his original Latin.) In the course of this biography, readers will have the opportunity to learn *about* Augustine and to learn *from* Augustine. For those interested in pursuing this fascinating, challenging, and still controversial ancient figure in greater depth, a select bibliography is provided for further study. This book has been profoundly shaped by the three biographies just mentioned—both positively and negatively. The pages of this book, in fact, could not have been written without an extensive use of their scholarship; they are present, as it were, in between the lines. Extensive notes or references have been avoided, as is fitting for volumes in this series.

Augustine dedicates an enormous amount of energy seeking to understand himself and exploring the "human." For him, being human is, in many ways, an "interior reality"; in that perspective he agrees with and continues the biblical view that "human beings" were created in God's image (*Gen.* 1:26-27). His efforts, therefore, follow an interior path—a fact which is most evident in his *Confessions*, but which permeates all of his writings. That intense interest in interiority has had a profound impact upon the West, leading commentators to attribute to Augustine the creation of the *"Western self."*[1] His unique way of

---

[1] C. Taylor, *Sources of the Self: The Making of the Modern Identity* (Cambridge: Harvard University Press, 1989), 130–132.

looking at and dealing with what it means to be human *seems* to place "the self" at center stage and to prize highly introspection and reflection as ways to come to appreciate that "self." Anyone reading Augustine at length and over time will be struck by his ability—even his need—to question "the human." He appears to want to keep us from taking ourselves for granted. In his *Confessions*, he remarks provocatively: *"factus eram ipse mihi magna quaestio, et interrogabam animam meam"*—*"I had become a great enigma to myself, and I questioned my soul"* (IV.4.9). His questioning of "the human" is not negative introspection or perverse, but it points the human in a definite direction—toward God (*ad Deum*). In Augustine's experience, the question of "the self" and the question of "God" are inseparable, a single question. As this work unfolds, it will be important to return often to Augustine's use of questioning himself and questioning God as ways to discover "the self."

There are many people whose help in bringing about this book must be acknowledged, too many, as always, to mention all of them by name. In particular, I* owe a debt of gratitude to Dr. Peter Stearns, distinguished historian and Provost of George Mason University, who kindly invited me to consider this project. I have benefited greatly from the hospitality and wisdom of the Augustinian community of Collegio S. Monica and the *Augustinianum* (Patristic Institute) in Rome. Those who reviewed the manuscript include Alexander Auerbach, Virginia Commonwealth University; Henry Chambers, California State University-Sacramento; Steven Fanning, University of Illinois at Chicago; Roy Hammerling, Concordia College; Kevin Herlihy, University of Central Florida; Art Marmorstein, Northern State University; and Robert Shaffern, University of Scranton. I am immensely indebted to Allan Fitzgerald and Barbara Agnew for their careful reading of the manuscript. They have saved me from many errors— those that remain are the products of my own stubbornness! But in a very particular way I want to acknowledge how much I have learned from my graduate and undergraduate students at Villanova University—my own reading of Augustine has been broadened and deepened by their shared reading, rich conversations, unexpected questions, and robust challenges. In countless ways they have opened up to me a new and unexpected Augustine. It is to them that I dedicate this work.

---

*Please note that these words were written by Fr. Thomas Martin; first person is therefore retained.

Acknowledgments

When available, the English text of Augustine's writings is, with kind permission from the Augustinian Heritage Institute, taken from *The Works of Saint Augustine: A Translation for the 21st Century*, New City Press, Hyde Park, New York. All other translations are by the author. The principal works in this volume cited are:

Expositions of the Psalms. Introduction by Michael Fiedrowicz, Translation and Notes by Maria Boulding, O.S.B. Editor, John E. Rotelle, O.S.A. Hyde Park, NY: New City Press, 2000–2004.

Letters. Translations and Notes by Roland Teske, S.J. Editor, John E. Rotelle, O.S.A. Hyde Park, NY: New City Press, 2001–2005.

Sermons. Introduction, Cardinal Michele Pellegrino, Translation and Notes by Edmund Hill, O.P. Editor, John E. Rotelle, O.S.A. Hyde Park, NY: New City Press, 1990–1997.

The Confessions. Introduction, Translation, and Notes, Maria Boulding, O.S.B. Editor, John E. Rotelle, O.S.A. Hyde Park, NY: New City Press, 1997.

Instructing Beginners in Faith. Translation, Introduction, and Notes by Raymond Canning. Edited by Boniface Ramsey. Hyde Park, NY: New City Press, 2006.

Soliloquies: Augustine's Interior Dialogue. Translation and Notes by Boniface Ramsey, O.P. Edited by John E. Rotelle, O.S.A. Hyde Park, NY: New City Press, 2000.

On Genesis: A Refutation of the Manichees, Unfinished Literal Commentary on Genesis, The Literal Meaning of Genesis. Translation and Notes by Edmund Hill, O.P. General introduction and other introductions by M. Fiedrowicz and translated by Matthew O'Connell. Editor, John E. Rotelle, O.S.A. Hyde Park, NY: New City Press, 2002.

"On True Religion." In *On Christian Belief*. General introduction and other introductions by Michael Fiedrowicz, translated by Matthew O'Connell. Editor, Boniface Ramsey. Hyde Park, NY: New City Press, 2005.

"On Christian Doctrine." *Teaching Christianity: De Doctrina Christiana*. Introduction, Translation, and Notes by Edmund Hill, O.P. Editor, John E. Rotelle, O.S.A. Hyde Park, NY: New City Press, 1996.

The Trinity. Introduction, Translation, and Notes by Edmund Hill, O.P. Editor, John E. Rotelle, O.S.A. Hyde Park, NY: New City Press, 1991.

"The Gift of Perseverance." In *Answer to the Pelagians IV: To the Monks of Hadrumetum and Provence*. Translation, Introduction, and Notes by Roland J. Teske, S.J. Editor, John E. Rotelle, O.S.A. Hyde Park, NY: New City Press, 1999.

"The Punishment and Forgiveness of Sins and the Baptism of Little Ones." In *Answer to the Pelagians. I*. Introduction, Translation, and Notes by Roland J. Teske, S.J. Editor, John E. Rotelle, O.S.A. Hyde Park, NY: New City Press, 1997.

"Marriage and Desire." In *Answer to the Pelagians. II*. Introduction, Translation, and Notes by Roland J. Teske, S.J. Editor, John E. Rotelle, O.S.A. Hyde Park, NY: New City Press, 1998.

I would like to thank Dr. Frank Galgano of Villanova University for his rendering of the map of "Augustine's Journeys."

Abbreviations

conf. = The Confesssions.
exp. ps. = Expositions of the Psalms.
mor. = On the morals of the Catholic Church.
ord. = On Order.
Trin. = The Trinity.
CCL = Corpus Christianorum Series Latina.
Punishment and Forgiveness of Sins = On the Punishment and Forgiveness of Sins and the Baptism of Infants.
Aen. = Vergil, Aenid.
ser. =Sermons

1

Augustine's World

On November 13, 354 CE, in a somewhat obscure corner of the Roman Empire, a son was born to a Roman official of modest means named Patricius and his wife Monnica (as a diminutive of a local Punic deity). They named their son, Augustine, not a very common Roman name in Roman Africa where they lived, but one that paid homage to the imperial title *Augustus*. Their choice of that name suggests that, from the outset, they had great hopes for their son. We do not know if he was their first-born, only that he was one of three, sharing home with an unnamed sister and a brother, Navigius.

The Roman world in 354 CE, both East and West, was not a tranquil world. It was threatened from within and from without by strife. Usurpers eager to claim at least a portion of the imperial crown had to share the battlefields with northern tribes, hungry for land and spoils. And, as a shadow over its easternmost boundaries lurked Sassanian armies, Persia never ceased to be Rome's number one fear—and enemy. Perhaps in remote and rural Thagaste, the *municipium* of Augustine's birth, there was little awareness of these distant threats, for Roman Africa was enjoying a period of prosperity, disturbed only occasionally by local unrest.

Augustine's father Patricius owned property and bore a minor civic title. By all accounts the title offered little reward and much responsibility in the highly regulated and taxed Roman world of Late Antiquity of the later fourth century. Nonetheless, their little estate put Augustine's family in a position of advantage when compared to the vast majority of the poor and slaves who made up the greater part of the Roman world's population; they would always have food on the table and slaves to serve it. We know very little in detail about Patricius except that the name is thoroughly Roman. Punic Africa had, in the centuries before Christ, challenged Roman superiority and lost. Beginning in 146 BCE, with the final and complete defeat of their Punic enemies, Rome declared Africa a Roman province and undertook to erase all things Punic and remake Africa into Roman Africa. *Delenda est Carthago*—thus did Cato the Elder, we are told, say to the Roman Senate—"Carthage must be destroyed," and so it was. The city was burned to the ground, its remaining inhabitants sold into slavery, and where the Punic city once stood a new Roman Carthage was eventually built. Africa's capital became a thoroughly Roman metropolis, its grid of streets and clusters of temples and baths were deliberately intended as a perpetual monument to the complete and total erasure of all things Punic. By 354 CE those events were a distant but powerful memory. Africa was Roman and had been for centuries. But what held for the capital and the new cities Rome built is less certain for the hinterland. The streets and layout of Thagaste, a non-Roman name, probably remained as they were in pre-Roman, Punic days. And in those hinterlands, Punic was still spoken—as it had been for untold ages. Debate continues about what the dominant influence ("Roman" or "African") in Augustine's world really was—a topic so complex and controversial that it must be left for another study. In fact, Augustine learned Latin from the cradle, but he had no trouble viewing himself as *homo afer*—an "African." It may be best to acknowledge the complex cultural, national, and linguistic dimensions of his world where "Roman" and "African," at least for Augustine, were not contradictory but had a range of interconnected connotations.

Africa's security and prosperity were intertwined. Safe seas, for example, guaranteed that its abundant grain and oil could feed and light Rome, and the results can be seen in the archaeological remains of luxurious estates and epigraphic testimonies to urban building projects. Most recent scholarship suggests that a flourishing and stable economy in Africa produced both private riches and urban benefaction. A passing comment by Augustine in one of his early works (*ord.* 1.3) suggests that in Africa "burning the midnight oil" was a luxury many simply took for granted; that is in contrast with Italy's dark nights because of the high cost of lamp oil (in fact, Augustine tells us, Italy tended to use "animal fat" for their lights, [*mor.* 2.16.42]). Once conquered, Africa had become Rome's breadbasket and during the navigation season ships laden with grain and other products crisscrossed the Mediterranean between Africa and Italy. Its elegant and distinctive pottery, African Red Slip ware, found its way to the farthest corners of the Roman Empire, a clear indication of the range and scope of its commercial activity. Despite the ever-present danger of shipwreck (see, e.g., *s.* 335.2), those hungry for profit and riches were regularly willing to risk life and limb to make the crossing. The distinguished French scholar Claude Lepelley, in a comprehensive study of Roman African cities during the time of Augustine, has used archaeological evidence from the period to argue for a civic life marked by vitality and prosperity. This and similar findings have overturned popular theories dating back to Gibbon's *The Decline and Fall of the Roman Empire* (1776–1788 CE), namely that the rise of a public Christianity was marked by the demise of much that was good and beautiful from the classical world. The picture is much more complex: Even though Christianity was increasingly public, much of Augustine's world remained deeply rooted in ancient traditions and values.

Rome kept close watch on Africa since it was so vitally important to its well-being. The Roman civil diocese of Africa comprised six provinces, its most prominent being Africa Proconsularis, with Carthage as the seat of government. Augustine, himself, was born in the province of Numidia, agriculturally rich and with a fierce streak of independence. The network of Roman roads through the provinces ensured communication and commerce—although this did not always meant that roads were safe (see, e.g., *conf.* III.8.16). Two parallel administrations governed Roman Africa, one civil, the other military. The Vicar of Africa (*Vicarius Africae*), one might call him the chief civilian officer, was directly accountable to the emperor, though his immediate supervisor was the Praetorian Prefect of Italy, Illyricum and Africa who resided in Italy. His primary task was to oversee the provincial governors and all related administration of the provinces. He also served as a final court of appeal for all the provinces with the exception of Africa Proconsularis. The Count of Africa (*Comes Africae*) was the chief military officer, appointed by the emperor and directly accountable to him. These two parallel administrations were matched by accompanying bureaucracies and hundreds of minor officials. Along with these two imperial nominees, the Proconsul of Africa, governor of the most important province, Africa Proconsularis, always a senator and likewise an imperial appointee, enjoyed special authority, and was assisted by two legates. Unlike the other governors who were under the Vicar, he was directly accountable to the emperor and often was entrusted with specific imperial tasks. Imperial officers were required to be in close communication with high-ranking administration officials, although periodically they took matters into their own hands and were quickly viewed as pretenders to the throne. Added to these formal offices, there were local chieftains, leaders of indigenous tribes that clung to their ancient identities and often posed a threat to Roman authority.

It is generally conceded that Roman government in Late Antiquity reached deeply into every aspect of daily life. Two other major officials were supraprovincial: the Count of the Treasury and the Prefect of Provisions. The former oversaw tax collections and other financial matters; the latter had responsibility for imperial grain shipments to Rome. Despite the long arm of government, it is clear that there was much variation on the local level as officials could "look the other way" when it came to laws they did not wish to enforce. It was also not uncommon for an occasional high official to use the prestige of the office to engage in a local revolt against the central government. (One can find abundant data regarding all of these issues throughout Augustine's sermons and letters.)

However, despite the apparent prosperity, life in Roman Africa and elsewhere in the ancient world was always precarious, both for the rich and for the poor. Nearly everything taken for granted today regarding fundamental hygiene and basic medicine would have been effectively unknown in the ancient world—at least in the sense that they had no idea what a "germ" was. Although there is a great deal of speculation involved in projecting ancient statistics, some sociologists claim that average life-expectancy was somewhere around 35 years of age. At the same time, since infant mortality was exceedingly high, this general statistic is misleading. Many did live to be much older—Augustine dies at age 75. More than a few could confidently dream of a blessed old age. In reading Augustine, and this is anticipating somewhat, it is striking to see how common "early death" is. In *Confessions,* Augustine recounts the death of a young friend, perhaps in his late teens; his own son dies as a teenager; his best friend Nebridius, despite being wealthy, dies as a young man; his mother, Monnica, dies in her early 50s. In many of the accounts surrounding their deaths, a fever figures prominently; one can only guess about the specific illness. Augustine's preaching reveals a keen interest in medicine on his part—it was perhaps an ancient obsession, given the fragile nature of life. On the other hand, Romans were fiercely attached to the baths—cleanliness did matter and Roman engineers were masters of water management, constructing elaborate aqueducts and sewer systems. The waters of the baths were seen as cleansing and healing and the presence of the Roman bath in city and town, estate and villa, attests to the importance that world paid to maintaining health of body—even though we might be dismayed at some of their methods. Surgery was practiced (no anesthesia), special diets were prescribed, and *amulets* were the rage. These latter (*ligurata*) were worn to cure headaches, fevers, bodily aches and pains—usually accompanied by the recitation of certain prescribed incantations. Where life was precarious, the measures seemed to be all the more desperate and extravagant—at least by modern standards.

These last comments are a reminder that Augustine's world was a deeply religious world—while there was not always consensus regarding the makeup and operation of religion, few disputed its value. Broadly speaking Augustine's religious world consisted of Christians, Jews, and those Augustine regularly called "pagan." This last label would have been offensive to those it was used *against*—and *against* is deliberately emphasized here. The term in Latin, *paganus*, referred to a "country person"—it could have the same complimentary effect of calling someone a "hillbilly" or "hick" in English. It ultimately came to mean someone who worshipped multiple gods (polytheism) or *a* God other than *the* God of the Judaeo-Christian tradition—one way or another, the *pagan* was someone who maintained ancient religious practices over and against Christian practices. To call a wealthy, educated, aristocratic Roman senator a *paganus* was provocative—he would have thought of himself as simply *romanus*, a true Roman who practiced what his ancestors practiced. The fact is that to call someone a "*pagan*" told you very little about that person's actual religious beliefs and practices; it meant, rather, that he or she was not Christian. As a young boy, and probably with little impact upon Augustine's world, the Emperor Julian formally abandoned Christianity and set about the mechanisms to restore traditional religion to the place of prominence it had before Constantine. That effort (360–363 CE) was cut short when Julian lost his life during a military campaign against the Persians, and it may have had the effect of hardening Christian attitudes toward "pagans." While the Jewish community in Roman Africa would have been a minority community, they were not an invisible community. They will often appear in Augustine's sermons—though more often than not these references are generic, giving little indication of actual social location and interaction. They were the "other," over and against which the Christian community could define itself. How this "theological identity" related to day-to-day life is not easy to say, though Augustine offers no indication that they were socially marginalized or physically threatened.

Regarding Christianity in Roman Africa, perhaps its most prominent feature was division and disunity of a most unfriendly sort. In North Africa, Christianity was divided into groups called *Catholic* Christianity and *Donatist* Christianity. When Augustine called himself *Catholic*, he was accepting a tradition of division with roots in the early fourth century. The details of that particular controversy will be treated in Chapter 8. At this point, it is another reminder that religion in Augustine's world was an all-too-normal part of daily life and social existence, an experience that was often a source of conflict. Atheism was neither a practical nor theoretical threat to religion in the ancient world—the question always was "what religion?" not "whether religion?"

With the ascent of Christianity, what became of the traditional cultural and intellectual life that had nourished Roman minds and hearts for centuries? The school curriculum remained as it had always been, except for the fact that its Greek component seemed to have weakened substantially in the West. Vergil and Vergil's Latin remained the standard. Augustine read Cicero, Varro, Horace, Livy, Sallust, Seneca—the list could be extended to include all the major Latin authors of the classical period. Their vocabulary, values, and images were synonymous with being educated and cultured in Augustine's world. They echoed not only in the classrooms, but also in the amphitheaters—the great public shows and performances (Augustine calls them *spectacula theatrica*) attracted huge crowds, mesmerized by the action on the stage (often "X-rated"). Books were plentiful for those who could read and afford them, grand paintings dazzled in public squares, and those paintings made their way into many households as true-to-life portraits of the householder (see, e.g., *s.* 9.15). Roman Africa was famous for its mosaic art that graced the houses of the wealthy, a marvel still to behold in the great Musée du Bardo of Tunis. Yet even the common folk could behold mosaic art in the public baths and other civic buildings. Art, literature, painting, sculpture, theater . . . Roman Africa and especially its capital city Carthage offered abundant cultural riches for those so inclined.

Family life, from everything we can gather from Augustine's own remarks, followed a very Roman model. Home life was not experienced as many know it today. It would, perhaps, be better to use a term, such as "household" to describe most people's living situations. Families were "extended"—one could imagine growing up surrounded not just by parents and siblings but by relatives, servants, and slaves. For this extended family everything converged upon the *paterfamilias,* the Latin term for the father as head of the household. His authority was sole and ultimate. Thus "officially" it was a male-dominated world—but it is not easy to know how this was translated into practical reality. It seems clear that the *paterfamilias* did not attend to many of the day-to-day details of raising the family, but spent his time with other men, doing business, engaged in civic matters, attending the baths together—a public life. Women were "confined" to domestic roles, raising the children, feeding the household, seeing to the various tasks and responsibilities that would keep all those living under the same room fed, clothed, in good health, and so on. We know from a comment by Augustine in his *Confessions*, regarding Monnica, (his mother), that many wives were victims of physical abuse by their husbands. But, Augustine tells us (*conf.* IX.9.19), it was not that way for Monnica. She knew her husband well-enough to know how to avoid such abuse, saving what needed to be said for a time when it could be spoken without fear. Relationships between husband and wife in Augustine's world must be framed within a context very different from contemporary models. Marriages were frequently pragmatic arrangements between families who realized the mutually beneficial nature of these unions. We do not have any ancient wedding contracts, but a passing comment by Augustine in the passage noted above suggests that in the wedding "contract" the wife is referred to as a "handmaid" (*ancilla*) and the husband is referred to as her "master" (*dominus*): At least in terms of the accepted cultural norms, the marriage relationship was not one of parity. The use of corporal punishment on the part of the *paterfamilias* regarding *all* the members of the household was simply taken for granted.

These final comments remind us that the world we are entering, the world of Augustine of Hippo, is vastly different from our world. Readers encountering him in his writings will find much that strikes them as familiar, even contemporary; but they ought not be surprised when they encounter the unexpected and the incomprehensible. Regarding the latter, modern encounters with this ancient man are aided by a vast literature produced over the past half-century regarding life in Roman Africa. The reasons for the almost dizzying quantity of writings about Roman Africa are manifold and complex, and the resulting body of literature reflects that complexity. One reason is Augustine himself. Given his importance in the history of western thought as well as the size of his body of writings, recent scholars have tried to understand, as much as possible, the world he lived in as an entry into his challenging writings. This quest has been further stimulated by remarkable recent findings of previously unknown or lost texts of Augustine. In 1981 CE, Johannes Divjak brought to light a series of newly discovered letters of Augustine, many of them treating social and political issues of the day. The discovery of these letters in turn stimulated many scholars to reexamine a host of issues regarding the social world of Augustine. Beginning in 1990 CE, François Dolbeau began to publish a new series of lost sermons that, like the previous letters, shed much new light on the world of Augustine. This discovery has likewise had the effect of stimulating much new research and exploration of the Roman Africa of Augustine's day, as well as its pre-Roman history (in many ways we know much more of that pre-Roman history than Augustine did, a direct result of the intense archaeological activity over the past century, into the present). And, 2008 saw the announcement of the discovery of further new sermons in Erfurt, Germany—with every prospect that such findings are far from over.

These recent discoveries of new letters and sermons and the subsequent research and discussion they produced built upon a substantial body of literature regarding Roman Africa that saw the light especially in the second and third quarters of the twentieth century. There were specific reasons for the volume of research and writing. In 1930 CE, the 15th centenary of Augustine's death was marked by major conferences, replicated in 1954 CE by international conferences associated with the anniversary of his birth. Throughout that period Augustine's Roman Africa, present-day Tunisia and Algeria, was under French colonial rule. It must be frankly admitted that many of the studies of Roman Africa carried on during this colonial period were ethnocentric, simply assuming that colonial rule restored Roman Africa's ancient greatness—after a cultural vacuum of more than a millennium. Much archaeological and historiographical work suffered from this colonial bias. Not surprisingly, after the revolutions that saw Algeria and Tunisia gain independence, there was an equally strong postcolonial reaction, that could not view Roman Africa on its own terms either, but only in the light of the recent colonial experience. What emerged were conflicting analyses with diametrically opposing conclusions. Hypotheses could be multiplied: The Africans always resisted Roman rule and Roman Africa was in constant (if often disguised) rebellion (was the Donatist controversy nothing more than an anti-Roman movement?); or, many Africans became thoroughly Romanized and had no trouble twinning the adjectives Roman and African (in fact, *Romanization* had been remarkably effective and embraced by the vast majority of the populace); or, Africa was enslaved and exploited by the Romans; or, Africa was brought to previously unimagined cultural and economic development by the Romans. Many scholars today resist such dichotomous analyses, suggesting that Roman Africa was diverse and complex—single-labels, especially modern ones, do not readily apply. In some areas there remained strong native, and in this sense "anti-Roman" traditions; in others, Romanization was aggressively pursued, but with a distinctively "African" flavor. What should become ever clearer to the modern reader as this work proceeds is that Augustine's world was every bit as diversified and complex as our own—and that should both attract and challenge.

Reading Augustine:

The following excerpt from a sermon preached by Augustine sometime after the Sack of Rome in August of 410 CE offers a window into his world:

> Isn't it the case that a few years ago, under the emperor Arcadius at Constantinople – perhaps some people are listening to what I am saying who know about it, and some who were present there at the time are now in this congregation – God decided to terrify the city and by terror to correct it, by terror to convert it, by terror to cleanse it, by terror to change it; so he came in a revelation to a faithful servant of his, a military man so it's said, and told him that that city was going to perish in fire coming from heaven, and instructed him to tell the bishop? He did so; the bishop didn't make light of it, he addressed the people.

The city was converted to mourning and repentance, as once upon a time that Nineveh of old.

However, in case people should suppose that the man who had told them this had been misled by a misunderstanding, or had wished to mislead them deliberately, the day came which God had threatened; everybody was very tense, and in great fear expecting to be destroyed, when at the beginning of the night as the world was already growing dark, a fiery cloud appeared from the east, small at first, and then it gradually grew as it approached over the city, until it hung, terrible and huge, above the whole city Horrid streamers of fire were seen to hang from the sky, and the stench of sulphur was not lacking either. All took refuge in church, and the place couldn't hold the multitude. Everyone was extorting baptism from anyone they could. Not only in church, but in houses, streets, squares, the saving sacrament was being demanded; in order to escape, obviously, not the present threat, but the wrath to come.

Still, after that great tribulation (Rv. 7:14), in which God confirmed the truth of his words, and of the revelation made to his servant, the cloud began to diminish just as it had grown, and gradually it disappeared. The people, feeling a little safer now, again heard that they must all quit the city, because it was going to be destroyed the following Saturday. The whole city moved out, together with the emperor; nobody stayed at home, nobody locked his house. They withdrew a good distance from the walls, and looking back at their sweet dwellings, with tearful voices they said farewell to the beloved homes they had left. And when that vast crowd had gone a few miles, stopping together, though, in one place to pour out prayers to God, they suddenly saw a great column of smoke, and cried out with a loud shout to the Lord. At length, when the sky cleared they sent some scouts to bring back news. When the anxious hour foretold had passed, and the messengers reported that the walls of the city and all the houses remained intact, they all returned with great relief and thankfulness. No one lost anything from his house, everybody found his open house just as he had left it. (On *the Sack of Rome* 7 = *Sermon* 397.7)

CHAPTER

2

Augustine's Childhood—A Son of Great Promise (*conf.* I.16.26)

> At that time I knew only how to suck and be deliciously comforted, and how to cry when anything hurt my body, but no more. After this I began to smile, at first only in my sleep and then when I was awake. So I have been told, and I believe it on the strength of what we see other babies doing, for I do not remember doing it myself. Little by little I began to notice where I was, and I would try to make my wishes known to those who might satisfy them; but I was frustrated in this, because my desires were inside me, while other peoples were outside and could by no effort of understanding enter my mind. So I tossed about and screamed, sending signals meant to indicate what I wanted, those few signs that were the best I could manage, though they did not really express my desires. (*conf.* I.3.6–7)

Augustine has made a lasting impression upon centuries of readers through his own reflections upon his infancy, childhood, and what, today, would be called "adolescence" in his first chapters of a work that defies easy categorization, the *Confessions*. For this reason alone, the work stands apart from other ancient literature, since infancy and childhood were virtual states of "nonexistence" in Augustine's world—at least as far as Roman literature is concerned. Cicero could write his famous work *On Old Age* (*De senectute*), but to write a work on childhood (*De pueritia*) would have been unthinkable.

Born into a Roman Empire that seemed to have existed forever, one can read in between the lines of his *Confessions* to imagine Augustine's milieu: a world of midwives and nursemaids, doting relatives and neighbors, pungent aromas, sights and sounds to dazzle the senses. Thagaste, the town of Augustine's birth, was small and surrounded by agriculture. One could also expect to find there all the expected markers of Roman culture: a forum with its monuments to the rich and famous, a town hall (*curia*), a law court (*basilica*), religious buildings (Christian churches now replaced pagan temples), public baths and fountains, luxurious walled villas, and more. Nearly 40 miles inland in eastern Numidia, it was not large enough to have a secondary school, but was home to some prominent families with their vast estates. In fact, Augustine's father will succeed in securing the benefactions of one of these renowned families for the education of his promising son.

Augustine's remarkably original work, *The Confessions*, showers the reader with abundant autobiographical details about his early years and offers tantalizing but fleeting glimpses of a world that might seem to have little in common with contemporary experiences of home and school. Before entering into that sometimes dismayingly elusive world of Augustine's early years it will be helpful to make some comments on his *Confessions*, since this work is the source for much of what we know about the young Augustine.

Augustine wrote the work probably between 397 CE and 401 CE and, even though the *Confessions* is not an autobiography, he does tell us much about himself, his upbringing, his education, his friends, his adventures, and wanderings. The narrative takes the form of an extended and eloquent (his Latin is rhetorically refined) prayer to God, that is, not the format one would normally associate with autobiography. In some ways, we his readers/listeners (as with most ancient works, this was written to be read aloud and *heard*) are invited to listen in on Augustine's prayer/conversation with his God, to "eavesdrop"; in the course of that conversation we learn much about Augustine, and also about the God Augustine addresses. The very first lines of the work come from Augustine's Christian Bible, from the Psalms to be exact, and Augustine will continue to cite that Bible throughout the work. It is often not easy to delineate where Augustine's own discourse ends and Scripture begins, since along with formal quotations he has allowed his narrative to be filled with biblical paraphrases, images, and allusions. If autobiography is discourse about oneself, Augustine has become so fully steeped in the Scriptures that his speech has become imbued with biblical discourse.

The work itself is divided into what he calls 13 "books," and each "book" is somewhat equivalent to a modern "chapter." Books I through IX take the reader from Augustine's childhood to his adult conversion to Christianity, ending with the death of his mother, Monnica, outside of Rome in Ostia Antica in 387 CE. Book X takes the reader to Augustine's present as a writer-bishop, offering much about the state of his conscience—*What does life mean? What is life all about*? Books XI to XIII are a prayerful yet dense exploration of the meaning of the first chapters of *Genesis*, the days of creation—considered not in an academic way but as raising fundamental questions about mysteries of time, knowledge, and truth. Again, this is not what one would expect in an autobiography. The term *confessions* has become synonymous with "tell all." The Latin term *confessiones*, however, has a delightful ambiguity. To confess can mean to acknowledge one's faith, one's sin, or one's God; it is profession, confession, or praise. In this work, Augustine turns everything, even his faults, into praise of God. Thus, one of the many reasons why the *Confessions* as a work is considered a "masterpiece" is that it defies easy categorization—why the literature about the work is staggering. Masterpieces always provoke commentary, often contradictory. Debates continue to rage about how to read the work and what is its unity and intention. It is important to keep this in mind as we begin to unfold Augustine's life—that this critical source for Augustine's life is itself a never-ending source of speculation and controversy.

The exact social standing of Augustine and his family is not a matter of scholarly consensus; especially since Augustine will later insist that he came from a poor family (see sermons 355–356 where he has to explain that a member of his community had personal possessions and a will when he died). While "poor" can be a relative word, there is little indication that Augustine grew up in poverty. His family owned fields and property, the household had nurses and servants, the pantry seemed to be well-stocked (*conf.* I.19.30), and especially, advanced education seemed to have been envisioned early on. In the ancient world, these were not signs of poverty but of relative well-being. This is not to deny that families such as that of Augustine's, and of Patricius in particular, did not feel pressured and perhaps even threatened by financial concerns and doubts about future security, but the world Augustine grew up in knew neither hunger nor destitution.

Augustine tells us that he was breast-fed by his mother and his nurses. As he describes his upbringing, nurses and household servants always seem to be in the background. He reports that his initial efforts at language and communication and the tears and wailing that are every child's lot were witnessed by an adult audience who looked on with both amusement and compassion. He, of course, did not remember these things but based his comments on what he heard from others and on his own observations; his writing about it shows a fascination with human experience which will only increase as time passes.

Augustine's household seems to have been typical—not just the nuclear family of modern times but an assortment of immediate family, relatives (*maiores*), servants, and possibly even boarders, all living under one roof (see his *Commentary on the Gospel of John* 10.9 where Augustine takes such a "crowd" for granted). Patricius, his father, would have been responsible for feeding all those mouths—and in return, was owed absolute obedience on the part of all, from wife, children, and servants. Readers of Augustine's *Confessions* are often struck by his differing portrayals of Patricius, "a distant and blatantly nonreligious father," and Monnica, a "hovering and very religious mother." There was nothing unusual about this in the Roman world; each had a lasting impact on Augustine.

Patricius, Augustine's father, owned property, probably modest holdings, and would have belonged to a class called the *honestiores*. The ownership of property resulted in both an honorary title and civic obligation. He was a *curialis*, meaning he was involved in local government, whose seat was called the *curia*. As a member of the town council his main responsibility would have been directed toward tax collection, though it is easy to imagine that he and his fellow *curiales* would have frequently dealt with the host of ongoing practical as well as impromptu tasks and unexpected happenings ever associated with civic life. Both the demands of caring for household and property as *paterfamilias*, as well as civic responsibility as *curialis* would have insured that Patricius' daily life was lived outside the home, in forum, curia, basilica, and the baths (going to them would have been a daily ritual where he would meet with his fellow *honestiores* and do business or just "be with the boys"). In his early days Augustine would probably have spent little "quality time" with his father, that task was left to the women of the household. We learn from Augustine, as well as other writers of the period, that within the household the "rod" (*verga*) was a normal way of maintaining discipline. Augustine notes in one of his sermons: "It is better to be corrected by a father's rod than to perish through the smooth talk of a robber" (*exp. ps*. 88.2.2).[1] It was a seemingly unquestioned and yet dismaying fact of life, though Augustine never offers evidence that he himself was thus disciplined that is, from his father; teachers were another question. Thus the Roman father, at least in theory, was someone a young boy would fear more than love. While Patricius had *neither* a positive nor a lasting impact upon his son in terms of religion and perhaps even less so as a role-model, he did everything he could to secure the best possible education for Augustine. Patricius died when Augustine was 16, that is, before it would have been possible for them to develop an adult relationship with one another.

Monnica emerges much more forcefully and provocatively as a formative presence in Augustine's account of his childhood, youth, and young manhood. She was 23 when she gave birth to Augustine. It may come as a shock to people today to know that in Roman society a girl was marriageable once she reached 12 years of age, though 14 has been argued as the median age. Given high mortality rates, especially surrounding childbirth, the thinking seemed to be "the earlier the better." However, a comment by Augustine that Patricius married Monnica "*plenis annis nubilis*" (*conf.* IX.9.19), perhaps it could be translated "a ripe age for marrying," suggests she was not a "child bride." Patricius will die when Monnica is 39 or 40. The portrait Augustine offers of Monnica, not only in the *Confessions*, but also in some of his early dialogues, is of a strong and intelligent woman, despite her lack of formal education. It seems she "managed" Patricius as much as he "commanded" her. Her religious beliefs were strong, and she eventually converted her husband to Christianity; with Patricius, she had great hopes for their gifted son. There was indeed great affection between Augustine and his mother—even if these two strong-willed people were often in conflict. There were periods of estrangement, but they were never enduring. It is clear that Monnica began to raise Augustine from his earliest years as a Catholic Christian, though it is important to think of the term *Catholic* in ancient rather than modern terms. The term meant *universal, worldwide*. Thus will Augustine often refer to "the Christian church spread throughout the world." While North African Catholic Christianity had a close working relationship with the bishop of Rome, one should not project back into Augustine's

---

[1] Note that Augustine's Book of Psalms followed the numbering of the psalms in Latin Bible. It differs from the numbering found in the Hebrew Bible where Psalms 10–147 are one digit higher than those of Augustine's Pslams.

times notions of a medieval papacy or a modern Vatican. Relations among bishops at that time were all about the delicate balance of respect and unity; the legal definition of those relationships would only come later.

Augustine tells us that Monnica did her best to impart to him her own piety, with both positive and negative effect. From his descriptions of Monnica's Christian piety, it is clear that, as an adolescent, he found some of her practices to be matters of piety rather than adapted to his intellectual pretensions. From his mother as well as from the example of others (*conf.* I.9.14), he learned to pray and took in the name of Christ and received notions of God that he found grossly materialistic—and not merely as a young man. But the greatest proof of the impact of his mother's faith upon him at that stage of his young life may be found in an experience that he recounts in Book I of his *Confessions* (I.11.17). Sometime during his childhood he fell gravely ill with a stomach ailment—so grave that he drew close to death. He begged to be baptized and Monnica was prepared to allow it, even though adult baptism was still the normal experience in fourth-century Christianity. Interestingly, Augustine made a sudden recovery and his baptism was postponed—as was any real faith commitment on Augustine's part. That would set the stage for a series of religious crises that would mark his next decades. From this event, we begin to get an inkling of the religious sensitivity Augustine carried within from his earliest years, and we also get a hint of the fragility of ancient life.

Even though the Christian church of Augustine's Africa was bitterly divided for most of the fourth century, the city of his birth, Thagaste, had overcome that division under the heavy-handed pressure of imperial legislation not many years before Augustine's birth. The schism that has come to be referred to as Donatism (see Chapter 8) was absent from the Thagaste of Augustine's youth. This helps to explain why there is no mention of it at this stage of his life. Equally important is the fact that Monnica's faith does not appear to have been marked in any way by that division.

Augustine offers in *The Confessions* a vivid and often unflattering account of the late antique Roman educational system as it operated in Roman Africa. A sorrowful road of toil and torture (*conf.* I.9.14) is how he describes his earliest immersion into the ancient school system. Just as Augustine offers a vivid impression of ancient child raising, so too with late Roman pedagogy. In many ways we learn more about the punishments meted out to unruly students than we do about the actual curriculum Augustine and his peers would have undergone at the primary school in Thagaste, where Augustine was sent to "learn to read" (literally, "to learn letters" [*discere litteras, conf.* 1.9.14]). What does Augustine tells us about his early school experiences? Along with frequent mention of beatings, prompted both by neglect of schoolwork and playful misbehavior, we learn that they spent time "reading, writing, and thinking" (*scribendo, legendo, cogitando*) (I.9.15). Archaeology has been very helpful in this regard since writing tables and exercise books have been unearthed. Repetition, imitation, and memorization formed the heart of the learning exercises. Tablets with permanent letters would be traced over by young students until they would be allowed to trace them on their own on wax tablets. Short sentences would be written on tablets and students would learn to copy them *exactly*. This gives some idea of the learning progression: from letters, to words, to sentences—that would eventually take the students to actual literature.

"'One and one make two, two and two make four' was hateful to me" (*conf.* I.13.22). Along with learning their letters, Augustine and his classmates learned their numbers. Once again, repetition and memorization were the cornerstones of the learning process, as Augustine learned not only to read, and write, but also "to count" (*scribere, legere, numerare,* ibid.). Augustine's schooling was an oral world and one can imagine passing by the ancient schoolroom only to hear the sing-song repetition of letters and numbers on the part of its young learners. Augustine recounts that one more subject formed an integral but most unpleasant part of the curriculum: Greek. He leaves us with no doubt that he hated the subject, though as an adult he is puzzled over such a violent emotional reaction:

"Why was it, then, that I hated studying Greek literature, which had similar songs to sing [the reference is to his reading of Latin literature, Vergil in particular]? Homer was just as skilled at weaving stories, and he too was empty in a thoroughly entertaining way, yet as a boy I found him distasteful. I expect Vergil is equally distasteful to Greek boys, when they are forced to study him as I was Homer. It was so difficult; and the difficulty of thoroughly mastering a foreign language seemed to sprinkle bitterness over those fabulous narratives for all their Greek sweetness, because I knew none of the words, and the threat of savage terrifying punishments was used to make me learn them" (I.14.23).

For a student as promising as Augustine it is somewhat surprising to hear of his visceral aversion to learning Greek. Was it precisely because all other subjects came so readily, but not Greek? Or did it have something to do with the shape of Greek instruction or with a particular teacher? Or was it simply laziness? Augustine himself does not seem to have an answer, but, later, as a bishop, thinker, and public figure, he will feel the burden of never having mastered Greek.

As education moved beyond rudimentary instruction and he found himself under the tutelage of what the ancients called "the grammarians," Augustine did fall in love with Latin literature. The *grammatici*, the term Augustine and his world used, are not well-described by the contemporary term *grammarians* since for us it would have a restricted understanding of imparting the technicalities of a language. In Augustine's scholastic world, the term encompassed the teaching of Latin literature and all the varied learnings that would flow from an encounter with the great Latin writers. Vergil was the bedrock of this curriculum, though Augustine and his classmates would have also read Cicero, Terence, Sallust, and beyond. Such authors, and especially Vergil and the *Aeneid*, were read aloud, investigated and explored grammatically and stylistically, memorized, and then recited. Gradually they would be trained to think of themselves as "little Vergils":

> An exercise was set for me which was fraught with worrying implications, for I hoped to win praise and honor if I succeeded, but if not, I ran the risk of being caned. I was required to produce a speech made by Juno expressing her anger and grief at being unable to repulse the Trojan king from Italy (see *Aen.* 1.38), but in words which I had never heard Juno use. We were obliged to follow the errant footsteps of poetic fantasies and to express in prose what the poet had said in verse. That boy was adjudged the best speaker who most convincingly suggested emotions of anger and grief and clothed them in apt words, as befitted the dignity of the person represented. What did it profit me, O God, my true life, that my speech was acclaimed above those of my many peers and fellow students? (*conf.* I.17.27)

What the teachers had in mind is obvious: Students were to demonstrate such a command of the text in question that they could declaim it in an original way, even as they remained true to its original meaning. Augustine's severe judgment, writing decades later of this and other experiences, is especially directed toward the cutthroat nature of such exercises. Winning was the goal, outdoing one's schoolmates. The reward was either crowning or caning. It was through exercises, such as this that Augustine and his fellow students memorized and absorbed the canon of Latin classics, perhaps a relatively small list by contemporary standards, but one that was available for recall and reworking at a moment's notice. Such learnings (well after leaving Thagaste) will serve Augustine well as a professional orator.

> . . . I am nearly always dissatisfied with the address that I give [to my students]. For the address I am so eager to offer is the superior one which I enjoy again and again in my inner being before I begin to formulate it in spoken words. And when I find that my actual address fails to express what I have before my mind, I am depressed by the fact that my tongue has been unable to keep up with my intellect. For all the insight that I have I want to pass on to my hearer, and I become aware that, speaking as I am, this is not going to happen, mainly for the reason that that insight floods the mind as with a sudden flash of light, whereas speech is slow-moving and drawn-out and of a very different nature. And while speech is still spinning out the words, that intellectual insight has already vanished into its secluded domain. . . . (*Instructing Beginners in Faith*, Prologue 2.3)

Thagaste was indeed a small municipality – it had no equivalent of a secondary school, but Patricius and Monnica were not prepared to have their promising son short-circuit his future by lack of educational opportunity. They provided for their son to pursue further education at Madaura, about a day's journey or some 20 miles distant. Augustine would probably have been around 11 years of age when he found himself away from home and family, to advance his study of literature and begin the study of rhetoric. Madaura was even further inland than Thagaste, and from all indications it was no great metropolis; however, it did have a claim to fame as the birthplace of Apuleius, perhaps the best known Latin author of the second century. Almost two centuries later, Madaura was still living off the reputation of its favorite son and became well-known as an educational center. It was probably at Madaura that Augustine won his literary crown mentioned above, though in his *Confessions* he maintains almost total silence about any details of his sojourn there. Years later he can recall its forum and its two statues of Mars, one naked, the other in battle dress (*Letter* 17.1). Did he stay with relatives? Or with his tutors? Was he homesick? He does not tell us. Scholars remind us that Madaura remained a stronghold of traditional religion (*pagan* is not a very helpful descriptive for the many and diverse forms of religion that were neither Christian nor Jewish). What impact did a sojourn in such a city have on a young, bright, and impressionable boy, such as Augustine? One thing for sure is that there he discovered that the Christian religion was not alone in claiming the spiritual allegiance of his fellow Africans. It is also clear that as he pursued education he set himself apart from even his own family; his cousins, for example, did not have the opportunity that he had (*The Happy Life* I.6). Augustine had begun to climb the social and cultural ladder.

Augustine also tells us that his education came to an abrupt halt during his 16th year when the funds were lacking, and he returned home to the family house in Thagaste. He dramatizes this adolescent interlude with tales of sexual awakening: "What was it that delighted me? Only loving and being loved" (*conf.* II.1.1). He recalls an incident of father and son suddenly encountering one another in the public baths (*conf.* II.3.6ff). Patricius, unexpectedly seeing his son naked, realizes he is fast becoming a man—and begins to brag of imminent grandchildren. A celebration seemingly ensues with the father consuming much wine and Monnica terrified that his son will get involved with someone else's wife. As Augustine recounts the incident decades later, it certainly made a deep impression—and once again we are treated to a slice of ancient life that is, perhaps, both foreign and enticing. Augustine goes on to talk about the adolescent bragging of illicit exploits, often made up so as not to be outdone by his friends. What is clear is that Augustine and his gang created their own world— and lived in it with total abandon: "I roamed the streets of Babylon" (*conf.* II.3.8).

But, something other than the sexual escapades of that year of idleness warrants the most attention. He recounts how, with his gang of friends, he stole pears from an orchard near the family's own vineyard. It was, as Augustine describes it, not a very enticing plunder; his family's own pear trees were healthier and its fruit tastier. He and his friends plundered that orchard for the sheer pleasure of doing so. Nothing more than a wanton act. After the theft they tossed the unwanted fruit to the pigs. This inelegant act becomes, for Augustine, an occasion to reflect eloquently upon human motivation and willingness. Those reflections are among the most impressive in the *Confessions*. "There was no motive for my malice except malice," he says (*conf.* II.4.9). Augustine, the promising young man, engages in a petty but ultimately disturbing act of theft and vandalism purely for the sake of doing it. "I would not have done it alone" Augustine said (*conf.* II.8.16). For him it reveals something, not only about his human heart, but also about an insidious quality that can be found at the heart of many human communities. There is no doubt that, as Augustine relates his experience to us, he also sees his life as revealing something about all of us, whether individually and collectively. Scholarly debate has raged about the historicity of Augustine's recounting of these adolescent events—and opinion remains divided. However, Augustine's own acquaintances read these accounts at that time—and he would have known if anyone was going to doubt his narrative. Augustine has shared a story of both turmoil and turbulence that many adults looking back at their own adolescence can resonate with; it manifests the often-painful and chaotic quest for human identity and purpose. We have here one reason why this unique and provocative writing that is Augustine's *Confessions* remains a best seller that has never been out of print.

Reading Augustine:

Years later, looking back at his youth when he wrote to a friend, Honoratus, about some of the things they shared, Augustine tries to explain what motivated him in his lifelong search for truth—a desire that Honoratus shared with him at the beginning.

> I felt I should not keep from you my thoughts about finding and holding to the truth. This, as you know, has been our burning passion since early youth. It is, however, a subject far removed from the thoughts of shallow-minded persons, who have gone to extremes with material considerations and fallen into thinking that nothing exists except what they perceive with those five well-known sources of information of the body. . . .
>
> There is nothing easier, dear friend, than to say one has discovered the truth, and even to think it, but from what I write here I am sure you will appreciate how difficult it really is. I have prayed to God, and I pray now, that it will be helpful, or at least not harmful, for you and anyone else at all into whose hands it chances to fall. This is what I hope for, knowing within myself that, in putting pen to paper now, I do so in a spirit of duty and devotion and not in pursuit of passing fame or shallow display.
>
> 2. My object then is to prove to you, if I can, that, when the Manicheans attack those who, before they are capable of gazing on that truth that is perceived by a pure mind, accept the authority of the Catholic faith and by believing are strengthened and prepared for the God who will bestow light, they are acting irrationally and sacrilegiously.
>
> You know, Honoratus, that the only reason we fell in with them is because they declared with awesome authority, quite removed from pure and simple reasoning, that if any persons chose to listen to them they would lead them to God and free them from all error. What was it that for almost nine years drove me to disdain the religion that had been instilled in me as a child by my parents and to follow those people and listen attentively to them except that they said that we were held in fear by superstition and that faith was imposed on us before reason, whereas they did not put pressure on anyone to believe without first discussing and explaining the truth? Who would not be enticed by promises like

that, especially if it was the mind of a young man yearning for the truth and made proud and outspoken by the debates in the classes of certain scholars? That is how they found me at that time, scornful of the "old wives tales" and keen to have and to imbibe the open, uncontaminated truth that they promised. What considerations held me back, and kept me from fully committing myself to them, and made me stay at the stage they called "listener," not yet putting aside the hopes and concerns of this world except that I noticed that they themselves were for the most part full and lengthy in their refutation of others rather than steadfast and assured in rational support of their own position? (*On the Advantage of Believing* I, 1-2)

3

Augustine's Youth—Sizzling in Carthage (*conf.* III.1.1)

C arthago—sartago (Carthage—a sizzling frying pan): with a clever play on words, certainly intended to capture the imagination of his Latin-reading audience as he begins Book III of the *Confessions*, Augustine enters into a turbulent period of his life as a young university student in Carthage. He would have been 16 going on 17 when he left the relatively rustic confines of Thagaste for a city that was, in many ways, a rival to Rome. Scholars estimate that Carthage, the third largest city in the Roman Empire and the second largest in the West, had a population somewhere near 200,000 inhabitants in Augustine's day. When Augustine arrived there in 370 CE, Carthaginians may have still remembered the total destruction by the Roman army in 146 BCE, which brought a centuries-long animosity between the Punic and Roman capitals to a devastating conclusion. Now, a half millennium later, there were no longer any traces, at least on the surface, of the ancient Punic metropolis. Carthage was remade into a totally Roman city, its parallel and perpendicular streets imposing Roman order on its flamboyant past. The journey from his hometown to African capital, a distance of some 165 miles, would have taken a few days, but we know nothing of the journey, nor where Augustine lodged when he arrived there. His father had recently died and Monnica handled the administration of his "scholarship," regularly sending him money (*conf.* III.4.7) from the generous benefaction of Romanianus, a distinguished and wealthy Thagastan. We might call this assistance Patricius' lasting gift to his son, a gift with untold and enduring impact. Since Romanianus had a spacious residence in Carthage, it is not unthinkable that Augustine initially found lodging there.

Carthage had everything to offer an inquisitive, bright, and driven young man. New friends, "university" lectures (we must not think of ancient higher education as having much in common with its modern counterpart), the theater, the Baths of Antoninus (only in Rome would there be a more spectacular edifice), even the ancient equivalent of a modern gang ("wreckers" [eversores]), and above all, new ideas. In Carthage, he will finish his rhetorical studies with great success; he will enter into a lengthy relationship with an unnamed companion and together they will raise an unexpected son; he will undergo a kind of spiritual-intellectual crisis that will culminate in his adherence to the religion of Mani, a Persian prophet of the third century. Carthage did indeed sizzle for Augustine.

Augustine tells us little about his education in Carthage: "My studies, which were called honorable, were directed to the practice of law, so that I might excel in them . . . I was already the leading student in the school of rhetoric" (*conf.* III.3.6). We know from other sources, however, what that education likely consisted of. Building upon his previous lessons, especially those he attended in Madaura, he and his fellow-students would have continued their reading of Rome's most eminent authors, with particular emphasis now on what Augustine calls the "books of eloquence" (*conf.* III.4.7). We know, and it comes as no surprise, that numbered among those authors was the great Cicero. Augustine makes specific reference to reading his Hortensius (a work that is lost, except for the quotes that Augustine preserved) and recounts the profound impact it had upon him. Given the nature of rhetorical training, which always went from "theory to practice," that is, reading was followed by delivering mock speeches, court defenses, historical reenactments, and the like, Augustine and his fellow students would have dedicated much attention to both literature and history to equip themselves for such exercises. He mentions working his way through the "standard order of learning" (*conf.* III.4.7), a progressive reading list that would expose students to a wide range of Latin literature. He also mentions "contests" or competitions that required detailed knowledge of these classical authors (*conf.* III.6.11). There must have been many such competitions—and it seems that more often than not, Augustine came out on top.

The portrait Augustine paints of his student days in Carthage is of intense learning by a tight-knit circle of friends, dividing their time between study, public displays of oratory, theatergoing, and "partying." He says, "We pursued trumpery popular acclaim, theatrical plaudits, song-competitions and the contest for ephemeral wreaths, we watched trashy shows and indulged our intemperate lusts" (*conf.* IV.1.1). Despite the disparaging mature retrospective, there is no doubt that Augustine's life, if not that of his companions, was not all play. There was an intense engagement with the liberal arts: grammar, rhetoric, dialectic, geometry, music, and arithmetic are specifically noted by him (*conf.* IV.16.30). And there was philosophy, since he makes particular mention of reading Aristotle's The Ten Categories (*conf.* IV.16.28) at this time. In bringing up this precise episode in his life he smugly notes that he studied and learned the work on his own and grasped it easily and comprehensively. He contrasts his experience with that of his "rhetoric master at Carthage" who could recite by memory the categories but did not have a clue to their meaning. Interestingly, he does not name his instructors in Carthage; his "rhetoric master at Carthage" remains a famous unknown. Once again, Augustine offers precious little detail about his Carthaginian studies—he is more interested in "providence" than in "history," but their impact was certain. He portrays himself as the capital's most promising young rhetor—for the entire effort was directed toward "performance." Augustine indeed seems to have excelled above all his peers in the art of performing. None of this was in vain, for it will eventually lead him to the municipal chair of rhetoric in Carthage.

Despite his emphasis on outside "show," it is clear that much more was going on inside this promising young student of rhetoric. As his *Confessions* recount, there remained within him an acute spiritual sensitivity, though often of a conflicted nature. Despite being away from home and from his pious mother, he did, at least occasionally, attend church. In cryptic words he tells of being "within the walls of your church" and using the occasion to indulge in "carnal desire and conduct" (*conf.* III.3.5). In a later sermon he offers clearer light:

> I as a lad used to attend vigils when I was a student in this city, and I kept vigil like that, all mixed up together with women, who were subjected to the impudent advances of men, which no doubt on many occasions put the virtue of even chaste people at risk. (*ser. Dolbeau* 2.5)

So much for his churchgoing. But Augustine suggests that such behavior, probably carried out with his circle of friends, left him interiorly a wreck: "For this you struck me with severe punishments, though none that matched my guilt" (*conf.* III.3.5). Interiorly his behavior haunted him. It will not be in church, however, that this spiritual core of his will suffer a true jolt. A book of Cicero, the *Hortensius*, can claim that distinction.

> In the customary course of study I had discovered a book by an author called Cicero, whose language is almost universally admired, though not its inner spring. This book of his is called the *Hortensius* and contains an exhortation to philosophy. The book changed my way of feeling and the character of my prayers to you, O Lord, for under its influence my petitions and desires altered. All my hollow hopes suddenly seemed worthless, and with unbelievable intensity my heart burned with longing for the immortality that wisdom seemed to promise . . . (*conf.* III.3.4.7)

All that remains of this work by Cicero are fragments and so it is no longer possible to judge it by its content. It belonged to a philosophical genre called protreptic [explain] that can be traced back to Aristotle, a model that Cicero takes up to defend and encourage the study of philosophy. It had that desired effect on Augustine; we might say it led him to decide against a career in law and directed all his attention to the liberal arts, with a strong spiritual underpinning that followed upon his reading of the Hortensius. He says that he began by turning to the Bible—what better place to look for wisdom. But it had the exact opposite effect. Well-trained in the art of language and literature, he set the Bible aside in disgust: "When I studied the Bible and compared it with Cicero's dignified prose, it seemed to me unworthy" (*conf.* III.4.8). Augustine would have read what is now called an "Old Latin" (*Vetus Latina*) translation of the Bible. The term "Old Latin" refers not to a single Latin version of the Bible but to a whole series of translations of varying degrees of accuracy and elegance that predate what would eventually be called the Vulgate—a more accurate and more elegant Latin version of the Bible that would emerge at the end of the fourth and the beginning of the fifth century. It would seem that along with a clumsy or inelegant translation that perhaps rendered the narrative opaque, Augustine may have further compounded his difficulties by taking up one of the more daunting books of the Christian Bible. Thus, what he read seemed mythical to him. That would have added to his difficulty.

It may be helpful to realize that in Augustine's world the Bible was a multi-volume work, composed of many separate tomes: for example, Genesis, Prophets, Psalms, Gospels, Paul's Letters, and so on. He probably turned first to one of the more difficult books of the Old Testament—perhaps the book of *Genesis* which will be a frequent focus of his attention later. One way or another, his reading of the Bible failed to have any significance for him, and that failure to find answers in his biblical encounter only seemed to intensify his spiritual quest, his searching for "true wisdom." That quest led him into the arms of the Manichees.

At the age of 18, Augustine encountered the religion of Mani—and it seemed as if his prayers were answered. What was it about Manichaeism that he found so attractive? It is clear that they engaged in clever preaching, promising enlightenment and guilt-free purity. What the Hortensius awakened in him, what he failed to find in the Bible, and the yearning that churned in his heart— somehow all of these converged in his new-found religion. Augustine had been raised by Monnica as a Christian, a Catholic Christian to be precise, though this upbringing seems to have provided him with little in terms of intellectual content. What he thought he found in the Manichees was the truth of Christianity that he had always been looking for.

The subject, "Augustine and Manichaeism," has already produced enough literature and commentary to fill a library. The many reasons will become clearer as we go develop our considerations of Augustine's life and thought. Before proceeding, however, it will be helpful to comment on this newly discovered religious community which traced its origins to a Persian charismatic figure of the third century and swept across the Roman world and beyond with such intensity that it evoked violently hostile reaction from both pagan and Christian emperors, beginning with Diocletian at the turn of the fourth century and well into Augustine's own day.

Mani was born in Persian-controlled Babylon in 216 CE and manifested deep religiosity while still young. He then experienced two life-transforming revelations, one at age 12, and another at age 24. The latter convinced him that what had been revealed to him surpassed all previous religious claims. He now was the bearer of the fullness of revelation, and his vocation was to bring what was to be called the "Religion of Light" to the entire world. Its religious message was equally grandiose and intimate, explaining both the cosmos and the human soul. Mani's second revelation set him on a religious journey that took him as far as India. When he returned, he presented himself to the Persian King Shapur who allowed Mani to preach the new religion, seemingly with great success.

From the outset, he also sent forth missionaries who preached east and west—we know that before long these missionaries were also found in Egypt. The traditional religion of Persia and its priests reacted with hostility to Mani and when a new king came to the throne, Bahram I, Mani was imprisoned and cruelly executed on February 26, 277 CE. His death did not stop the "Religion of Light" but only seemed to intensify it and to stimulate further missionary efforts. Followers made their way throughout the Roman Empire: Syria, Cappadocia (in present-day east-central Turkey), Africa, and even to Rome. Manichaeism's success in the Roman world also sparked Roman hostility. Persia had the distinction of being Rome's archrival, thus a Persian religious movement was automatically viewed with suspicion if not hostility.

What was Mani's revelation? What did he preach? What was the "Religion of Light"? What was its relationship to Christianity? Why did Augustine—and many others—find it so attractive? Scholars have engaged these questions with a remarkable intensity for the past 250 years, sparked by the interest of European scholars in non-Western religions and religious movements. The study of Manichaeism took on a new intensity in the twentieth century with the discovery of a series of ancient Manichaean texts that shed much clearer light on the teaching and practices of the "Religion of Light." It is clear that its origins owed much to Christianity, or at least to some Christian ideas, though it also borrowed ideas from Buddhism and Zoroastrianism, the traditional religion of Persia.

The "Religion of Light" that Augustine encountered offered both doctrine and experience. Its doctrine sought to explain the present human experience of distress and toil, the answer to the perennial question: If God is good, then why does evil exist? The experience, shaped by moving religious ritual and what seems to have been an intense community life, affirmed and secured the teaching in an affective and effective way. Manichaeism is traditionally referred to as a dualistic religious system: Reality consists of opposing forces of good and evil, locked in mortal combat, with the human soul as the present arena of that conflict. Goodness (or the Father of Light, God) is engaged in combat with Evil (the Prince of Darkness, Satan), and, at their respective sides, are hosts of like-minded helpers and collaborators, all engaged in the struggle, all committed to their respective Lord. Perhaps to a modern mind all of this sounds like an ancient version of Star Wars, but to the ancients it was deadly serious—something to die for.

Augustine would have learned this story by means of an elaborate narrative with exotic names, cosmic copulations, accounts of celestial battles and catastrophic deceptions, heavenly rescue plans and more. This is not the place to explore the elaborate Manichaean mythology because it is too complex for a concise treatment; but it is important to emphasize that it offered both a narrative about creation and about redemption. The material world (as we know it) and present human bodily existence are the results of a primordial chaos and conflict; divine light became trapped in material reality, including human bodies.

> They think that the souls not merely of human beings but also of animals
> are derived from the substance of God and are actually parts of God. They also

say that the good and true God fought with the nation of darkness and mingled a part of himself with the princes of darkness, and they claim that this part, which has been defiled and imprisoned throughout the whole world, is purified through the food of the elect and through the sun and the moon, and that what will not be able to be purified from that part of God will at the end of the world be bound with an eternal chain of punishment. In that way God is not only believed to be violable, corruptible, and subject to contamination, since a part of him can be reduced to such evils, but he cannot be entirely purified from such defilement, impurity, and evil, even at the end of the world. (*Letter* 236, 2)

That was the Manichaean message that Augustine would have heard. To come to this knowledge is to enter the path of salvation. In this sense Manichaeism fits under the broad umbrella of ancient Gnosticism that linked esoteric religious knowledge with redemption. Mani, so the "Religion of Light" taught, is the Revealer of this Knowledge. Mani presented himself as "Apostle of Jesus Christ," and Augustine initially embraced Mani as if he were a Christian prophet/teacher. For a religiously sensitive young man that Augustine was, Manichaean instruction offered him a doctrine that was both affirming and intellectually challenging: his soul was a "part of God." This conferred upon him a dignity that was not bodily centered; in fact, it virtually disposed of the body. It also promised that if one but nurtured that "part of God" that was the soul, the result would be an ascent to unimaginable religious heights. It seems clear that Augustine was deeply into "bodily pursuits" at this time, and he felt pangs of guilt and remorse for his carnal habits. In so many ways the "Religion of Light" absolved him of this guilt by telling him that they did not reflect the real Augustine—that Augustine was found in his soul which was a "part of God." In any case, he learned that Evil bore the guilt for his actions.

Along with this elaborate narrative there was an aggressive effort against the principles of Judaism, something that was common among many Gnostic movements. The "god" of the Old Testament, the creator "god" of Genesis, played right into the hands of the Prince of Darkness. Anyone familiar with the Old Testament is aware of its often earthy narrative: when Noah is portrayed as drunk and naked in front of his daughters or when Jacob lies to his father Isaac who then disinherits Esau. The Manichees loved to mock what they considered to be the sordid history of Israel that was enshrined in the Old Testament. It was for this reason that they considered the "God of Israel" an incompetent bumbler—at best. This was not a holy book, they insisted, but stories of perversion and ignorance. Augustine, unable to respond to such arguments, accepted their alternative narratives—at least initially. They presented themselves as offering reason rather than faith as the true avenue to God, but they demanded unquestioned acceptance and affirmation for their "foundational narrative."

But those who are called hearers among them eat meat and cultivate fields and, if they wish, take wives; the elect do none of these things. But the hearers kneel before the elect in order that not only their priests or bishops or deacons but even any of the elect may impose hands on these supplicants. They also adore and pray to the sun and the moon with the elect. On the Lord's day they also fast with them, and they believe along with them all the blasphemies because of which the heresy of the Manichees should be detested. That is, they deny that Christ was born of a virgin and do not confess that his flesh was real but false. And for this reason they claim that his passion was not real and that there was no resurrection. They blaspheme against the patriarchs and prophets. They say that the law given by means of Moses, the servant of God, did not come from the true God but from the prince of darkness. (*Letter* 236, 2)

All of this was enshrined in elaborately written and decorated books and celebrated, it seems, in moving rituals. Added to this was an intense awareness that once you entered their community you entered into Truth; from that position, the rest of the world was seen as doomed. The experience seemed to offer a sense of security—at least by its opposition to everything outside the group. One of the striking impressions that Augustine gives us in his *Confessions* is of the sense of community that Manichaeism seemed to engender. Even once Augustine began to be suspicious of the Manichaean account of reality, he clung to the sense of community they offered.

> There were other joys to be found in their company which still more powerfully captivated my mind – the charms of talking and laughing together and kindly giving way to each other's wishes, reading elegantly written books together, sharing jokes and delighting to honor one another, disagreeing occasionally but without rancor, as a person might disagree with himself, and lending piquancy by that rare disagreement to our much more frequent accord. We would teach and learn from each other, sadly missing any who were absent and blithely welcoming them when they returned. Such signs of friendship sprang from the hearts of friends who loved and knew their love returned, signs to be read in smiles, words, glances and a thousand gracious gestures. So were sparks kindled and our minds were infused inseparably, out of many becoming one. (*conf.* IV.8.13)

What Augustine found in the Manichaean community was a deep bond of friendship and intimacy, enhanced perhaps by the realization that they belonged to something "forbidden" (Augustine specifically mentions at *conf.* IV.1.1 that their Manichaean allegiance was "*occulte*—in secret"), a feeling that would have intensified the bond they shared.

That was not the only bond Augustine nurtured. In Carthage, Augustine began a live-in relationship with a young woman that would continue for nearly fifteen years. Augustine was about 18 at the time and deeply engaged in his studies. He tells us next to nothing about her: neither how, nor when nor where they met—not even her name. It is not likely that she followed him into his new religious community since their son seemed not to have been raised as a Manichaean. What is known is that they violated a fundamental tenet of the "Religion of Life" by generating another "body"—together they unexpectedly had a son whom they named Adeodatus, meaning "Gift of God." The Manichees disapproved of marriage because of its "carnal implications," but they tolerated it as long as it did not produce offspring—to add other "bodies" to the world was simply to introduce more darkness into it. Augustine does not hesitate to paint himself in the worst possible light when speaking of the relationship. At least from his side it was a selfish affair, oriented toward taking care of his physical desires. But even those desires have unexpected consequences:

> At this time too I lived with a girl not bound to me in lawful wedlock but sought out by the roving eye of reckless desire; all the same she was the only girl I had, and I was sexually faithful to her. This experience taught me at first hand what a difference there is between a marriage contracted for the purpose of founding a family, and a relationship of love charged with carnal desire in which children may be born against the parents' wishes – though once they are born one cannot help loving them. (*conf.* IV.2.2)

Augustine's long-lasting relationship can perhaps be best described as a quasi-marriage (the Romans would have called it "concubinatus") and such relations were not uncommon in Augustine's Roman world. In fact, Roman law was careful to regulate them, especially regarding heirs and inheritances. We know nothing of her social class (a lower social status would automatically preclude marriage but Augustine does not allow us to decide one way or another), but we do know that Adeodatus (the name is not uncommon in Roman Africa and is Punic in origin: Iatan-baal, gift of God) would have been regarded as illegitimate under Roman law, with no legal claim to his father's inheritance. All of this becomes murkier when Augustine tells us (*conf.* VI.15.25) that pressure from Monnica finally ended their long relationship since it was proving an obstacle to a socially acceptable marriage. Was it her social status? Augustine is silent. Ultimately, it seems certain that his unnamed companion had little or no protection under the law given the nature of their relationship—everything favoring the male, his family, and his fortune.

Augustine certainly leaves the impression that this unnamed woman meant much to him—when the relationship ended he describes her as being "ripped from my side" and his heart as "torn and wounded and trailing blood" (*conf.* VI.15.25). But, for now, that had to be left aside; the young Augustine found himself almost a husband and already a father; he was responsible for a household, but still pursuing his rhetorical studies. Monnica, who had been appalled and dismayed by the course her son's religious life had taken in the beginning, had distanced herself from Augustine for a time—but not for long. Augustine says, "She agreed to live with me and share my table, under one roof" (*conf.* III.11.19), telling us that a dream had convinced her that her son would eventually find the right path to God. In all of these matters, Monnica had never lost sight of her hopes for her son's future. She would have been the first to make sure that his career aspirations were not shipwrecked by domestic or familial burdens.

Augustine finished his studies and began teaching, initially at Thagaste. Just why he returned to Thagaste is not clear. It has been suggested that Romanianus, his benefactor, may have funded the endeavor. The only clue we get is

Augustine's terse statement: "when I first began to teach in the town where I was born . . ." (*conf.* IV.4.7). It is also a disputed question whether the "domestic reunion" between Monnica and her son took place in Thagaste or in Carthage (it must be frankly admitted that a precise chronology of these years is not possible—the primary source for our information, the *Confessions*, offers a narrative that is always more theological than strictly chronological). Augustine tells us nothing of this first teaching endeavor, but he does talk about how a deep friendship with a childhood schoolmate revived when he returned home to Thagaste.

> . . . when I first began to teach in the town where I was born, I had a friend who shared my interests and was exceedingly dear to me. He was the same age as myself and, like me, now in the flower of young manhood. As a boy he had grown up with me; we had gone to school together and played together. He was not then such a friend to me as he was to become later ... I did love him very tenderly and similarity of outlook lent warmth to our relationship; for I had lured him from the true faith, which he had held in a thoroughly immature way and without conviction, to the superstitious and baneful fables which my mother deplored in me. Already this man was intellectually astray along with me and my soul could not bear to be without him. . . . (*conf.* IV.4.7)

Augustine seems to have managed to lure all of his close friends into the Manichees. Suddenly, his friend became seriously ill and hung between life and death.

> As my friend struggled with fever he lay for a long time unconscious and sweating at death's door; and as hope for his recovery dwindled he was baptized without his knowledge. I cared little for this, since I took it for granted that his mind was more likely to retain what he had received from me, irrespective of any rite performed on his unconscious body. How wrong I was; for he rallied and grew stronger, and immediately, or as soon as I possibly could. . . . I attempted to chaff him, expecting him to join me in making fun of the baptism he had undergone while entirely absent in mind and unaware of what was happening. But he had already learned that he had received it. . . . (*conf.* IV.4.8)

Augustine was convinced that his friend would laugh with him. The exact opposite happened, however, as the unnamed young man responded to Augustine's derision harshly. Talking aloud to God, he wrote:

> . . . he recoiled from me with a shudder as though I had been his enemy, and with amazing, new-found independence warned me that if I wished to be his friend I had better stop saying such things to him. I stood aghast and troubled, but deferred telling him of my feelings in order to let him get better first, thinking that once he was in normal health again I would be able to do what I liked with him. But he was snatched away from my mad designs, to be kept safe with you for my consolation: a few days later the fever seized him anew and he died. And I was not there. (*conf.* IV.4.8)

What follows in Augustine's account are some of the most remarkable lines about the power of friendship in all of ancient and perhaps even modern literature (see below). The fact that Augustine chose to reveal this side of himself, his need for deep bonds of friendship, acceptance, and intimacy, surely offers insight into the depths and complexity of his personality. His pursuit of wisdom and truth was inexorably tied together with his pursuit of love and security. These two inseparable sides of Augustine, mind and heart, will become his trademark.

Reading Augustine:

Augustine's life was always filled with close relationships—some of which brought him great joy, others filled him with sorrow. On a number of occasions he pondered the mystery of human friendship. These are two examples.

> But good human beings seem even in this life to provide no small consolation. For, if poverty pinches, if grief saddens, if bodily pain disturbs, if exile discourages, if any other disaster torments, provided that there are present good human beings who know not only how to rejoice with those in joy, but also to weep with those who weep (Rom 12:15) and can speak and converse in a helpful way, those rough spots are smoothed, the heavy burdens are lightened, and adversity is overcome. He who by his Spirit makes them good does all this in them and through them. If, on the other hand, riches abound, no death occurs, bodily health is present, and one lives in a country safe from attack, but evil human beings also dwell there among whom there is no one who can be trusted . . . are not those former things bitter and hard without anything joyful or pleasant in them? Thus in no human affairs is anything dear to a human being without a friend. (*Letter* 130.2.4)
>
> I admit that I find it easy to abandon my whole self to the love of them [friends], especially when I am wearied by the scandals of the world, and I find rest in that love without any worry. I, of course, feel that God is in that person to whom I abandon myself with security and in whom I find rest in security. And in that security I do not at all fear that incertitude of tomorrow stemming from the human fragility that I lamented above. For, when I perceive that a man is aflame with Christian love and has become my loyal friend with that love, whatever of my plans and thoughts I entrust to him I do not entrust to a human being, but to him in whom he remains so that he is such a person. For God is love, and he who remains in love remains in God, and God in him (1 Jn. 4:16). (*Letter* 73.10)

4

Augustine, a Young Man—In Pursuit of a Future

"So I left Thagaste and came to Carthage" (*conf.* IV.7.12): The time in Thagaste may have been a time of idleness, but the death of his friend convinced him to return to Carthage, the African capital. Augustine took up teaching, probably sometime in 376 CE. Serge Lancel comments in his remarkable study of Augustine (p. 45): "not just anyone could teach rhetoric in the African capital." Lancel suggests, based upon a comment by Augustine in the *Confessions*, that he had a public position (*conf.* VI.7.12), an appointment to a "municipal chair." If Lancel's supposition is correct, it would mean that Augustine now possessed a coveted civic post, a significant first step on the road to success. How he secured the post is unknown to us. Carthage would have offered him a salary and also provided him with a location—he likely offered public lectures in rhetoric in some official building designated for this purpose, and from some comments concerning a close friend and student, Alypius, the location was likely near the African capital city's main forum. Augustine was now about 25, not that much older than his students, but with a reputation well advanced. He had already won oratorical contests and now had a public office—Augustine began to move in influential circles.

He must have been an effective teacher in more ways than one—he managed to bring many of his students to Manichaeism. Given Augustine's bitter accounts of his rough treatment at the hands of his first school masters, we might surmise that he effectively sought to win his students over by invitation rather than by intimidation. He recounts how a student, Alypius, soon-to-become intimate friend, was "cured" of his addiction to the blood sport of the amphitheatre by a few biting comments in the course of a class lecture (*conf.* VI.7.12). Also during this period he took on as a student a wealthy young man by the name of Nebridius. They too were to develop a bond of intimate and deep friendship. Both Alypius and Nebridius had the potential to introduce Augustine into high society and their teacher undoubtedly took advantage of the new doors that were opened up to him. A further opportunity came when he entered a civic competition in poetry and took first prize. It was the proconsul of Africa, Helvius Vindicianus, who placed the victor's crown on Augustine, and he then began to take an interest in the fortunes of the young public professor of rhetoric, meeting with him on several occasions (*conf.* IV.3.5).

Augustine, however, was not only a teacher; he also remained a student. On the one hand, this would seem to have been fully a part of the demands of being a good teacher—something to which Augustine was deeply committed. On the other hand, his voracious appetite for knowledge in search of wisdom was as strong as ever. Augustine tells us that he did much reading in the liberal arts and in philosophy, though he does not name the authors nor the books he read. Not only did these scholarly pursuits further inflame his quest for knowledge, they also served to increase his doubts about Manichaeism. His reading of certain books on astronomy forcefully contradicted everything the teachings of Mani proposed regarding the sun, moon, and stars. His Manichaean allegiance was becoming intellectually ever more precarious. It is perhaps surprising to note that these academic pursuits included a fascination with the study of astrology, a pursuit which Vindicianus—and his close friend Nebridius—discouraged in Augustine to no avail.

What did a mind as sharp as Augustine's find attractive in astrology? First of all, it was a very popular practice in Augustine's world (see, e.g., *exp. Gal.* 35); for many, in fact, the practice of "reading the stars" was taken for granted. But for Augustine, it seems that there was something that attracted him to the practice of astrology. Still seething inside his mind were unsettling questions regarding human responsibility and destiny, the scope of human freedom and the power of the will, the origin and nature of evil and these questions will remain with him throughout his life, though they will assume different formulations as time goes on. Astrology offered one set of answers to these questions; it seemed to absolve human beings of moral responsibility, as if to say, "It's all in the stars." Augustine tells us that he both consulted astrologers and offered horoscope readings for his friends.

Did Augustine see astrology as a complement as an alternative to his Manichaean allegiance? Perhaps there was a bit of both in his pursuit of the stars. In the meantime, his allegiance to the "Religion of Light" increasingly dimmed. Nebridius pointed out some real concerns about the sect's account of evil, so serious that these questions fundamentally undermined the Manichaean account of God. Augustine also witnessed the successful debates of a certain Catholic controversialist against his fellow Manichees regarding troubling biblical questions. Augustine was not impressed by the Manichaean response: they would only answer the challenges in private, not in public. But religion was not the only thing on Augustine's mind. During this period Augustine began to think about writing a series of books on the liberal arts—probably as a result of teaching his students about these subjects. Although his project was never completed, what does remain from it sheds some light on his interests and intellectual concerns during this important Carthaginian sojourn. It also prompted the writing of his first book, a lost work called "On the Beautiful and the Fitting" which he dedicated to a famous Roman rhetor of the time, Hierius. Greek speaking from the beginning but then famous for his Latin eloquence, Hierius represented everything Augustine esteemed and sought to achieve. If the work were extant it probably offered precious insight to the mind of Augustine during this critical stage in his development. One thing is clear: his wide and varied intellectual pursuits were not yet strong enough to pull him away from Manichaeism completely. His list of doubts, however, seemed to increase by the day.

He continued his participation in Manichaean rituals and practices (e.g., he recounts how he and his friends engaged in "food-rituals," *conf.* IV.1.1). If Manichaean doctrine raised nagging questions, we get no impression that his day-to-day sharing in the Manichaean community life was in jeopardy. The affective bonds of friendship and community that he had developed with his co-religionists seemed to prove stronger than the intellectual doubts. When he asked the deeper questions, he was often offered two responses: only the Elect, the full-fledged members, received the deepest revelations; he, therefore, had to await that moment patiently. The second response would prove to be more devastating: he was told to await the arrival of Faustus, a Manichaean bishop with a renowned reputation among members of the sect. They said, "Wait for Faustus, he will answer your questions, wait for Faustus" (*conf.* V.6.10). Augustine must have heard this innumerable times—so much so that his hopes and expectations were at fever pitch when Faustus did eventually arrive:

> 6.10 All through that period of about nine years, during which I was spiritually adrift as a hearer among the Manichees, I had been awaiting the arrival of this Faustus with an expectancy that had been at full stretch too long. Whenever I had been in contact with others of the sect, and their replies to the questions I raised on these topics failed to satisfy me, they would put me off with promises about him. Once he had arrived, they assured me, and I had an opportunity to discuss things with him, these points, together with any more serious problems I might raise, would quite easily be sorted out and resolved. When he came, then, he did indeed impress me as a man of pleasant and smooth speech, who chattered on the usual themes much more beguilingly than the rest. A man adept at serving finer wines, then; but what was that to me in my thirst? My ears were sated with such offerings already. The content did not seem better to me for being better presented, nor true because skillfully expressed, nor the man wise of soul because he had a handsome face and a graceful turn of speech. Those who had held out promises to me were not good judges; to them he seemed wise and prudent merely because they enjoyed the way he talked. . . .
>
> For some time, though, you had been teaching me in wondrous, hidden ways, my God . . . ; so I had already learned under your tuition that nothing should be regarded as true because it is eloquently stated, nor false because the words sound clumsy. On the other hand, it is not true for being expressed in uncouth language either, nor false because couched in splendid words. . . .
>
> 6.11 After waiting so long and so eagerly for this man, I was certainly delighted with his lively and spirited style in debate, and by his apt choice

of words to clothe his thought, words that came to him readily. Yes, I was delighted, and along with others I praised and extolled him; indeed I was in the forefront of those who did so. But I was annoyed that amid the crowd who went to hear him I was unable to catch his attention or share my anxious questionings with him in intimate conversation and the give and take of discussion. If ever I did succeed in gaining a hearing with him in the company of intimate friends and at a time which was not unsuitable for an exchange of ideas, and I put to him some of the problems that preoccupied me, then, before even coming to anything deeper, what I found was a man ill-educated in the liberal arts, apart from grammar, and even in that schooled only to an average level. . . .

6.12 Once it had become sufficiently clear to me that he was poorly informed about the very disciplines in which I had believed him to excel, I began to give up hope that he could elucidate and clear up for me the problems with which I was concerned. To be sure, he could have been ignorant about these and still have had a grasp of religious truth, but only on condition of not being a Manichee. Their books are full of interminable myths concerning sky, stars, sun and moon, and it had been my earnest wish that by comparing these with the numerical calculations I had read elsewhere he would demonstrate to me that the phenomena in question could be more plausibly explained by the account given in Mani's books, or at least that an equally valid explanation could be found there; but now I no longer deemed him capable of explaining these things to me with any precision.

I must say, however, that when I raised these points for consideration and discussion he refused courteously enough, reluctant to risk taking on that burden; for he knew that he did not know about these matters, and was not ashamed to admit it. He was not one of the talkative kind, of whom I had suffered many, who tried to teach me but said nothing. His heart was, if not right with you, yet not without discretion. He was not altogether unaware of his own lack of awareness and was unwilling to enter rashly into argument that might leave him cornered, with no way out and no easy means of retracting. This attitude endeared him to me all the more, for the restraint of a mind that admits its limitations is more beautiful than the beautiful things about which I desired to learn. I found him consistent in this approach to all the more difficult and subtle questions.

6.13 The keen attention I had directed toward Mani's writings was therefore rebuffed, for I felt more hopeless than ever in respect of their other teachers now that this man, for all his reputation, had turned out to be so incompetent in many of the subjects that mattered to me. I began to spend much time in his company on account of his ardent enthusiasm for the literature that I, as a master of rhetoric, was teaching to the young men of Carthage, and thereafter I fell into the habit of reading with him any works which he had heard of and wished to study, or which were, in my judgment, suited to his ability... since I had found nothing better than this sect into which I had more or less blundered, I resolved to be content with it for the time being, unless some preferable option presented itself.

Thus it came about that this Faustus, who was a death-trap for many, unwittingly and without intending it began to spring the trap in which I was caught, for thanks to your hidden providence, O my God, your hands did not let go of my soul. Through my mother's tears the sacrifice of her heart's blood was being offered to you day after day, night after night, for my welfare; and you dealt with me in wondrous ways. You, my God, you it was who dealt so with me; for our steps are directed by the Lord, and our way is of his choosing. What other provision is there for our salvation, but your hand that remakes what you have made? (*conf.* V.6.10–13)

Faustus did not answer Augustine's questions, Augustine, rather, was the one answering Faustus' questions. Augustine spoke well of him and found that he was an avid student, but it is clear that the result of this decisive encounter was disappointment: Augustine's intellectual doubts about Manichaeism were not resolved . . . nor would they be.

Augustine did not find his regular students quite as enthusiastic as Faustus. In fact, he increasingly found the unruly behavior and lack of interest among his young students to be less and less tolerable. He paints an unflattering portrait of his Carthaginian students:

. . . the unbridled licentiousness of the students [in Carthage] is disgusting. Looking almost like madmen they burst in recklessly and disrupt the discipline each master has established to ensure that his pupils make progress. With boorishness that defied belief they commit many acts of violence which would attract legal penalties if custom did not seem to plead in their defense . . . (*conf.* V.8.14)

Augustine is writing some 15 years after the fact but writes in such a way as to indicate that little had changed in Carthage in this regard. At some point he decided that he had probably gotten all that he could from Carthage and that he had given Carthage all that he had to offer: the time had come to move on. Friends who knew told him that Rome was the place to go. Students there were under imperial supervision and so much more disciplined. His dear friend Alypius had already traveled to the capital city to take up a public position there. It also seemed that the Carthaginian authorities had begun to put pressure on the Manichees, still officially a forbidden sect whose members could be punished under the law. We have to surmise that Augustine saw this as a potential threat to his future. Behind the move there must have equally been the realization that being in Italy brought him one step closer to the imperial government (at this point in history the Western emperor was resident in Milan, not Rome). If he secured an imperial post, comfortable wealth and long-term security would not be far behind. Thus, it likely was a convergence of disparate motives that convinced Augustine to seek his future on the continent and to begin preparations accordingly.

It seems clear that Augustine intended to travel alone, leaving behind his companion and their son Adeodatus. Did he intend that once settled in Rome he would send for them? Augustine is silent on the matter. And, while we learn nothing of his companion's reaction to this decision, Augustine leaves no doubt about his mother Monnica's response to the news. Strong woman that she was, she resisted Augustine's departure with all her might. One can only imagine the scene his announcement created—but to no avail. Augustine's mind was made up, and he had to resort to subterfuge to escape his mother's grasp. On the night he was to set sail he announced, in fact, that he had no intention of sailing. He was awaiting, so he told her, the departure of a friend to another port and the winds were not yet favorable for that voyage. He advised her to seek rest and shelter in a nearby church for the night, one dedicated to St. Cyprian, promising her that, in the meantime, he would await the morning with his friend. Instead, he used this cover to make his escape.

> So the wind blew for us and filled our sails, and the shore dropped away from our sight as she stood there at morning light mad with grief, filling your ears with complaints and groans. (*conf.* V.8.15)

Anyone, past or present, familiar with Vergil's Aeneid would be struck by the similarities between the epic's portrayal of a distraught Dido weeping at the departure of Aeneas from Carthaginian shores to Italy and Augustine's painting of Monnica, mad with tears of grief on the same sea shore. He, deliberately and provocatively, draws upon these images to describe his own epic departure from Africa and from Monnica for new adventures in Rome.

The account of his departure for Rome has given rise to some debate about the historicity of Augustine's account of his intellectual and spiritual journey as told in the *Confessions*. Indeed, that story was one of the most remarkable of the ancient world, and it wielded an enormous influence after Augustine died, especially in the West. Once again it bears repeating that this author is among those convinced of the fundamental accuracy of Augustine's account, especially since some key players in the narrative were living and would have read the *Confessions*. Alypius, for example—at the time of Augustine's writing of the *Confessions*—was still a close friend and had also become an active collaborator with Augustine. While allowing for the literary license readers would expect that actual events would be placed in a cohesive and artistic narrative. Given the reality of anyone's retrospective and subjective analysis of past events, it could be argued that there were too many living eyewitnesses who would have read this work for Augustine to offer an account that did not fundamentally match reality. And not all those readers were necessarily friendly.

Be that as it may, it is worthwhile to note that the Augustine setting sail for Rome has now reached the age of 30, with a life already marked by both great promise and equally great disappointment. At each step along the way he seemed to reach a pinnacle: wholeheartedly embracing the Manichees and their promise of spiritual fulfillment, only to be deeply disillusioned; being top in his class, starting as a teacher supported by a patron, winning a municipal chair, only to be sadly disappointed by unruly students. At this point was there a premonition that Rome might be no different—was this the price of success? As

Augustine looked back toward the ever diminishing African horizon, his heart may have been heavy.

When Augustine arrived in Rome sometime in 384 CE, it was still the cultural center of the Roman Empire, even though the political winds had begun to shift to the East. Constantinople was now the "New Rome." Rome was still the home of the Senate, a city of remarkable monuments that exemplified what seemed to be an eternal history and a divine destiny; Rome still saw itself as the largest and most remarkable city in the world, and it remained the home of an ancient Roman aristocracy that was intransigently resistant to an ascendant Christianity. As a result, scholars are often disappointed by how little Augustine tells us about the Rome he encountered in 384 CE: nothing about its monuments, public spaces, its palaces, not even its churches. Subsequently, when he uses an example of an actual memory of a city in contrast to "imagining a city" the pair is always Carthage/Alexandria. Did Rome awaken in Augustine the awareness that he was, after all, an African, that is, neither Italian nor Roman in a specific sense of those words? He does say that, in Italy, people made comments about his African accent. Did that remind him in some way of the long animosity between Rome and Carthage that eventually led to the Punic wars and the destruction of Carthage in 146 BCE? Such a comment is speculative, and Augustine did not, in fact, stay in Rome very long. Upon arrival, he became seriously ill and almost died. The Manichaean community he found there nursed him to health. Even though he had begun to drift away from them, his connection to that movement was real—and it would, before long, again be useful for his next career move.

Even though he had found it personally satisfying when they had taught him that his immoral actions were not his fault, but the fault of an evil force within him (*conf.* V.10.18), he had begun to distance himself—intellectually—from Manichaeism and from the moral hypocrisy of some of its hierarchy. But he still had nowhere else to go. In the midst of his settling in, he returned to his philosophical reading with intensity, perhaps for the sake of his classes, but at least as part of his continuing effort to satisfy his own driving inquisitiveness. The philosophy he encountered, called the New Academy, privileged a sophisticated skepticism, a seemingly refreshing alternative to a doctrinaire Manichaeism. It offered him the comfortable philosophical refuge of open doubt, and he decided to make this doubt his intellectual home for the time-being. In the meantime, he gathered students and, while he did initially find them more to his liking than in Carthage, he quickly became disillusioned:

> I now set myself to work at teaching rhetoric in Rome, the task for which I had come. My first move was to gather students together at my house, and I began to make a name for myself among them and more widely through them. But what did I then discover, but that abuses prevailed in Rome which I had not been obliged to contend with in Africa? It was obviously true that acts of vandalism by young hooligans did not occur there, but, I was told, "A crowd of these young men conspire together, and in order to avoid paying their fees to

their teacher suddenly leave him for another. They betray their good faith, and because they hold wealth so dear they account justice cheap." (*conf.* V.12.22)

A pattern has clearly emerged: Augustine found himself just as dissatisfied and disappointed as he was in Carthage he fled, his only comfort a somewhat weary skepticism.

In the midst of such persistent darkness a new light unexpectedly broke through with a promise of hope. Symmachus, prefect of Rome, a dedicated adherent to Roman ancient religion and tradition, was approached by Milanese officials to procure for the city a municipal rhetor. Not only would the office be the equivalent of a publicly funded chair in rhetoric, but since Milan was also the residence of the western imperial court, the holder of the position would also be entrusted with declaiming imperial panegyrics on appropriate occasions.

> A message had been sent from Milan to Rome, addressed to the prefect of the city, asking for a master of rhetoric. A pass had also been issued, authorizing the person chosen to use the official post-horses. Against the background of unsatisfactory student behavior I therefore canvassed support among citizens drunk on Manichaean nonsense, in the hope that after having prescribing a subject for a trial discourse the prefect Symmachus would recommend and dispatch me . . . (*conf.* V.13.23)

Symmachus had everything to gain by sending a protégé to Milan who would not only be beholden to his patron, but would also be clever enough to withstand the mounting Catholic influence embodied in the then Catholic Bishop of Milan, Ambrose. Though distantly related, Ambrose and Symmachus represented radically opposing world views. Both were highly educated, articulate, and experienced. Symmachus saw religion from a "Roman" perspective, that is, a perspective that sought peaceful coexistence with most religious perspectives. Ambrose recognized the limits of "Roman" tolerance and responded forcefully. Symmachus lost a major battle when Ambrose prevailed against him and a cohort of non-Christian senators who had sought to have the Altar of Victory restored to the senate house in Rome. That would have been tantamount to getting imperial approval for the restoration of the "ancient rites" that would be performed at that altar. To Ambrose this would have been an unforgivable surrender to paganism—and his interventions prevailed.

One can well imagine the strategy behind Symmachus' choice of Augustine. He knew nothing of Augustine's interior break with Manichaeism and must have taken great pleasure in filling the post of official orator with someone who was not only an accomplished rhetor, but who would also be an affront to Ambrose. And so, after only a short sojourn in Rome, Augustine once again moved on, eager to embrace what would, at last, guarantee him fame and fortune. He would now be moving in imperial circles, and he could set his sights on a prestigious government office—and on a wealthy wife as well (*conf.* VI.11.10). He could begin to dream of a life of aristocratic retirement where philosophical studies were pursued in comfort and security.

By the time Augustine came to the now imperial city in the fall of 384 CE, Ambrose of Milan was already a larger-than-life figure. Born into a distinguished Roman family, Ambrose began his life in Trier where his father had an imperial appointment. As it was all too common in that time, Ambrose's father met with a premature death, a death that was probably associated with imperial politics in some way. Ambrose, along with his mother, brother and sister, returned to Rome where he received a classical education in the liberal arts and in law; he soon found himself in an enviable position within the imperial circle of officials. He soon became the equivalent of a governor for the region around Milan. In about 373 CE, after the death of the bishop of Milan, Auxentius, his concern about a possible conflict over the choice of a new bishop of Milan led him to be present, ready to keep order.

Auxentius had represented a Christian faction which came to be called Arians by the Christians who opposed them. The Arian controversy, in fact, an intense and bitter intra-Christian dispute, raged for much of the fourth century. It was a dispute about how to understand the Father-Son relationship and how to describe it in everyday terms. The Arians held that Jesus Christ was distinct from and less than the Father, based on a quick reading of some phrases of the Scriptures (e.g., "The Father is greater than I" Jn. 14:28). Their opponents—often called Nicenes—probably represented the majority Christian view by this time. They based their opposition on the Council which was held in 325 CE in Nicea, a place not far from Constantinople, and which was composed of episcopal representatives from most Christian churches. The Nicenes proclaimed Jesus Christ as "one-in-being-with-the-Father," that is, Jesus Christ, the Son of God, was truly and fully God; they were able to show that those Scripture verses that seemed to suggest inequality only made sense when seen as a coherent part of a great mystery. This controversy began in Alexandria in the second decade of the fourth century and spread rapidly—at least in part because of the interest and involvement of emperors and Christians alike. It was eventually agreed that this was not an argument about words, but about the meaning of salvation in Christ. By Augustine's time, this complex dispute had become less a matter of passion and more of an occasion for teaching what it meant to believe that Jesus Christ is God, that is, that, by his life, Jesus Christ brought salvation to the world.

Ambrose, a Roman official in Milan, when he came to the church where rival Christian groups had faced off over the successor to Auxentius, sought to maintain order. All of a sudden (Ambrose's biographer claimed that the voice of a child cried "Ambrose, bishop"), the gathered crowd began to demand that Ambrose be chosen as the successor, most likely because he was seen as a neutral figure in the Arian-Nicene dispute. Ambrose—even though he came from a Christian family—had not yet been baptized. But his resistance was futile. He was baptized and, one week later, he was ordained as bishop of Milan.

Ambrose would become one of the most influential and eminent Christian bishops of the West; he consolidated Nicene faith in Milan, once-and-for-all; he also became a powerful theological voice for a Christianity that was now at center stage in the Roman Empire—capable of holding the emperors of his time to account when they acted in non-Christian ways. When Augustine came to Milan, still restless and searching, he could hardly ignore this formidable, highly visible figure. Ambrose had the reputation of being an excellent rhetor; Augustine went to hear him, hoping to advance his own career. Ambrose will become—for Augustine—a good teacher and not merely a convincing speaker.

We can precisely date Augustine's first official discourse in Milan, November 22, 384 CE. That day marked the tenth anniversary (*decennalia*) of Valentinian II's accession to the throne as Augustus, emperor of the West, sharing the crown with Theodosius I in the East. He was only four when he was proclaimed Augustus. Nine years later, a Roman "tenth anniversary" would be a contemporary "ninth anniversary," the boy emperor was 13 or 14 years old and hardly an imposing imperial figure. He was, rather, the puppet of his mother and of the imperial council, as well as the unfortunate subject of much court intrigue. The content of imperial panegyrics was well-defined (de rigueur); it had to address and acclaim imperial military prowess, wise government, benevolent laws, just judgments, and more. All of this would be declaimed in elaborate and ornate language suitable for an imperial occasion. While it seems that Augustine succeeded, even though he was aware of how some criticized his African accent, he tells us that the circumstances led him to have an interior crisis. For someone whose journey so far had been driven by a search for truth, he now found himself at the pinnacle of success, but at the cost of that very quest for truth. He was now a master of the eloquent public lie.

> I recall how miserable I was, and how one day you brought me to a realization of my miserable state. I was preparing to deliver a eulogy upon the emperor in which I would tell plenty of lies with the object of winning favor with the well-informed by my lying; so my heart was panting with anxiety and seething with feverish, corruptive thoughts. As I passed through a certain district in Milan I noticed a poor beggar, drunk, as I believe, and making merry. I groaned and pointed out to the friends who were with me how many hardships our idiotic enterprises entailed. Goaded by greed, I was dragging my load of unhappiness along, and feeling it all the heavier for being dragged. Yet while all our efforts were directed solely to the attainment of unclouded joy, it appeared that this beggar had already beaten us to the goal, a goal which we would perhaps never reach ourselves. With the help of the few paltry coins he had collected by begging this man was enjoying the temporal happiness for which I strove by so bitter, devious and roundabout a contrivance . . . (*conf.* VI.6.9)

The discourse has not come down to us. If it had, we might have a striking picture of imperial rhetoric and of Augustine at the height of his secular career. His public role was to be exercised again, a short time later, on January 1, 385 CE, when Flavius Bauto acceded to the office of Consul. Since Augustine stood before a real military hero, the lies did not need to be quite so prominent. But, in that process, Augustine began to get a first hand view of imperial politics, the caliber of some of the empire's leading statesmen, and the inevitable intrigue that permeated the imperial palace.

If Augustine suddenly found himself depressed in Milan, he did not necessarily find himself lonely. Alypius and Nebridius, now his two closest friends, joined him there and with them he shared his joys and sorrows. Monnica, his companion and their child Adeodatus, now approaching adolescence, joined Augustine in Milan, along with some young relatives. Augustine had left Africa, but Africa came to him. We get a glimpse of how Augustine's success was a benefit to him and to his "extended family."

Perhaps at this point it is important to pause and note that we are able to know so much in detail about Augustine's personal life and journey because of the remarkable story about himself that he tells in the *Confessions*. This remarkable work was—in so many ways—without precedent. The story that Augustine tells is never about himself alone. The cast of characters who journey with him are as much a part of his story as Augustine himself is. The fact that they play such a vital role in moving his own journey forward, and the fact that some of these "journeyers" were still alive and able to read about themselves—Alypius is a case in point, ought to remind us that "Augustine's story" is never just his story, and his close friends read what he wrote—a fact that would have helped Augustine tell the story accurately. He was, in fact, being shaped by them, some of whom were quite remarkable in their own right—Monnica and Ambrose are the most prominent, but Alypius and Nebridius will contribute significantly to his life. It is not possible to imagine "Augustine's self" without these other "selves."

Reading Augustine: *Conf.* VI.7.11–10.17

Halfway through Book VI of the *Confessions*, Augustine pauses to talk about two of his best friends. They shared his journey, but each of them was a friend in a different way:

> 7.11 Those of us who lived as friends together sighed deeply over these experiences, and I discussed them most especially and intimately with Alypius and Nebridius. Alypius and I had been born in the same town, where his parents were leading citizens. He was younger than I, and had been among my students when I began to teach in our town. He studied under me again at Carthage and held me in high esteem, because I seemed to him good and learned, while I for my part was fond of him on account of his great nobility of character, which was unmistakable even before he reached mature years. However, the whirlpool of Carthaginian immoral amusements sucked him in; it was aboil with frivolous shows, and he was ensnared in the madness of the circuses. At the time when he was being wretchedly tossed about in it, I as a professor of rhetoric had opened a school and was teaching publicly, but he did not attend my courses on account of a quarrel which had arisen between me and his father. I had discovered that he loved the circuses with a passion likely to be his undoing, and I was extremely anxious because he seemed to me bent on wasting his excellent promise, if indeed he had not already done so. I had, however, no opportunity to

restrain him by any kind of pressure, either out of goodwill as a friend or by right as his teacher, for I presumed that his attitude to me was the same as his father's, though in fact he was not like that. Accordingly he disregarded his father's wishes and took to greeting me when we met; he also began to frequent my lecture hall, where he would listen awhile, then go away.

7.12 . . . One day when I was sitting in my usual place with my students around me he came, greeted me, sat down and applied his mind to the subject we were studying. I chanced to have a text in my hands, and while I was expounding it an apt comparison with the circuses occurred to me, which would drive home the point I was making more humorously and tellingly through caustic mockery of people enslaved by that craze. You know, our God, that I did not think at the time about curing Alypius of this bane. Yet he took my illustration to himself, believing that I had used it solely on his account; and what another person might have regarded as a reason for being angry with me this honest young man regarded rather as a reason for being angry with himself and loving me more ardently. Long ago you had told us, weaving the advice into your scriptures, Offer correction to a wise man, and he will love you for it. Yet I had not corrected him myself. You make use of all of us, witting or unwitting, for just purposes known to you, and you made my heart and tongue into burning coals with which to cauterize a promising mind that was wasting away, and heal it.

If anyone is insensitive to your merciful dealings, let such a person silently withhold your praise, but from the marrow of my being those same dealings cry out in confession to you; for after hearing my words he wrenched himself away from that pit in which he had been willfully sinking, and finding incredible pleasure in his blindness. With a strong resolve of temperance he shook his mind free, and all the filth of the circuses dropped away from him. Never again did he go there. Then he overcame his father's opposition to his taking me for his teacher; his father gave in and gave him leave.

Once he had begun to study with me again, he became entangled in the same superstition as I, for he loved the display of continence put up by the Manichees, believing it to be real and authentic. In fact it was insane and seductive. It captivated precious souls who were still too ignorant to penetrate the depth of virtue and liable to be deceived by the superficial appearance of a virtue that was but feigned and faked.

10.16 I had caught up with him in Rome, and since a very strong bond of friendship kept him close to me, he set out for Milan in my company; for he did not want to leave me, and he also hoped to make some use of the legal expertise he had acquired, though this was in response to his parents' wishes rather than his own. Three times already he had acted as assessor, and aroused the amazement of others by his integrity, though for his part he found it still more amazing that they could value gold above honor. . . .

Almost the only source of temptation for him lay in literary studies, for he had the opportunity to have books copied for his own use at palace prices; but after considering the claims of justice he changed his mind for the better, judging that equity, which forbade him so to act, had more to recommend it than the privilege of office, which enabled him to. This was a trifling matter, but anyone who is trustworthy in a small thing is trustworthy in a great one too, and that saying uttered by your Truth can never be without force: If you have not proved trustworthy over dishonest money, who will give you what is real? And if you have not been trustworthy over what belongs to another, who will give you any of your own? This is what he was like, this man so closely united with me, the friend who concurred with me as we debated the right way to live.

10.17 Nebridius too shared our aspirations and was tossed to and fro along with us, for he was an ardent fellow-seeker of the happy life and an exceedingly keen researcher into the most difficult questions. He had left behind his home territory near Carthage, left Carthage itself where he had spent most of his time, left his father's fine estate, his home and his mother (who did not attempt to follow him), and come to Milan for no other purpose than to live with me and share in our fiercely burning zeal for truth and wisdom. So then there were three gaping mouths, three individuals in need, gasping out their hunger to one another and looking to you to give them their food in due time. By your merciful providence our worldly behavior always brought bitter disappointments, but whenever we sought to discern the reason why we should suffer them, we met with only darkness. So we would turn away, moaning, "How long are we to go on like this?" We were perpetually asking this question, but even as we asked it we made no attempt to change our ways, because we had no light to see what we should grasp instead, if we were to let go of them.

5

Augustine's Conversion— The Doctors Call It a Crisis! (cf. *conf.* VI.1.1)

Perhaps anyone looking at Augustine from the outside would have judged him to have truly arrived. He held the post of municipal professor of rhetoric in the now imperial city of Milan. He attracted wealthy and capable students; he delivered court orations; he made the rounds of distinguished households, contacts that proved invaluable for a future that was bound for the stars. We know that one of the first formal contacts he made was with the Bishop Ambrose, who received Augustine warmly, though we must imagine that the Milanese bishop was on his guard, especially given this young rhetor's Manichaean background and his connections with Symmachus.

> I regarded Ambrose as a fortunate man as far as worldly standing went, since he enjoyed the respect of powerful people; it was only his celibacy which seemed to me a burdensome undertaking. I had not begun to guess, still less experience in my own case, what hope he bore within him, or what a struggle he waged against the temptations to which his eminent position exposed him, or the encouragement he received in times of difficulty, or what exquisite delights he savored in his secret mouth, the mouth of his heart, as he chewed the bread of your word. Nor was he aware of my spiritual turmoil or the perilous pit before my feet. There were questions I wanted to put to him, but I was unable to do so as fully as I wished, because the crowds of people who came to him on business impeded me, allowing me little opportunity either to talk or to listen to him. He was habitually available to serve them in their needs, and in the very scant time that he was not with them he would be refreshing either his body with necessary food or his mind with reading. . . . (*conf.* VI.3.3)

> This man of God welcomed me with fatherly kindness and showed the charitable concern for my pilgrimage that befitted a bishop. I began to feel affection for him, not at first as a teacher of truth, for that I had given up hope

of finding in your Church, but simply as a man who was kind to me. With professional interest I listened to him conducting disputes before the people, but my intention was not the right one: I was assessing his eloquence to see whether it matched its reputation. I wished to ascertain whether the readiness of speech with which rumor credited him was really there, or something more, or less. I hung keenly upon his words, but cared little for their content, and indeed despised it, as I stood there delighting in the sweetness of his discourse (*conf.* VI.13.23).

Augustine's initial attitude toward Ambrose, at least as presented in the *Confessions*, was strictly "professional." He made the necessary courtesy call required of his new position. But there was more. Augustine was interested in what kind of orator Ambrose was and, out of curiosity, was at times present for Ambrose's preaching. The young rhetor certainly appreciated Ambrose's kindness and welcoming attitude, and he also admired his eloquence; but he had little or no time for the bishop's religious world. Despite his departure from Manichaeism, there was still a profound distrust if not a strong anti-Catholic strain that ran deeply through his heart; that served to limit Augustine's contact with Bishop Ambrose. Convinced that Ambrose had nothing true or spiritual to offer him, he did not really pay attention to what Ambrose had to say; he was, after all, only interested in how he spoke. Deep down, Augustine was also deeply attached to the skepticism he has recently embraced: "despairing as I did that any way to you [God] could be open to humankind" (*conf.* V.14.24).

But if Augustine distanced himself emotionally and spiritually from Ambrose's faith, such was not the case with Monnica. Upon her arrival in Milan, she quickly became a devoted member of Ambrose's church—and, it seems clear, a devoted fan of Ambrose himself. She gave herself wholeheartedly to church-going and pious practices—some of the latter she brought with her from Africa. Comments by Augustine offer not only a glimpse of Monnica's piety, but also of the kind of religious practices that were not uncommon in the Christianity of the late fourth century.

> In Africa she had been accustomed to make offerings of pottage, bread and wine at the tombs of the martyrs. When she attempted to do so here [in Milan], she was prevented by the doorkeeper; but as soon as she learned that it was the bishop who had forbidden the practice she complied in so devoted and obedient a spirit that I marveled at the attitude she had so readily adopted. . . . (*conf.* VI.2.2)

Augustine then explains Monnica's religious practices at the cemeteries, noting how she brought with her a heavily diluted wine.

> She would bring her basket containing the festive fare which it fell to her to taste first and then distribute; but she would then set out not more than one small cup, mixed [with water] to suit her abstemious palate, and from that she would only sip for courtesy's sake. It happened that there were many shrines of the dead to be honored in this manner she would carry round this same single

> cup and set it forth in each place. She thus served to her fellow-worshippers extremely sparing allowances of wine which was not only heavily diluted but by this time no more than lukewarm. What she sought to promote at these gatherings was piety, not intemperance. (*conf.* VI.2.2)

What Augustine is describing is a ritual that had been present in Africa long before Christianity arrived on its shores, a ceremony of honoring the dead by gathering at tombs and sharing wine and food. Not only did the living celebrate there, but also some of the refreshment was sent down a kind of tube into the tomb. The ancient rite of remembrance and communion with the dead had certainly received a Christian transformation, but it is important to appreciate its still intoxicating potential. At a Christian cemetery with multiple martyrs' tombs it is easily to imagine the effect of round after round of "passing the cup" in sacred toast to each and every martyr. It seems Monnica had no difficulty putting these practices aside and becoming a "front pew" member of Ambrose's congregation.

> Her spiritual fervor prompted her to assiduous good works and brought her constantly to church; and accordingly when Ambrose saw me he would often burst out in praise of her, telling me how lucky I was to have such a mother. Little did he know what a son she had: I was full of doubts about all these things and scarcely believed it possible to find the way of life. (*conf.* VI.2.2)

Augustine tells us that he began to attend Ambrose's preaching on a regular basis and that, slowly, not just his use of words but their content began to impact upon him.

One sure residue of his long association with Manichaean beliefs was their summary dismissal of the Hebrew Bible, that is, of the Old Testament. Despite Augustine's religious upbringing at the hands of Monnica, he knew little of the Bible, in particular of the Old Testament. When the Manichees engaged in their systematic derogation and derision of the sacred text, Augustine was ill-equipped to do anything more than accept their interpretation. The ancient narrative was filled with anthropomorphisms regarding God, moral practices that seemed abhorrent, "holy ancestors" who seemed, at least on occasion, anything but holy. Augustine had agreed with the Manichaean position that Catholic Christians blindly accepted a crude text that affirmed an even cruder god. Ambrose's preaching gradually deconstructed such perceptions and prejudices; Augustine learned that the Old Testament needed to be understood spiritually, that is, not in a literal way. He also learned that Catholics did not believe in a crudely material god, but in a God who was much different from the phantasms of human projection. Thus, the text in Genesis that says humans were created "in God's image" did not, as the Manichees taught, reduce the divine to a bodily existence but, to the contrary, lifted humans to a transcendent spiritual identity. He explains how Ambrose helped him:

> . . . I listened to him straightforwardly expounding the word of truth to the people every Sunday, and as I listened I became more and more convinced that

it was possible to unravel all those cunning knots of calumny in which the sacred books had been entangled by tricksters who had deceived me and others. I came to realize that your spiritual children, whom you had brought to a new birth by grace from their mother, the Catholic Church, did not in fact understand the truth of your creating human beings in your image in so crude a way that they believed you to be determined by the form of a human body. Although I had not even a faint or shadowy notion of what a spiritual substance could be like, I was filled with joy, albeit a shamefaced joy, at the discovery that what I had barked against for so many years was not the Catholic faith but the figments of carnal imagination. (*conf.* VI.3.4)

What Ambrose conveyed in his preaching and what Augustine learned from him was indeed about how to understand religious texts and religious faith. It came to represent a method of reading texts Ambrose demonstrated in his preaching. This intellectual-cultural method of reading had played a prominent role in Greco-Roman literary criticism for centuries, an allegorical approach which set cultural and religious texts in a more-than-literal and spiritually enriching context. That method began with the interpretation of the epics of Homer, making sure that the stories or events recounted there not be dismissed as scandalous or meaningless, but be set within a larger context of meaning. The battles among the gods became interior battles; the strivings of the heroes became moral strivings, and so on. An allegorical approach to the text made such readings possible.

An important step was made when Philo of Alexandria († ca. 50 CE), a prominent intellectual and a devout Jew, adapted this method to the reading of the Old Testament. On the one hand, he wanted to offer the Hellenistic world a port of entry into Jewish sacred texts that a cultivated Greek or Roman would find familiar. On the other hand, he wanted his own Jewish community to feel more comfortable and at home in the world of Hellenism. Interestingly, this approach did not require that the literal meaning be abandoned. For example, when the Hebrew Bible spoke of the adornment of the Temple and of all its precious accessories, it had in mind a real temple. But it also had in mind the "interior temple of the soul" as the dwelling place of God. A bridge was established between an ancient historical religious text/event and the contemporary religious experience of the believer. Early on Christian interpreters of the Bible embraced Philo's method and adapted it to Christian use. One of the most prominent to do so was Origen of Alexandria (†256 CE) who wrote in Greek and profoundly shaped the subsequent Christian theological tradition. Ambrose, fluent in Greek, was able use this method in his preaching, culling valuable insights from Greek Christian thinkers, such as Origen, and translating them into an eloquent Latin.

Augustine was intrigued, impressed, and slowly convinced that there lay before him a treasure trove of meaning hitherto unimagined in the very texts that the Manichees had taught him to scorn. Here was a world where the intellectual and the spiritual converged—just what Augustine had been longing to find for so long. Augustine tells us that, as a result of Ambrose's preaching and the intellectual-spiritual impact it had upon him, he decided to enroll himself formally as a catechumen (a candidate for baptism) in the Catholic church in Milan. That process that had already begun at his birth when his mother Monnica brought him to church as a baby and had him blessed—but not baptized. When he became a catechumen, it marked his official abandonment of Manichaeism, although he was still a long way from becoming a practicing Catholic Christian. During this period of Christian history, many remained life-long catechumens, putting off baptism until their death bed, thus postponing the spiritual and moral demands that came with baptism. Christian preachers of the period frequently emphasized the unpredictable nature of life and death as a spur not to postpone baptism. For Augustine, becoming a catechumen seemed to have served as a public statement that would be well-received by his mother and, no doubt, by Ambrose. It also afforded him a secure "space" where he could continue to pursue his complex and still unresolved quest for a true spiritual home.

There was another outcome of this still tentative religious step, one that may strike the modern reader as tragic and cruel. In the eyes of some segments of the Milanese aristocracy Augustine's decision would have accorded him a respectability formerly precluded by his Manichaean connection. As a catechumen he could find a welcome in devout Christian households previously withheld. Not only was Monnica delighted with her son's religious advance, but it also opened the way for her to find a "suitable" wife for her now prominent son. Although Augustine and his companion had now been together for a decade and a half, their relationship had no legal standing. Some speculate, and indeed it can only remain speculation, that Monnica would have strenuously resisted any attempts on Augustine's part to turn the relationship into a formal marriage. Some also argue that the class status of his companion precluded the possibility of a valid legal marriage—but Augustine himself never states this. Speculative questions about this relationship could be multiplied indefinitely, but there is not enough information to offer a good answer to the questions: Why Augustine did not marry his companion? Why did he look elsewhere for a marriage partner? What Augustine tells us is striking:

> Insistent pressure was on me to marry a wife. Already I was asking for it myself, and a marriage was being arranged for me, thanks especially to my mother's efforts ... and an offer for a certain girl was made on my behalf; but she was about two years below marriageable age. I liked her, though, so we decided to wait ... the woman with whom I had been cohabiting was ripped from my side, being regarded as an obstacle to my marriage. So deeply was she engrafted into my heart that it was left torn and wounded and trailing blood. She had returned to Africa, vowing to you that she would never give herself to another man, and the son I had fathered by her was left with me. But I was too unhappy to follow a woman's example: I faced two years of waiting before I could marry the girl to whom I was betrothed, and I chafed at the delay, for I was no lover of marriage but the slave of lust. So I got myself another woman, in no sense a wife. . . . (*conf.* VI.13.23–15.25)

He deliberately offers a most unflattering portrait of himself, but Monnica the matchmaker does not really fare much better. As mentioned earlier, marriages in this Roman world share little in common with contemporary understandings of the relationship of husband and wife. It was not a question of two people "falling in love" (that could always happen later) but of two families seeking mutual benefit. Negotiations would be conducted between the respective parents and this parental agreement initially would have formed the basis for the relationship. There are, indeed, striking portrayals of loving couples in the world of that time (on funerary images), but that would have occurred after the ceremony, not before. One can speculate that one of the by-products of Monnica's churchgoing in Milan was personal contact with other pious women—and their families. She kept her eyes and ears open and at some point found what she had been looking for: a marriage partner for her son. A conversation could then be initiated and that would lead to formal agreement. Perhaps one of the clauses insisted on by the other family (or by Monnica?) was that "the other woman" must go. On some levels neither Augustine nor his companion seemed to have had much of a voice in the arrangements. This was "family business," but Augustine went along with the process. What the girl's family would gain was someone close to the imperial court with good promise for future high office. What Augustine gained was an entrance into an aristocratic family and wealth. What is remarkable is that Augustine dares to recount the whole affair. He could, after all, have left it out altogether. That narrative—especially in relation to the woman who was torn from his side—has fueled some present-day accounts of Augustine as "antiwoman." To this author, however, that way of thinking misses the heart of his retelling of the sad affair. Augustine portrayed the unnamed woman as truly noble; she, in fact, is the only one who is thus praised.

Augustine was about 30 years of age at this time, and his bride-to-be was two years below a marriageable age. We know that 12 was the minimum age for a legal marriage in Augustine's world and most young women were married by age 16. While we cannot be absolutely certain of the age of Augustine's betrothed there is no doubt that she was very young by modern standards. High infant mortality rates surely led the ancients to think differently about the age of those who married.

Although publicly Augustine was seen as "having it all," and by his own account, he maintained a strong public persona; within himself, however, a disturbing revolution was underway. He had already abandoned Manichaeism and was now a catechumen, but the concerns that had driven him to the Religion of Mani were still there—and still unresolved. What is happiness? What is truth? What is evil? Who is God? These and still other questions were boiling just below the surface as haunting questions. While Augustine had begun to realize that Catholic Christianity might offer him credible answers, this was still rather vague, not something practical or concrete. His own thinking was still scarred by the "materialism" and the "dualism" of Manichaeism: God appeared to be an extended ethereal body, and evil was felt as a relentless threat to anything good.

All of these questions ultimately echoed back to Augustine himself: What about me? What will make me happy? Will I ever come to the Truth? Why am I so bound to evil deeds? Where is God in all this? Who is this God? Augustine was, as usual, a questioner and a dedicated student who could not be content with simplistic answers to the questions that long tormented him. Providentially, it seems that Milan was experiencing a veritable intellectual-religious renaissance at the time of Augustine's sojourn there; that experience proved decisive for his exit from the intellectual quagmire that held him fast. Frequent attendance at Ambrose's preaching gradually chipped away at his materialistic categories of thinking. He also encountered other intellectually gifted thinkers (whether Christian or not) who exposed him to what scholars today call "Neo-Platonism" (Augustine and his colleagues would have called it "Platonism"). The thinker whose writings were most closely associated with this philosophical renaissance was Plotinus (†270 CE). Although he wrote only in Greek, he eventually settled in Rome and became renowned for his original reinterpretation of Plato. By the time Augustine arrived in Milan his works were available in Latin translation. The Platonism of Plotinus had a deeply spiritual dimension and a developed "method of interiority" that invited the wisdom-seeker to undertake a journey "within." Some aspects of Plotinus' thought seemed to resonate well with certain Christian doctrines, such that a bishop like Ambrose could bring Plotinus into dialogue with Christian thinking and with the Scripture. One way or another Augustine would have discovered Plotinian ideas was by listening attentively to Ambrose. To Ambrose's voice would have been added that of the Milanese priest Simplicianus, Ambrose's spiritual father. It was Simplicianus who initiated Ambrose into the faith, both spiritually and intellectually (see *conf.* VIII.2.3). He had an important role in Augustine's spiritual and intellectual development in Milan—perhaps as much or even more than Ambrose had. A holy man and dedicated scholar, although he left us no writings, he was very much at home with the writings of Plotinus, and he acted as a guide and mentor for Augustine's own reading and study. Someone else had provided Augustine with what he calls the "books of the Platonists" (*conf.* VII.9.13), books that Augustine seemingly devoured with the same intensity as that of the Hortensius during his student days in Carthage. This reading, Augustine will tell us, and his subsequent conversations with Simplicianus, had a conversion-like impact on Augustine. He began to be able to conceive of spiritual reality, such that God did not have to be thought of as an "immense body," and he began to get behind the haunting question of "whence evil." Those efforts opened him to fundamental questions about human freedom and responsibility.

Especially in Books VI through VIII of his *Confessions* Augustine offers a description of an intellectual-spiritual itinerary that is intense, if not overwhelming; those books have provided a classic example of conversion and religious experience. It is marked by heights of spiritual insight and depths of painful frustration, narrated with a passion and beauty in a mesmerizing and carefully constructed Latin narrative. Scholars have found here a veritable gold mine, and many have tried to draw from the pulsing narrative a more precise outline of the unfolding of ideas and experiences Augustine underwent. Philosophers, in particular, interested in how Neo-Platonism and Plotinian thought were ingested by Augustine, have sought to unpack and dissect the narrative to argue for finding there a precise content of philosophical concepts and a fixed path of spiritual unfolding. But, in many ways, the narrative resists such precision. One should perhaps think of Augustine in this period as being bombarded with new ideas and intense moments of spiritual insight in a "zigzagging and spiraling" kind of way that resists any overly precise linear narrative or specific formula: "What agonizing birth-pangs tore my heart, what groans it uttered, O my God!" (*conf.* VII.7.11). More than a decade later, as Augustine remembers that period of intellectual and spiritual rebirth in Milan, it is clear that it was a time of great pain and great promise, no merely academic exercise. What happened was transformative:

> Advised by these [Platonic] writings that I must return to myself, I entered under your guidance the innermost places of my being; but only because you had become my helper was I able to do so. I entered, then, and with the vision of my spirit, such as it was, I saw the incommutable light far above my spiritual ken, transcending my mind: not this common light which every carnal eye can see, nor any light of the same order but greater, as though this common light were shining much more powerfully, far more brightly, and so extensively as to fill the universe. The light I saw was not this common light at all, but something different, utterly different, from all these things. Nor was it higher than my mind in the sense that oil floats on water or the sky is above the earth; it was exalted because this very light made me, and I was below it because by it I was made. Anyone who knows truth knows it, and whoever knows it knows eternity. Love knows it. (*conf.* VII.10.16)

It may be surprising to think that philosophical texts can stimulate such religious and mystical outcomes. Augustine eloquently exhibits in this excerpt why Neo-Platonism was so attractive to highly sophisticated thinkers who were looking for something more than clever philosophical theories. Their writings proposed a pathway to transcendent union and spelled out the steps toward such union, one that required a disciplined mental attentiveness that proceeded step by step to dizzying heights of contemplation. Augustine provides a vivid account of his own efforts to undertake this pathway:

> Thus I pursued my inquiry by stages, from material things to the soul that perceives them through the body, and from there to that inner power of the soul to which the body's senses report external impressions. The intelligence of animals can reach as far as this. I proceeded further and come to the power of discursive reason, to which the data of our senses are referred for judgment. Yet as found in me even reason acknowledged itself to be subject to change, and stretched upward to the source of its own intelligence, withholding its thoughts from the tyranny of habit and detaching itself from the swarms of noisy phantasms. It strove to discover what this light was that bedewed it when it cried out unhesitatingly that the Unchangeable is better than anything liable to change; it

sought the fount whence flowed its concept of the Unchangeable – for unless it had in some fashion recognized Immutability, it could never with such certainty have judged it superior to things that change. And then my mind attained to That Which Is, in the flash of one tremulous glance. Then indeed did I perceive your invisible reality through created things, but to keep my gaze there was beyond my strength. I was forced back through weakness and returned to my familiar surrounding, bearing with me only a loving memory, one that yearned for something of which I had caught the fragrance, but could not feast upon. (*conf.* VII.17.23)

His incredible powers of description evoke the image of someone ascending on a path that winds through fascinating landscapes; each step along the way requires a bold step forward and upward, and around each bend he kept encountering an ever more dazzling panorama, climbing higher and higher. Somehow the summit—That Which Simply Is—is reached, presenting a view that is both unanticipated and overwhelming. Its stunning impact propels the seeker back to everyday reality—with only a burning memory of a fleeting moment of ecstasy. Recent scholars have coined a precise label to describe what these philosophical writings Augustine encountered were about: spiritual exercises. These texts spoke of transformation and of union with ultimate reality and, to that end, offered a kind of spiritual road map to guide the seeker along the way to the desired destination. They not only talked about ultimate reality, but they also presented a way to encounter it. Augustine was clearly enthralled by what he had discovered and experienced.

Enthralled, he was—but frustrated as well. As Augustine recounts it, his efforts to experience the reality of God only take him so far; then, he finds himself dragged back to reality by the weight of his own habits and unruly desires. Both the philosophy and the Christianity he found in Ambrose's Milan were highly spiritualized; both the philosophical life proposed by the writings he was devouring and the Christian life preached by Ambrose manifested little concern for bodily pleasures and material success. Both a flowering career and an impending marriage were the flip side of a life unthinkable without comfortable wealth and bodily intimacy. In the Christianity that Augustine encountered in the late fourth-century pleasures of the body and riches in the bank held little sway among those who wished to excel spiritually; that stance was reaffirmed by the texts he read and the Ambrosian sermons he heard. Augustine did not envision a path for himself other than the most excellent one. It was not possible for him to stop with or be content with the "new knowledge" that had given him a new outlook on life. That knowledge had to become, in some way, a way of life, a lifestyle. All of those factors brought him to a crossroads-experience, but he found himself unable to make a decision—and that is when the real crisis began for him.

Augustine recounts a series of "events" which plunged him into a deep spiritual turmoil. Augustine invites his readers, especially in his *Confessions*, into his inner struggle in ways that are unprecedented; as people read that inner story again and again, it has had an ongoing, even lasting impact upon Western attitudes toward the self, that is, toward an understanding of the individual person. Writing about that which may seem like a series of events, Augustine was able to reflect on them as moments of bright insight and sudden rupture, as happenings which became dilemmas and turning points with spiritual consequences. Augustine's personal experiences thus became an invitation to subsequent generations to pay attention to the discernment of individual motives and values.

The "events" that Augustine described included theological matters, such as the nature of God or beliefs about Jesus Christ, anthropological questions about what "truly human" means, and moral dilemmas relating to human willing and happiness. At the time of a previous crisis, which had been precipitated by his reading of Cicero's Hortensius and had inspired a thirst for wisdom, Augustine had turned to the Bible. At that time, he was "put off" by its lack of any literary elegance. Now, nearly fifteen years later, he once again turned to the Bible. Much had changed since those youthful days in Carthage:

> It was therefore with intense eagerness that I seized on the hallowed calligraphy of your Sprit, and most especially the writings of the apostle Paul. In earlier days it had seemed to me that his teaching was self-contradictory, and in conflict with the witness of the law and prophets, but now as these problems melted away your chaste words presented a single face to me, and I learned to rejoice with reverence. So I began to read, and discovered that every truth I had read in those other books [of the philosophers] was taught here also, but now inseparable from your gift of grace, so that no one who sees can boast as though what he sees and the very power to see it were not from you [God] – for who has anything that he has not received (see 1 Cor. 4; 7). (*conf.* VII.21.27)

As always, it must be kept in mind that Augustine's account is a decade-later retrospective. But he does present this "turning-point" in a striking way. His choice of language in the Latin is anything but neutral: "I seized on" (*arripui*) describes his approach to the Bible, and especially to the Letters of St. Paul. This was no casual reading adventure; the language conveys ardor and intensity (arripui may be described as the frenzied tearing open of a long-awaited letter from a dearly beloved to seize its contents). But Augustine is not speaking about the Bible in general; he mentions the Letters of St. Paul quite specifically. This marks the "beginning" of a relationship with the apostle Paul that will profoundly shape his subsequent thought and, in turn, profoundly condition the role of Saint Paul in all of Western Christianity, down to the present. "Beginning" was deliberately placed in quotes because, as Augustine notes in his narrative, there was another, earlier reading of Paul, most likely when he was one of the Manichees; they set Paul against the Old Testament (the witness of the law and prophets) so as to deny the its value. When Augustine also notes that, previously, he had found Paul's teaching to be self-contradictory, he is probably referring to Manichaean efforts to show various Pauline inconsistencies; at that time he could not refute their arguments (see the classic example of this difficulty at work in Augustine's *Contra Faustum* 11.4). Now it all began to fit together under the guidance of Ambrose's preaching and from the "religious instruction" he was receiving from Simplicianus and other members of the Milanese community.

Added interior pressure came from another distinct source, that is, from stories and examples of dramatic Christian conversions. Augustine learned from friends and acquaintances of three such accounts, and in each instance something touched his heart deeply. Simplicianus told him the story of the public conversion to Christianity of the distinguished intellectual and Neo-Platonist, Marius Victorinus. Then, a friend, Ponticianus, recounted two stories in one: it was about two imperial officers who found a copy of *The Life of Antony of the Desert* by chance and were converted to the monastic life it described.

This *Life of Antony*, written by Athanasius of Alexandria and published in Greek shortly after Antony's death in 356 CE, was quickly translated into Latin and immediately become an ancient equivalent of a "best seller." It had a profound impact throughout the Roman world as many found themselves overwhelmed by the story of Antony abandoning all things to live as a desert monk. Many followed suit—abandoning worldly careers and living lives of celibacy and withdrawal from the world. That is precisely what the two friends of Ponticianus did, and Augustine was profoundly touched by their story. A call to a life of celibacy and withdrawal began to gnaw at Augustine, but he had neither the will nor the courage to take such a step. As Augustine recounts it, Ponticianus' account ignited within him a furious internal dialogue and debate filled with challenge and reproach:

> My conscience gnawed away at me in this fashion, and I was fiercely shamed and flung into hideous confusion while Ponticianus was relating all this. Having brought the conversation to a close and settled his business with us, he [Alypius] returned to his place, and I to myself. Was anything left unsaid in my inner debate. (*conf.* VIII.7.18)

All this had been ignited by an impromptu visit by Ponticianus to Augustine and Alypius, and, when Ponticianus left, Augustine plunged ever more deeply into crisis. He finally had reached his breaking point, and ever close at hand was Alypius, his "heart brother" (*conf.* IX.4.7). Tears accompanied by emotional distress and the kind of bodily turmoil that often accompanies such intense internal upheaval overtook Augustine, as Alypius stepped back but not away. Augustine wrote, "All this argument in my heart raged only between myself and myself. Alypius stood fast at my side, silently awaiting the outcome of my unprecedented agitation" (*conf.* VIII.11.27).

What follows are perhaps the most read and studied 536 words of Western religious literature: Augustine's recounting of his "conversion." The term is deliberately put between quotation marks because of the various and diverse interpretations given to it especially over the past century or so by scholars, whether they are devoutly religious or fervently areligious. Augustine's agitation took him into the inner garden of his house in Milan where he threw himself on the ground under a fig tree. Then, amid his own cries and tears, he heard a voice coming from nearby: Tolle! Lege! Tolle! Lege! or "Pick up and read! Pick up and read!" He heard those words, he recounts, as a divine call, and, returning to where he had been, he snatched up the Letters of Paul (once again he arripui) and opened it at random. His eyes fell on Romans 13:13-14 where Paul asks his readers to abandon a life of vice and sensuality, adding "Put on the Lord Jesus Christ." In Augustine's day, that text was associated with Christian baptism. Paul's words finally accomplished what all of his searching and striving failed to accomplish for the past decade and a half. As he recounts it, the decision to "live totally for God" exploded upon him and so he resolved to do. Subsequently, he would break off his engagement to marry, resign his imperial position, give up his desire for "worldly honor and success," and live as a servus Dei, a servant of God. He told Alypius what had just happened within, and Alypius told Augustine what was happening to him as well. Alypius then took the book from him and read the verse which followed. The result was the same. Together they went in to Monnica and told her that her prayers have been answered. No marriage, no career . . . Convertisti enim me ad te (VIII.12.30) is how he states it: You [God] converted me to you!—and not, I converted to you God! Augustine would never be the same—nor would Western Christianity.

Reading Augustine: *Conf.* VIII.12.28-30

Augustine tells the story of the moment of crisis which he shared with Alypius and which finally gave him peace.

> But as this deep meditation dredged all my wretchedness up from the secret profundity of my being and heaped it all together before the eyes of my heart, a huge storm blew up within me and brought on a heavy rain of tears. In order to pour them out unchecked with the sobs that accompanied them I arose and left Alypius, for solitude seemed to me more suitable for the business of weeping. I withdrew far enough to ensure that his presence – even his – would not be burdensome to me. This was my need, and he understood it, for I think I had risen to my feet and blurted out something, my voice already choked with tears. He accordingly remained, in stunned amazement, at the place where we had been sitting. I flung myself down somehow under a fig-tree and gave free rein to the tears that burst from my eyes like rivers, as an acceptable sacrifice to you. Many things I had to say to you, and the gist of them, though not the precise words, was: "O Lord, how long? How long? Will you be angry for ever? Do not remember our age-old sins." For by these I was conscious of being held prisoner. I uttered cries of misery: "Why must I go on saying, 'Tomorrow... tomorrow'? Why not now? Why not put an end to my depravity this very hour? I went on talking like this and weeping in the intense bitterness of my broken heart. Suddenly I heard a voice from a house nearby – perhaps a voice of some boy or girl, I do not know – singing over and over again, "Pick it up and read, pick it up and read." My expression immediately altered and I began to think

hard whether children ordinarily repeated a ditty like this in any sort of game, but I could not recall ever having heard it anywhere else. I stemmed the flood of tears and rose to my feet, believing that this could be nothing other than a divine command to open the Book and read the first passage I chanced upon; for I had heard the story of how Antony had been instructed by a gospel text. He happened to arrive while the gospel was being read, and took the words to be addressed to himself when he heard, "Go and sell all you possess and give the money to the poor: you will have treasure in heaven. Then come, follow me." So he was promptly converted to you by this plainly divine message. Stung into action, I returned to the place where Alypius was sitting, for on leaving it I had put down there the book of the apostle's letters. I snatched it up, opened it and read in silence the passage on which my eyes first lighted: "Not in dissipation and drunkenness, nor in debauchery and lewdness, nor in arguing and jealousy; but put on the Lord Jesus Christ, and make no provision for the flesh or the gratification of your desires." I had no wish to read further, nor was there need. No sooner had I reached the end of the verse than the light of certainty flooded my heart and all dark shades of doubt fled away. I closed the book, marking the place with a finger between the leaves or by some other means, and told Alypius what had happened. My face was peaceful now. He in return told me what had been happening to him without my knowledge. He asked to see what I had read: I showed him, but he looked further than my reading had taken me. I did not know what followed, but the next verse was, "Make room for the person who is weak in faith." He referred this text to himself and interpreted it to me. Confirmed by this admonition he associated himself with my decision and good purpose without any upheaval or delay, for it was entirely in harmony with his own moral character, which for a long time now had been far, far better than mine. We went indoors and told my mother, who was overjoyed. (*conf.* VIII.12.28–30)

6

Augustine the Convert—
Comings and Goings

Eleven years after Augustine finished his rhetorical studies in Carthage (375 CE), he began a journey that took him home to Thagaste then back to Carthage and then to Rome and Milan. The event in the garden that brought those years to culmination took place sometime in early August, 386 CE. The eleven years that follow will be just as remarkable and challenging for Augustine, culminating in the Third Council of Carthage on August 28, 397 CE in which he participated as a bishop. His name is registered in the official acts of that council: "Augustine, bishop of the people of Hippo Regius" (*Augustinus episcopus plebis hipponensium regionum subscripsi*—CCL.149.341). One can mark the eleven years from August 386 CE to August 397 CE by highlighting four geographical locations: Cassiciacum, Ostia (Rome), Thagaste, and Hippo Regius. Each setting will provide Augustine with new opportunities and challenges; each in its own way was as decisive for his future as was the garden event in Milan.

Augustine took advantage of the vintage holidays, early in the fall of 386 CE, to resign from his official posts in Milan (for more, see *conf.* IX.1.1–4.7). A lung problem that afflicted him at this time allowed him to request a departure for medical reasons. That meant that he did not need to publicize his "new self" but could retire discretely. Along with the household for which he was responsible in Milan, his extended family, and some like-minded friends, Augustine sought refuge in the hills outside of Milan, a place he calls Cassiciacum. There he lived in a country villa that his wealthy friend and patron Verecundus offered him. So, in the fall of 386 CE, Augustine began a new life along with several others.

Cassiciacum

They formed a small, rustic community in Cassiciacum—located perhaps where present-day Cassago Brianza is found, that is, about 18 miles northeast of Milan. It was a rather disparate group: Augustine; his mother, Monnica; his son, Adeodatus; his brother, Navigius; two young cousins, Lastidianus and Rusticus, neither with very much education; two teenage students, Licentius, son of Romanianus, and Trygetius; and Alypius, his closest friend. During the few months he spent there, Augustine regained his health, settled his nerves after the spiritual and emotional turmoil he underwent in Milan, reflected on this life that had finally given him peace, began to think about his next step in life, and inaugurated a literary career. Because of the four books that are the product of this retreat-like sojourn, Cassiciacum has become a focus of intense interest, scrutiny, and, not surprisingly, controversy. The reasons for controversy are not limited to what Augustine wrote there. Rather, when he gives a retrospective account of the time at Cassiciacum in Book IX of his *Confessions*, there appears to be some tension between this latter narrative and what we find in the earlier four books. Since these were the first published works that have been preserved, they have been minutely and repeatedly dissected. Augustine never anticipated how these works would capture the attention of more than 1,600 years of scholarship.

Before speaking about the books themselves, however, something needs to be said about him in the Fall of 386 CE. Now 32 years of age, he was—according to Roman tradition—a young man (*juvenis*), that is, someone standing on the threshold of adult and public life. In many ways Augustine had already crossed that threshold when he held the public imperial position of rhetor; his prospective and advantageous marriage would have confirmed his status. All of that pointed to a promising future. But Augustine had crossed back over that threshold, seemingly leaving the promised fame behind.

Practically speaking, what did his "conversion" mean? He was no longer imperial rhetor; he was no longer engaged. He tells us that he was "no longer seeking a wife or entertaining any worldly hope, for you [God] had converted me to yourself" (*conf.* VIII.11.30). But that is a statement of what he no longer was, not a clear affirmation of what he had in mind. What exactly was he? This time away at Cassiciacum, a time of retreat and reflection, gave him the chance to begin to respond to that question. The intellectual dimension, as usual, had its usual, prominent place. This can be seen by reading the four writings that emerge from this rather short time span. But scholars, especially over the past 100 years, have asked how to characterize that dimension. Was Augustine a philosopher? A believer? What was the importance of philosophy and what was its relation to Christian faith for Augustine at this time?

In 1918 CE, a prominent French scholar by the name of Prosper Alfaric (*L'Évolution intellectuelle de Saint Augustin*, Paris, 1918 CE) asserted that Augustine's conversion was not really to religion but to philosophy. Augustine, he says, went to Cassiciacum as a Neo-Platonist, not as a Christian. Today, few, if any, subscribe to Alfaric's stark labeling, but most scholars recognize the strongly Neo-Platonic quality in these first writings. While these texts are highly intellectual, it must also be noticed that Monnica, a woman without formal education, emerges as one of the wisest voices in them. These texts take the form of philosophical dialogues, and the terms *philosophia* and *ratio*, occur prolifically.

But *Deus*, the Latin for God, is even more frequently used. Since Augustine would never have thought of opposing philosophy and faith, his view of the matter would not have understood how the believer and the thinker could be contrasted. But these works were intended for thoughtful readers, including those who believe or at least those Augustine wants to become believers. These four writings are named: *Against the Academicians*, *On the Happy Life*, *On Order*, and *The Soliloquies*.

Four Thoughtful Treatises

Begun first, but only completed later, Against the Academicians is a frontal assault on philosophical skepticism because of its compromising attitude toward the pursuit of truth. Augustine dedicates it to his patron Romanianus, whom he won over to the Manichees, and the work is an invitation to Romanianus to join Augustine in abandoning error and embracing the incarnate Christ (3.19). Augustine manifests his confidence about the attainment of truth, a possibility that he sees as inseparable from dedicated life-commitment. This stance is perhaps most powerfully evident in an appeal to Romanianus at the outset of Book II where Augustine recounts his own wanderings on the path of error and the amazement he experienced when he picked up the books of the Platonists and returned to himself. Throughout this work, the close link of truth and happiness is present, but the constant question asks whether that happiness consists in simply looking for the truth or requires that one actually attain that truth.

His book, *The Happy Life*, which was completed before *Against the Academicians*, has a more distinctly religious flavor to it. Thus, Monnica emerges as a central interlocutor in the dialogue. The happy life is none other than union with the God who is Truth, for which we must strive "with solid faith, lively hope, and ardent love" (4.35). The happiness of the soul, therefore, is to know— reverently and fully—who leads to Truth, what Truth brings rejoicing, and how Truth joins one to the One who is Supreme. His thoughtful exposition brings him, by the end of the dialogue, to that which the church already has: a Christian framework for understanding happiness.

On Order is Augustine's first written exploration of the problem of evil. The word "order" in the title refers to God's providential guidance of all God's own creation. Nothing is outside the pale of God's design, and so everything within creation must be understood within a divine framework, including evil. In his later writings, he pursued the question of evil with greater depth and philosophical acumen, but for now it is enough for him to assert, against the Manichees, that God is not the author of evil, nor is evil outside God's providential governance. To come to such knowledge requires more than intelligence and study, one must undergo "purification" and "ascent," that is, an inner transformation that draws strength from the liberal arts. One then begins by studying material things and gradually ascends to spiritual reality. That exercise prepares one to accept the authority of God. That process, therefore, is a clarion call to faith. In the embrace of this religious authority, in fact, reason (ratio) can begin to soar beyond its own capacity.

In these first three dialogues, Augustine intellectually engages and challenges his fellow sojourners at Cassiciacum—and they also challenge Augustine. The conversations, often rather daunting, take place indoors and outdoors, but they are interrupted for meals. There is joking, praying, reproving, and celebration. In presenting these conversations against such a backdrop, Augustine knows well that he is following a venerable Roman tradition that goes back to similar conversations enshrined in the writings of Cicero and Horace. Such gatherings were described with the Latin term *otium*. They were a kind of scholarly retreat into the countryside.

The final dialogue stands apart, as is clear from its provocative title, the Soliloquies. The title word is, in fact, invented by Augustine—a dialogue with himself. After Augustine, that word will enter into common usage. It takes the form of two books (a third was envisioned but never completed) and takes us deeply into Augustine's own inner self. There is a marked "spiritualizing" emphasis in the dialogue, a profound awareness that the body and bodily pleasures serve only to obstruct Augustine's desire to ascend to God. In some ways he is still haunted by the years of "intimate embrace"; he has left those experiences behind, but the memories are still with him. Readers of the work are almost always struck by the starkness of the dialogue: the interlocutors are himself and reason (*ratio*). Scholars are divided as to whether *ratio* refers to Augustine's reason or to "reason in general," that is, to the *ratio* which transcends any individual and is shared equally by every individual. One of the most commented upon parts of this dialogue occurs at the outset of Book II:

> Reason: What exactly do you want to know?
> Augustine: Those very things I've prayed for.
> Reason: Briefly, what are they?
> Augustine: God and the soul I desire to know.
> Reason: Nothing more?
> Augustine: Absolutely nothing. (Soliloques 2.1)

Nothing more than God and the soul Volumes have been written on this comment. Has Augustine fled into himself? Or do we have here the basis of all other knowledge?

Because of what they may reveal to us about Augustine as he stood at this life-changing junction, and because they are, in themselves, both provocative and perplexing, much has been written about these four works. Controversy still swirls around the question of their historicity: few describe them as pure fiction, and virtually all agree that some literary refashioning has taken place. They were recorded by a stenographer, and subsequently "edited" and "published." It seems that they were read by Augustine's friends in Milan within a few months of their writing. They manifest Augustine's heart and mind at the time just before his baptism.

Recent studies have demonstrated that, behind the narrative, there are indications that Augustine was already engaged in an intensive reading program of Christian literature and there was an ever-increasing presence of the Bible. It is not surprising that there are references to Cicero and Vergil throughout the dialogues, nor that the approach to the liberal arts that underlies much of these dialogues suggests the influence of Varro, nor that the philosophical writings of the Neo-Platonists lurk just below the surface. But some scholars see in these works an attempt by Augustine to articulate what might be called Christian philosophy as *the true philosophy*, one that demonstrates a sensitive compatibility between Platonism and biblical Christianity. It is, in fact, at the beginning of Book II of the *Against the Academicians* that Augustine's offers his very first scriptural reference, or perhaps better allusion, a discrete quoting of 1 Cor. 1:24 regarding Christ as the "power and wisdom" of God. The Latin terms are telling: Christ as *virtus* (it can mean both power and virtue), Christ as *sapientia* (and Augustine reminds his interlocutors in *Against the Academicians* that the term philosophy means "the love of wisdom—*amor sapientiae*" (2.3). Late in life, Augustine will look back at these writings and affirm them, cautioning his readers that he mistakenly saw too much "equivalence" between Christianity and philosophy, that his terminology was too secular, that in retrospect he detects the presence of a subtle pride, that is, he attributed too much to the human and not enough to the divine. As such, these works provide a profile of his "first steps," not of his "final steps."

Baptism

Sometime early in 387 CE, Augustine returned to Milan where he formally submitted his name for baptism, joined by Adeodatus and Alypius:

> The time arrived for me to give in my name for baptism, so we left the country and moved back to Milan. Alypius had decided to join me in being re-born in you, and was already clothed with the humility that befitted your mysteries . . . We associated the boy Adeodatus with us as well, my son according to the flesh, born of my sin . . . We included him in the group as our contemporary in the life of your grace, to be schooled along with us in your doctrine . . . And so we were baptized, and all our dread about our earlier life dropped away from us. During the days that followed I could not get enough of the wonderful sweetness that filled me as I meditated upon your deep design for the salvation of the human race. How copiously I wept at your hymns and canticles, how intensely was I moved by the lovely harmonies of your singing Church! Those voices flooded my ears, and the truth was distilled into my heart until it overflowed in loving devotion; my tears ran down, and I was the better for them. (conf. IX.6.14)

Some historians are disappointed that among Augustine's letters we do not have his request sent to Bishop Ambrose for baptism. Earlier in Book IX, Augustine tells us that he had sent several letters to Milan from Cassiciacum, one would have been addressed to city officials to announce his official resignation for health reasons. Since the Cassiciacum retreat began at the outset of a holiday period, there was no need for him to announce his departure at that moment. Another letter would have been to Ambrose, informing him of his intentions and requesting some reading advice (see *conf.* IX.5.13). Once back in Milan he would have sent another letter to begin the formal process of baptismal preparation. We do have other letters from the period, especially a remarkable correspondence between Augustine and intimate friend Nebridius, but Augustine remains quite discrete about those final months of his preparation for baptism.

Was Augustine exercising the "discipline of the secret," an early Christian practice of not talking publicly about sacramental rites nor allowing the unbaptized to witness them? We do know that his preparation for baptism was demanding: instruction, fasting, some prebaptismal ceremonies, and interrogations regarding the seriousness of one's intentions. His silence about his preparation for baptism, therefore, is most likely a sign of the very personal character of that process. It is possible to surmise that, in this time period, Augustine came into contact with a monastic foundation of Ambrose. He does not tell us what prompted his interest nor that contact, but some scholars see the beginning of an idea that blossomed when he returned to Africa: the monastic Augustine. Augustine was also quite restrained about his experience of baptism, but present day tourists and pilgrims can still visit the large baptismal pool that he and his companions descended into—a part of the excavations beneath the present-day Duomo of Milan.

In the midst of his preparation for baptism, Augustine did find time to write a draft of Book III of the *Soliloquies*. He named it *The Immortality of the Soul*. Late in life, when he looked back on this work, he found it quite unintelligible. In fact, he never intended to publish it; he did, however, want to continue the reflection that he had begun in the *Soliloquies*, and that shows that Augustine's interest in the nature and origin of the human soul was ongoing. It would, in fact, interest him for the rest of his life. Even in the midst of the intense religious dedication required of baptismal preparation, Augustine did not abandon his intellectual interests, presumably because of the importance he attached to understanding his faith.

One of his more intriguing works of the period is his *On Music*, begun in Milan but finished in Africa. Despite the title, it is not the kind of work that would lead a musician into the concert hall, but an esoteric work that deals with the nature of harmony, sound, rhythm, intervals, and the like. Underlying it is an attempt to lay out a pathway from the material to the immaterial, and that is, therefore, about the music of the soul.

If the waters of baptism in Milan brought peace to Augustine's soul, the time spent in Milan also seemed to bring clarity to Augustine's plans.

> You gather like-minded people to dwell together, and so you brought into our fellowship a young man named Evodius, who was from our home town. While serving as an administrative officer in the Special Branch he had been

converted to you before we were; he was then baptized and abandoned his secular career to enlist in your service. We stayed together, and made a holy agreement to live together in the future. In search of a place where we could best serve you, we made arrangements to return as a group to Africa. And while we were at Ostia on the Tiber my mother died. (*conf.* IX.8.17)

He and his party of fellow-Africans took leave of Milan, probably during the summer of 387 CE, to begin the long and demanding journey that would take them back to Africa.

Ostia

One of the most remarkably well-preserved cities of the ancient world is only a short distance from the center of present-day Rome, the archaeological site now referred to as Ostia Antica—Ancient Ostia. One can still see the mosaic floors of the ancient equivalent of a modern travel agency where travelers like Augustine and his party paid for passage to Carthage. They would have had to pass through Rome to reach Rome's port, Ostia, lodging there and not in Rome to recover from the effects of a demanding three-week journey from Milan, preparing themselves for their return passage to Africa. Two events intervened, one deeply personal, the other, political. The little community of Milan remained virtually intact for the journey home: it included Augustine, Monnica, Adeodatus, Navigius, Alypius, Evodius, and the two young cousins. Hospitality was probably offered by the Christian community at Ostia. Not long after their arrival there, Monnica took sick. But some days before that, as Augustine recounts in Book IX of the *Confessions*, he and his mother were engaged in deep conversation about spiritual matters. As they talked together, something special happened as they ascended to the heights of contemplation. Augustine describes the moment:

> 10.24 Our colloquy led us to the point where the pleasures of the body's senses, however intense and in however brilliant a material light enjoyed, seemed unworthy not merely of comparison but even of remembrance beside the joy of that life, and we lifted ourselves in longing yet more ardent toward *That Which Is*, and step by step traversed all bodily creatures and heaven itself, whence sun and moon and stars shed their light upon the earth. Higher still we mounted by inward thought and wondering discourse on your works, and we arrived at the summit of our own minds; and this too we transcended, to touch that land of never-failing plenty where you pasture Israel for ever with the food of truth. Life there is the Wisdom through whom all these things are made, and all others that have been or ever will be; but Wisdom herself is not made: she is as she always has been and will be for ever. Rather should we say that in her there is no "has been" or "will be," but only being, for she is eternal, but past and future do not belong to eternity. And as we talked and panted for it, we just touched the edge of it by the utmost leap of our hearts; then, sighing and unsatisfied, we left the first-fruits of our spirit captive there, and returned to the noise

of articulate speech, where a word has beginning and end. How different from your Word, our Lord, who abides in himself, and grows not old, but renews all things.

10.25 Then we said, "If the tumult of the flesh fell silent for someone, and silent too were the phantasms of earth, sea and air, silent the heavens, and the very soul silent to itself, that it might pass beyond itself by not thinking of its own being; if dreams and revelations known through its imagination were silent, if every tongue, and every sign, and whatever is subject to transience were wholly stilled for him —for if anyone listens, all these things will tell him, 'We did not make ourselves; he made us who abides for ever and having said this they held their peace for they had pricked the listening ear to him who made them; and then he alone were to speak, not through things that are made, but of himself, that we might hear his Word, not through fleshly tongue nor angel's voice, nor thundercloud, nor any riddling parable, hear him unmediated, whom we love in all these things, hear him without them, as now we stretch out and in a flash of thought touch that eternal Wisdom who abides above all things; if this could last, and all other visions, so far inferior, be taken away, and this sight alone ravish him who saw it, and engulf him and hide him away, kept for inward joys, so that this moment of knowledge — this passing moment that left us aching for more — should there be life eternal, would not *Enter into the joy of your Lord* be this, and this alone? And when, when will this be? When we all rise again, but not all are changed?"

10.26 So did I speak, though not in this wise exactly, nor in these same words. Yet you know, O Lord, how on that very day amid this talk of ours that seemed to make the world with all its charms grow cheap, she said, "For my part, my son, I find pleasure no longer in anything this life holds. What I am doing here still, or why I tarry, I do not know, for all worldly hope has withered away for me. One thing only there was for which I desired to linger awhile in this life: to see you a Catholic Christian before I died. And this my God has granted to me more lavishly than I could have hoped, letting me see you even spurning earthly happiness to be his servant. What now keeps me here?" (*conf.* IX.10.24–26)

The reader ought not to be surprised to learn that this little narrative has led to much speculation and commentary. It is virtually unique in ancient literature because it portrays a moment of mystical ecstasy that is not individual and private, but shared. Further, it involves a woman—which was certainly an unusual, even provocative, dimension of that story for the ancient, "masculine" world. In addition, the language of this narrative is both Neo-Platonic and biblical.

What Monnica and Augustine achieved a vision of God, enjoying God in a way that Augustine had found impossible when he spoke of his efforts in Book VII. The vision of Ostia allows them to find joy with God in anticipation of their final state of eternal association with him. The conversation that led to this contemplative ascension was about Christian ideas of the afterlife—one more aspect of the process whereby Augustine sought to give meaning to the events of his life. It is an account that tells Christians about the capacity for immediate knowledge of the divine—a statement by Augustine to his readers about the truth of Christianity. Augustine and Monnica encountered together and within themselves the Creator. Hence, Augustine is interested, not in a statement about his personal experience, but in a contemplation that is no mere platonic ascent but a touch of transcendent Wisdom.[1]

A few days after that event, Monnica succumbed to her illness; she was 56 years old. Book IX of the *Confessions*, written ten years later, gave Augustine the opportunity to remember that experience and to compose a remarkable literary epitaph to his mother. Over the intervening centuries, numerous artists have also chosen to represent that scene.

This deeply personal and unexpected loss delayed passage back to Africa. Political unrest—which may have hastened the departure of Augustine and his friends from Milan—further complicated matters. In the uncertainty that surrounded the political and military events, the sea lanes were no longer safe for travel. Augustine and his friends were forced to spend almost a year in Rome to await the resolution of those conflicts. We do not know where they lodged and what their contacts were during that time period.

This was Christian Rome, where Siricius was pope; it had become a place of pilgrimage because of the tombs of Peter and Paul. Basilicas had even been constructed over their tombs. But, years later, Augustine will only say that he and his companions had visited the shrine of St. Peter and were scandalized by the "sacred imbibing" that went on at the site of the tomb. Augustine continues to write during his ten-month or so stay.

It was perhaps in Rome that he made his final break with the Manichees. During this second sojourn there—keenly aware of the moral and spiritual hypocrisy of their leadership—he chose to write his very first anti-Manichaean treatise: the *Morals of the Catholic Church* (later to be complemented by *The Morals of the Manichees*). It contrasts the "lifestyle" (*mores* is the Latin term he uses) of the Catholic Church with that of the Manichees. Late in life he recounts that what prompted him was their bragging about exemplary living—he knew otherwise. This treatise was important for several reasons. Compared to his previous writings, it is more explicitly religious and biblical. Clearly, Augustine had studied more than the Neo-Platonists. It also has stunning comments about the centrality of love for the Christian religion and offers devout vignettes about the dedicated servants of God he encountered in some monasteries surrounding Rome. Augustine surely had the best interests of his former co-religionists firmly in mind, inviting them now to the true faith. For the first time, too, here are hints of "Augustine the Theologian."

A second work of the Roman sojourn, *The Greatness of the Soul*, is of a very different nature. In it, Augustine continues to explore a topic of great concern to him: the nature of the human soul. The work is a dialogue between

---

[1] The remarks in this paragraph depend on J. P. Kenny, *The Mysticism of Saint Augustine*, New York, Routledge, pp. 84–86.

Augustine and Evodius and shows how much the question remained a "work in progress" for Augustine. It reveals a still underling tension in Augustine regarding how "body and soul" can be a unity (although the soul definitely has priority) and lays out a program for progressive spiritual development by means of the soul's ascent away from the material and sensible to the spiritual and the intelligible.

A third book was begun, one that will not be completed until he returned home to Africa, *On Free Choice of the Will*. It is a serious attempt to confront head-on the haunting question that had kept him with the Manichees for so long: *whence evil*? The answer, Augustine argues, is to be found in human freedom, that is, in the choice of what is inferior, freely ignoring or rejecting what is superior, thus initiating a descending spiral of chaos and corruption with a host of death-dealing consequences. What Augustine insists upon most in this bold attempt to confront the question of evil is an affirmation already heard: God is not the author of evil, but its master. Evil does not and cannot threaten God's sovereign love for creature and creation. In fact, evil is not seen as a "something," but as the result of moving away from the One who is, from good. Augustine will thus call it the absence of good.

On August 28, 388 CE, with the defeat of Maximus and the end of the political crisis, preparations for the return voyage to Africa were set in motion. Sometime in early fall of 388 CE, Augustine and his party set sail for the return trip to his homeland, Africa, never again to leave it. After five years in Italy he returned as a different person, with a new life. The narrative that had, for nine books, described the progress toward his conversion and its immediate aftermath now shifts in tone and content. Book X gives some "hints" about subsequent unexpected happenings in his life; they will be recalled at the opportune time.

Thagaste: Home Again

If the winds were favorable, Augustine's ship could have arrived in Carthage in two to three days. Once they arrived there, they found hospitality with a friend Innocentius and made contact with the Catholic Christian community there. At the house of his friend he would have met a deacon named Aurelius. Before long, Aurelius will be the bishop of Carthage and his collaboration with Augustine will be close and effective. But neither of them would have suspected such an outcome at the time. Augustine re-established old relationships, for example, with a former student (*discipulus*) of his, Eulogius, who was now a teacher of rhetoric. Eulogius reminded Augustine about a dream he had in which Augustine helped him work out a vexing question he needed to teach about the following day. Augustine indeed had returned to a lively and spiritual world.

Everything indicates that he envisioned the sojourn in Carthage as provisional. Soon, he and his little group returned to the family property in Thagaste. It seems that Augustine did divest himself of that property by giving the title to

the local Church. He lived off the modest income generated from estate reve-
nues, that is, from receipts for the sale of sundry agricultural products.

That little community was made up of Augustine, his son, Adeodatus, Alypius, Evodius, and perhaps others. The life they lived together resembled Cassiciacum in some ways, though the setting was probably more humble. Today that
might strike people as "monastic," and in some ways it did resemble a monastery: celibacy, simple living, prayer, study, manual labor, conversations about
matters lofty and spiritual—such was the regimen at Thagaste. But, for Augustine, it was a matter of continuing his searching, together with friends.

Augustine, the author, added a second book to his *The Morals of the Catholic
Church*, this time dealing specifically with the morals of the Manichees. Also
preserved from this period is Augustine's correspondence with Nebridius—an
exchange of letters about a range of lofty topics: philosophy, the soul, the nature
of knowledge, religious belief. Those letters were sprinkled with many comments that reflect their deep friendship as well as the engaging dialogue of these
two friends. Nebridius pleads with Augustine to come join him at his country
villa outside of Carthage. Augustine responds with an invitation for Nebridius to
join the little community at Thagaste. Both seem poignantly aware that the geographical separation will not change, and that only intensifies the depth of
communication reflected in the letters.

In one of these letters, Nebridius somewhat chidingly remarks that the
townspeople of Thagaste need to be less demanding and more respectful of the
time and intellectual leisure of their neighbor. Augustine on his part seems unwilling to shut the door to them. Neither Augustine nor Nebridius go into detail
regarding the nature of these contacts, but it does seem clear that Augustine has
returned home with something like a celebrity status and that he is more than
willing to give his time. Was this assistance legal, religious, educational? There
is no way to know, but it does indicate that Augustine's "retirement" was of a
most energetic sort. Sometime during this period Nebridius, whose health always seemed to have been delicate, died. Clearly, that loss painful to Augustine;
the correspondence between them that has been preserved offers a lasting literary epitaph. He often referred to his friend as *meus Nebridius*, my Nebridius;
life in Augustine's world remained as fragile and precarious as ever.

At about this time, Augustine takes his writing another step with the composition of *On Genesis Against the Manichees*. Previously, Augustine's works
seem to have circulated privately. Hence, this appears to be Augustine's first
"public" writing. Significantly, it is a work of biblical exposition. He notes in
the introduction that he has been asked by some who have encountered his writings and found them too challenging to write something that the ordinary reader
could understand, especially in relation to "the perniciousness of the Manichees." Upon his return to Africa Augustine had encountered a vibrant Manichaeism that sought to proselytize in an aggressive way, broadcasting their
particular take on the Bible and on material creation. With this more popular
work, Augustine has not only attempted a new style of writing accessible to a
wider public, but he has also embarked upon new territory, attempting to com-

ment on a biblical text. There is clear indication that Augustine has been devoting extensive time to reading other Christian authors—even though he almost never tells us what author or work he is reading. There is something original and exciting about Augustine's engagement with the Bible. At this stage, he has begun to pay attention to the Book of Genesis, and one can presume that, in preparation for baptism, he heard or at least knew about the sermons preached by Ambrose on Genesis. He brings to the undertaking not only his expertise as a rhetorician and dialectician, but also a distinctive take on the biblical text that will leave his readers begging for more. A brief citation is suggestive:

> And God divided between the light and the darkness, and God called the light day, and the darkness he called night (Gen. 1:4-5). Here it does not say, "God made the darkness," because darkness as we have said above is just the absence of light. But still a distinction was made between the light and the darkness. Just as we make noise by shouting, while we make silence by not making a sound because silence is when the noise stops, and yet we distinguish by some kind of sense between noise and silence, and call one thing noise and the other silence, so just as we are rightly said to make silence, in the same way God is rightly said in many places of the divine scriptures to make darkness, because he either does not give light to times and places or else withdraws it from them, just as he chooses. This however is all said according to our way of understanding. In what language, after all, did God call the light day and the darkness night? Was it in Hebrew, or Greek, or Latin, or some other language? And so with all the other things he gave names to, you could ask what language he spoke. But with God there is just sheer understanding, without any utterance and diversity of tongue. (*On Genesis: A Refutation of the Manichees* 1.9.15)

Significantly, this is only the beginning of Augustine's labors with Genesis. He will return several times to writing a spiritual understanding of Genesis.

Two further works undertaken at Thagaste merit comment. Augustine's first work *Against the Academicians*, dedicated to his patron, Romanianus, was a concerted effort to lure him away from the Manichees. *On True Religion* has the same scope—it shows an Augustine who is maturing theologically and philosophically—always with a personal dimension that was his trademark. The work is an assault on Manichaean doctrine, especially their creation myth, as well as their method of biblical interpretation. Augustine's growing familiarity with the Christian Bible is evident. While the work manifests a robust philosophical sensitivity, there is also a stark criticism of any kind of philosophical practice that involves attempts to "contact the gods" through religious ritual—an effort that will be revived in his mature work, *The City of God*. The Neo-Platonist philosopher Porphyry is the apparent target here. He advocated the practice of theurgy, certain ritual practices that were believed to trigger religious encounters and personal transformation. There is a sensitive religious intensity throughout the text, as Augustine exhorts Romanianus to "go within":

> Do not go outside, come back into yourself. It is in the inner self that Truth dwells. And if you find your own nature to be subject to change, transcend even

yourself. But remember, when you are transcending yourself, that it is your reasoning soul transcending yourself. So then, direct your course to what the light of reason itself gets its light from. Where, after all, does every good reasoner arrive but at the truth. Since truth herself, of course, does not reach herself by a process of reasoning but is herself what reasoners are aiming at, see there the concord which cannot be surpassed, and put yourself in accord with her. Confess that you are not what she is – if in fact she does not seek herself, while you have sought her, and come to her, not by walking from one place to another but by the desire of your mind, so that the inner self might find in accord with its lodger not a carnal pleasure of the lowest sort but a spiritual pleasure. (On True Religion 39.72)

Do not go outside, come back into yourself. The interior method modeled in the previously written *Soliloquies* continues to develop. At Thagaste, he is certainly not simply an "intellectual" but begins to show himself a "spiritual master."

However, he was also father and teacher to his son Adeodatus. Perhaps the books on the liberal arts that Augustine had, while still in Milan, wanted to write were intended not just for a general readership, but most especially for his son. Tragedy struck, however, for Adeodatus died sometime around 390 CE. There is no way of telling the cause of death—an accident, there is no description of the cause of his death. However, Augustine leaves no doubt about the affection he had for his son and one can only imagine the sorrow. For a third time a literary epitaph took shape for one of Augustine's dearest, a book entitled *The Teacher*. It takes the form once again of a dialogue, this time between father and son. They discuss and explore the nature of language, learning, and knowledge—and Adeodatus excels as a student—and more: Augustine learns from his student, the student teaches Augustine.

> There is a book of ours entitled The Teacher, in which he [Adeodatus] converses with me. You know that all the thoughts there attributed to my interlocutor were truly his, although he was only about sixteen years old. Many other things even more wonderful did I observe in him. The brilliance he evinced filled me with awe, for who else but you could be the artificer of such prodigies? Very soon you took him away from this life on earth. . . . (*conf.* IX.6.14)

Augustine speaks warmly about his son, musing that he was gifted by God. It is striking that in the course of a few years Augustine lost three significant persons who were deeply imprinted upon his own heart and affections: Monnica, Nebridius, Adeodatus. In a work, *On True Religion,* which he wrote at this time, he says that "anyone who loves God with all their heart knows that those never perish who do not perish for God" (*True Religion* 47). If Augustine found consolation in his faith, humanly speaking, he must have found Thagaste filled with burdensome memories. It may be precisely for this reason that Augustine gave thought to relocating, and decided to pay a visit to near-by Hippo Regius, a bustling port city some 40 miles northwest of Thagaste. What he encountered in

Hippo Regius was absolutely unexpected—and once again, Augustine was forced to undertake a new life.

Hippo Regius

After his return to Africa from the Continent and his settling in Thagaste, how well-known was Augustine? He had already produced a remarkable number of writings, but this was the late fourth century when literacy was certainly not as developed as it is today and when "books" were hand-written and terribly expensive. Augustine makes a passing comment in writing to Romanianus about sending him *On True Religion* that reminds us that in his world "paper and post" was always problematic. But it almost seems that against such odds, Augustine's name and works began to circulate. In a sermon preached late in his life, and his first biographer Possidius echoed this, Augustine began to be circumspect in his travels, for fear of being unwillingly drafted into the clergy, an all-too-common practice of that time.

Augustine had, indeed, become a "man of the church" in many ways and in many eyes, but there is little indication that he sought to tie this to any official position; in fact, the contrary was closer to the truth. He referred to himself as a *servus Dei*, literally a servant of God, and in his world the title was slowly beginning to take on the meaning of monk, without implying anything official, formal, or overly organized. Every indication suggests that Augustine saw his future as an "independent" Christian thinker and intellectual, perhaps more a Christian philosopher than anything else—and judging from the volume of writings he had produced in the few short years after his conversion, he embraced this role with vigor and enthusiasm—and looked forward to an even more productive literary future. On a "business" journey to a not-too-distant Hippo Regius, that is, in search of a property for a religious community, all of this would suddenly be turned upside down.

Hippo Regius, a busy port city, was not Carthage, and it was certainly not Thagaste. Sailors could be heard cursing in Greek at the wharves where Africa's agricultural riches made their way to Rome and products from throughout the Mediterranean arrived in return. Augustine tells us he went there to try to recruit an acquaintance who not only indicated interest in Augustine's newly embraced way of life, but also because "I was looking for a place to establish a monastery, and live there with my brothers" (*serm.* 355.2). He also knew that Hippo Regius had a bishop already, so he thought that he could go there without fear. Augustine does not tell us why he was seeking to establish a monastery in Hippo Regius. One can only speculate. Augustine's conversation with the acquaintance became more complicated than expected and so he was obliged to stay longer than anticipated. While attending church in Hippo Regius one day, the elderly bishop, a man named Valerius, whose first language was Greek and who was less that fluent in Latin, told the gathered congregation that he was looking for a priest to assist him. What took place, as both Augustine and his first biographer Possidius recount it, was something in the nature of an "ambush." The people around Augustine began to shout his name and pushed him forward to the bishop—here was just the man Valerius and Hippo Regius needed. Augustine tells us that he cried and did his best to resist—but eventually gave in: "I was caught, I was made a priest, and from this office I eventually came to the episcopate" (*serm.* 355.2). Was Augustine set up? Did Valerius and others in the congregation know that Augustine was there and were they convinced he was just the man they needed? Or was it a kind of miracle? Perhaps for Augustine the answer did not matter—life had suddenly taken him where he never intended to go.

Reading Augustine: Possidius, Life of Augustine, Chapters 3 and 4

The Life of Augustine written by his contemporary, Possidius, provides a view of the events surrounding his conversion and return to Hippo Regius. The excerpts cited below deal with his desire for a reflective Christian life along with others and with his forced ordination as a priest:

Chapter 3, 1. Having received God's grace through the sacrament, Augustine decided that together with some fellow townsmen and friends who were likewise bent on serving God he would return to Africa and to his own house and property.

2. Thither he went and remained for about three years. He then renounced the property and, with those who had joined him, lived for God in fasting, prayer, and good works and in meditating day and night on the law of the Lord. The truths which God revealed to his mind in meditation and prayer he communicated to present and absent alike, instructing them in sermons and books.

3. It happened during this period that one of the people known as "imperial agents" was residing in Hippo Regius' and learned of his good reputation and teaching. The man was a good God-fearing Christian and had a keen desire to see Augustine, telling himself that if he were only privileged to hear the word of God from his mouth, he would surely be given strength to set aside all worldly lusts and attractions.

4. Augustine learned of this from a reliable person and because he wanted this soul to be delivered from the dangers of the present life and from eternal death, he immediately went of his own accord to Hippo. He met the man, spoke with him often, and exhorted him as persuasively as he could with God's help to fulfill his promises to God.

5. Day after day the man kept promising to do so, but as long as Augustine remained there, he did not carry out his promise. Surely, however, he derived some benefit and fruit from what divine providence was now everywhere accomplishing through this purified and ennobled instrument that was ready for the Lord's use in every good work.

Chapter 4, 1. The bishop of the Catholic Church of Hippo at this time was the saintly Valerius. The needs of the Church required him one day to speak urgently to the people about providing and ordaining a priest for the city. The

Catholics already knew of Augustine's way of life and teaching and they seized upon him as he stood peacefully in the congregation, unaware of what was to happen (for, as he used to tell us, when he was a layman he avoided only those churches that needed a bishop).

2. They therefore laid hold of him and, as is customary in these situations, brought him to the bishop to be ordained. With complete unanimity they asked that this be done, and demanded it with fervent cries. Meanwhile Augustine wept copiously; there were some, he himself told us, who attributed these tears to pride and tried to console him by telling him that though he was worthy of better things, priesthood was at least a step toward a bishopric.

3. In fact, however, the man of God, as he told us, was applying a higher standard and was grieving at the many great dangers which the government and administration of the Church would bring upon him; that was the reason for his tears. In the end, however, they had what they wanted.

7

Augustine the Priest—A Future Found, a Past Remembered

For sure, neither the old Valerius nor the stunned Augustine could appreciate at the time the implications of the seemingly impetuous happening of his unanticipated ordination. If Hippo Regius was a somewhat lackluster port town, its newest resident was anything but ordinary—and Augustine had a history wherein nothing he had done seemed to be ordinary. Did Valerius sense this and for that very reason gamble on this recently converted thinker, writer, and servus Dei? There is no way to know.

The Catholic church in Hippo Regius was in an uncomfortable position when it drafted Augustine late in 390 CE or early 391 CE. Their bishop was probably an outsider whose lack of familiarity with Latin made communication with his people difficult. The dominant Christian church in Hippo Regius was not the Catholic church but the Donatist church.[1] "Donatist" was not the term they used, but one that their rivals gave them at some point in the fourth century. They were Christians, mostly from North Africa, who had, for almost a century, claimed to be the true Church and criticized the Catholic leadership for infidelity in time of persecution and, then, for collaboration with civil authority. Few outside of that part of the world accepted their view.

Non-Christians were plentiful, and there seemed to be a small, thriving Jewish community as well. There were also Manichees, and they seem to have been as bold as ever. Thus, the Catholic community Augustine encountered in Hippo Regius was apparently anything but flourishing, and that may have made it possible and even necessary for Valerius to act boldly. When Augustine was visiting Hippo, Valerius made his presence known and the people called him to serve as priest. The old bishop now had a former imperial rhetor at his side, someone who knew the government from the inside, one of Africa's brightest

---

[1] Even though it would be chronologically correct to describe Donatism here, a fuller account of this movement will be found in Chapter 8 where it can be dealt with in an appropriate way.

orators and intellectuals. He would to use Augustine's talents to the full advantage of the Catholic church of Hippo Regius.

By wandering among the ruins of this ancient city today, located at the outskirts of the Algerian city called Annaba, one can still imagine the Hippo Regius of Augustine's day. There was an impressive forum and amphitheater, luxurious villas by the sea with rich mosaics, numerous public baths and, in the distance, farmland and verdant hillsides. It seemed to have been a fairly prosperous city, able to feed itself from its fertile surroundings; in addition, the port city had the rest of the Mediterranean world at its doorstep. However, it was no Carthage: no bookstalls filled with the latest writings, no scholarly circles where teachers of rhetoric, literature, and philosophy gathered with students. From Augustine's sermons, one has the impression that the people of Hippo Regius were practical and hard-working, not concerned about "ideas" but about "making a good living." How would the people accept their new priest who was at home with a lofty Christian Neo-Platonism? How would he deal with practical-minded shopowners, farmers, and dockworkers? What did Augustine, the intellectual who was accustomed to discussing the origin of the soul and the harmonies of the universe, have to say to the "everyday" people of Hippo Regius? In Thagaste, he was often asked to help others, and he appears to have been generous to a fault. That reputation may have preceded him.

If Augustine's few years had been remarkably productive in Thagaste, showing a growing biblical-theological maturation, it is no exaggeration to say that Augustine's surprise ordination set the course for the rest of his life. His literary output was complemented by a series of public initiatives that are integrally related to Augustine, the thinker and writer. Some distinctive aspects of those first years of ministry placed him on a public stage and forced him, again and again, to search the Scriptures.

We get a sense of his state of mind from a letter written to Bishop Valerius almost immediately after this life-altering event; he was requesting some time away to prepare himself for his new responsibilities. It is worth quoting some parts of that letter, since it reveals Augustine "from the inside" not long after the shock at what had happened to him. He begins with an acute awareness that he has been called upon to engage in a daunting task.

> Before all I beg you that with your devout wisdom you [Valerius] bear in mind that in this life, and especially at this time, nothing is easier, more pleasant, and more attractive for men than the office of bishop, priest, or deacon, if the task is carried out perfunctorily or in a self-serving manner, but that before God nothing is more miserable, more sad, and more worthy of condemnation. Likewise, nothing in this life, and especially at this time, is more difficult, more laborious, and more dangerous than the office of a bishop, priest, or deacon (*Letter* 21.1)

If he felt rather self-confident upon his arrival in Hippo Regius, trying to recruit a friend and looking to establish a monastery, he now found himself painfully aware of his own inadequacies in the face of the unexpected difficulty in his new responsibility.

> But I did not learn either from my boyhood or young manhood what this manner of service is, and at the time when I had begun to learn, I suffered violence because of the merit of my sins – I do not, after all, know what else I should think – such that the second post at the helm was handed to me who did not yet know how to hold an oar. (*Letter* 21.1)

In some ways, Augustine takes his new calling as a punishment from God—and proceeds to "confess" that upon his return to Africa he had been vocally critical of the clergy he encountered. His experience of the priest Simplicianus and of Bishop Ambrose in Milan had set a high standard and his disappointment was not all that surprising.

> But I think that my Lord wanted to correct me in that way precisely because I dared, as if I were more learned and better, to reprimand the mistakes of many sailors before I had experienced what is involved in their work. And so, after I was launched into the middle of the sea, I began to feel the rashness of my reprimands, though even earlier I judged this ministry to be filled with perils. And this was the reason for those tears that some of the brothers noticed that I shed in the city at the time of my ordination, and not knowing the reasons for my sorrow, they, nonetheless, consoled me with a good intention with what words they could, though with words having absolutely nothing to do with my wound (*Letter* 21.2)

God, he believed, had a sense of humor in thinking that he could use Augustine's experience to bring the bishop to deal with Augustine's feelings of inadequacy. "The Lord, however, laughed at me and chose to reveal me to myself by this experience." (*Letter* 21.2) Augustine appeals to Valerius' love.

> If he did this, not in condemning me, but in showing me mercy – for I certainly have this hope even now that I know my illness – I ought to examine carefully all the remedies of his scriptures and, by praying and reading, work that he may grant my soul health suited for such dangerous tasks. I did not do this before because I did not have the time. For I was ordained at the time when we were planning a period of retreat for gaining knowledge of the divine scriptures and wanted to arrange our affairs in order that we could have the leisure for this task. And the truth is that I did not yet know what I lacked for such work as now torments and crushes me. But if I learned through actual experience what a man needs who ministers to the people the sacrament and word of God with the result that I am now not permitted to pursue what I have learned that I lack, you are asking, Father Valerius, for my death. Where is your love? Do you really love me? Do you really love the Church that you wanted me to serve in this way? And yet I am certain that you love both me and the Church. But you think that I am well prepared, while I know myself better, and I would, nonetheless, not have known myself if I had not learned by experience (*Letter* 21.3)

Augustine even anticipates Valerius' objection to his request for some time off: but you are brilliant; your faith is clear; and you have already published books. What could you possibly need?

> But Your Holiness perhaps says, "I would like to know what is lacking in your instruction." There are so many things lacking that I could more easily list what I have than what I desire to know. For I would dare to say that I know and hold with complete faith what pertains to our salvation. But how am I to exercise this ministry for the salvation of others? (*Letter* 21.4)

"But how am I to exercise this ministry for the salvation of others?" That is the question that stands at the heart of Augustine's appeal. It is one thing to "write about God and salvation"; it is quite different to minister effectively to people, especially since the Catholics to whom he preached were in constant contact with a rival Christian community called "Donatist." This leads Augustine to specify his request for some time away to study the Scriptures:

> For this task I wanted to obtain through the brothers from your most sincere and venerable love a short time for myself, say, up to Easter, and I now ask this through these prayers . . . I implore your love and affection that you may be merciful to me and grant me as much time as I have requested for the purpose for which I requested it and help me by your prayers that my desire may not be unfulfilled and that my absence may not be without fruit for the Church of Christ and for the benefit of my brothers and fellow servants. (*Letter* 21.6)

Valerius must have given Augustine at least some time away, but, if the chronologists are correct, only until the beginning of Lent of 391 CE when the first of Augustine's sermons that has been preserved (Sermon 216) was preached to those who were preparing for baptism, the catechumens. It was but five years since Augustine had found himself in the same circumstances, preparing to be baptized at the hand of Ambrose.

> The commencement of my ministry and of your conception, your beginning to be begotten by heavenly grace in the womb of faith, needs to be aided by prayer, so that my sermon may contribute to your welfare and salvation, and your conception to my encouragement and consolation. We clergy instruct you with sermons; it is up to you to make progress in your conduct. We scatter the seed of the word; it is up to you to produce the crop of faith. Let us all run the course in the tracks of the Lord according to the vocation with which we have been called by him; none of us must look back. Truth, you see, who can neither be misled nor mislead, openly warns us: Nobody putting hand to plow and looking back is fit for the kingdom of heaven (Lk. 9:62). That you indeed long for this kingdom and are aiming at it with all the energy of your minds, is shown by your very name, your being called competentes. What else, after all, are *competentes* but people asking together? I mean, just as *condocentes, concurrentes, considentes* simply mean people teaching together, running together, sitting to-

gether, so the word *competentes* is made up from asking together, and aiming at one and the same thing. . . . (*ser.* 216.1)

The Latin text of the sermon is lofty and rhetorically polished, a style that his listeners were likely not accustomed to hearing. Alliteration, parallelisms, and carefully constructed sentences are evident throughout. Word-play, a standard feature of the rhetorician, is featured prominently at the outset as he unpacks the Latin term for those seeking baptism: *competentes*—"people asking together," for baptism, for salvation. He juxtaposes the term with words like *condocentes*, *concurrentes*, *considentes*—the prefix "*con*" highlighting and echoing "together"—together with them. If his listeners may have been raising their eyebrows just a bit, they would also have been struck by the fact that their "star priest" cannot emphasize enough the word "together." A few lines later he calls his listeners *contirones mei*—an expression not easily translated into English but meaning the equivalent of "my fellow beginners," "my fellow apprentices," "my fellow novices," "my fellow new recruits." That is exactly how he found himself: a beginner priest, new to preaching, an apprentice, a novice, a new recruit. Those precious weeks away from Hippo Regius on a Bible retreat seemed not only to have helped Augustine become reconciled with his "new future" but to embrace it wholeheartedly.

Once he had a clearer sense of what the Scriptures said about ministering to others, it was possible for him to know what the down-to-earth and simple folk were seeking from him when they forcibly kept him in Hippo. Augustine may have suffered "spiritual violence" at the hands of the Catholics of Hippo Regius, but he can now see himself as one of them—or at least as trying to become one of them. Valerius' gamble had been rewarded and Augustine is off to a good start.

A Garden Monastery

Augustine's unexpected ordination had occurred in the course of a visit to Hippo Regius, the purpose of which was to look for a place to establish a monastery. Already in Thagaste, Augustine was living a quasi-monastic existence, and it seems that in Hippo Regius he intended to take that project a step forward. While virtually all his plans underwent drastic change in Hippo Regius, one thing remained the same: In a sermon preached in Hippo Regius in 426 CE, Augustine looked back over some 35 years and recounts how his monastic vision did not die with ordination.

I brought nothing with me; I came to this Church with only the clothes I was wearing at the time. And because what I was planning was to be in a monastery with the brothers, Father Valerius of blessed memory, having learned of my purpose and desire, gave me that plot where the monastery now is. I began to gather together brothers of good will, my companions in poverty, having nothing just like me, and imitating me. Just as I had sold my slender poor man's property and distributed the proceeds to the poor, those who wished to stay with me did the same, so that we might live on what we had in common. But what would be our really great and profitable common estate was God himself. (*ser.* 355.1)

Terms such as monastery and monk have, in the course of history, taken on very distinct profiles. At this point in Western Christianity, 391 CE, this terminology was still developing; so it is important not to project later developments back into that time or onto Augustine. The "monastic movement" that Augustine entered into was on the one hand not well-organized and certainly not institutionalized. On the other hand, it was much more radical and daring simply because, at least for Western Christians, it was "new." Augustine continued to see himself as both *servus Dei* and priest, and even to recognize and talk about the tension. As priest, he was constantly in the public light; as a servus Dei, he found refuge and solace from those cares—at least in theory. Augustine the priest lived in community with fellow servants of God, and they lived simply, prayerfully, celibately. They lived in the heart of the city and yet lived in contrast to "city life," since they did not marry, did not own property, and their work and labor was consciously in the service of God.

When Augustine will become bishop he will find it necessary to leave that garden monastery and take up residence in the bishop's house, at least as a way to protect the monastery from the turmoil and comings and goings that were part of episcopal life. However, even there, one of his first household reforms was to turn the bishop's house into what he called a "monastery of clerics." He sought, once again, to join others in a common task. Augustine's subsequent life, his intense theological and literary activity, his involvement in numerous debates and controversies, his pastoral activity as preacher and leader of worship, will always have in the background his identity as a *servus Dei* living in spiritual communion and sharing common life with fellow servants of God. While his companions were sometimes cause for heartache and disappointment, more often than not they provided him with support and relief, an oasis of peace in the midst of a life of activity that was anything but peaceful.

Public Disputation

Perhaps Augustine's earliest high profile event in Hippo Regius was a public debate with a Manichaean priest named Fortunatus. Since stenographers were present for the debate and recorded virtually every word of the proceeding, the subsequently published acts, which bear the title *Against Fortunatus the Manichaean*, offer the modern reader a window into the activity of Augustine the young priest, but, just as importantly, into the important role public disputation and debate played in the ancient world. The event took place over two days, August 28 to August 29, 392 CE. The venue was not a church but "the baths of Sossius." Baths in Augustine's world were not simply a place to swim, get clean, and engage in sport; they also functioned as community centers. Along with athletic and aquatic facilities, they also had meeting spaces for large gatherings, such as formal, public debates. Those who gathered there would have been significantly more diverse than those in a "church crowd." Now, less than two years since Augustine's ordination, Augustine hardly seems like a beginner. Fortunatus responded to Augustine's direct assaults with questions rather than answers. Augustine's frustration was evident throughout the first day; he often chided his opponent but never lost his control. Fortunatus kept sidestepping Augustine's questions, and those in attendance finally broke into the ancient equivalent of boos and jeers. That forced the gathering to adjourn until the next day.

On the second day Augustine succeeded in landing a disputational knockout by getting Fortunatus to admit that "his God," the God of Manichaean theology, is "bound by necessity." Technically, that meant that he was not all-powerful. Fortunatus was suddenly incapable of responding further to Augustine's arguments. Left speechless, he conceded defeat. The gathered crowd then acknowledged the victor, and Fortunatus quickly left town.

Augustine had struck a mighty public blow against the Manichaean movement that had, until then, boldly proselytized African Christians, both Donatist and Catholic. This highly visible anti-Manichaean debate also signaled to everyone in Hippo Regius that Valerius, the Catholic bishop, had at his side a formidable assistant priest—something truly new was now happening in Hippo Regius: making religion a matter of public debate surely opened the way to other discussions.

Augustine, however, was not content with this result; crowds were fickle—memories faded. During these early days of his priesthood he also wrote a series of works directed to individual Manichees, always aware that such writings had a larger audience. *On the Usefulness of Belief* is in many ways a friendly little work, addressed to Honoratus, someone Augustine had known during his own Manichaean days. Its warm tone to an old friend politely conceals its rigorous deconstruction of the Manichaean religion. This little pamphlet (in English about 33 pages) was the tip of an iceberg of anti-Manichaean writings throughout the period, some gentle, some harsh, but all of them were intended to cleanse Augustine of his Manichaean past and persuade his former coreligionists to do the same.

If both the Catholic minority and the Donatist majority cheered Augustine's victory over a mutually shared opponent, however, it is likely that the Donatist leadership was also beginning to feel uneasy. The Catholic church in Hippo Regius and Numidia now had a public and convincing voice. If Augustine was able to sway a crowd against the Manichees he might just as easily persuade a crowd against other opponents, for example, against the Donatists. It does seem that Augustine had little personal experience with the Christian conflict that had been rocking Roman Africa for almost a century. Chapter 8 will be dedicated to this thorny history, but, at this point it is important to note that Augustine was already publicly challenging the Donatists in several ways. The Donatists seemed to have been experts at tapping popular sentiment, to Catholic disadvantage, through crowd-pleasing song and slogan; they were able to generate the kind of crowd activity one might see at a contemporary sports event, filled with emotion and chanting.

It comes as no surprise, therefore, that Augustine's first surviving anti-Donatist work had a popular form, probably a first for this former imperial rhetor. In the *Psalm Against the Donatist Sect*, composed in 393–394 CE, Augustine abandons the formal and elaborate canons of Latin poetic composition in favor of what might be called an a-b-c-darius, that is, the first verse begins with A, the second B, third C, and so on. It was, as it were, composed alphabetically. The verses follow the accent of popular language rather than the fixed traditional method of Latin poetic compositions, which were based upon various combinations of long and short syllables. With some exaggeration it might be compared to abandoning the form of Shakespearian sonnet for a modern ballad, at least in terms of form. It was written to be easily memorized and chanted or sung by Catholic crowds; the Donatist crowds were already using such techniques against the Catholics. But it was not empty verse, for it was intended to be a concise rhyming summary of the Catholic position on the religious conflict, held together by a recurring refrain: you who take joy in peace, judge now the truth (*vos qui gaudetis de pace, modo verum iudicate*). Augustine calls it a psalm (*psalmus*), not a song, since his model is biblical. He knew that some of the psalms (e.g., Psalm 118) followed the "a-b-c" format. Augustine works his way through the history of the controversy, establishing as any lawyer might, the background for his criticism. He had come to realize that few people had a conscious awareness of that history, and he knew that his adversaries often used that lack of information to prey upon peoples' fears. By the time he reached the end of his psalm, he is no longer summing up the case, but he has become the voice of the church, chiding Donatists to decide for Christ—*pro Christo* or to choose Donatus—*pro Donato*. He asks, "Will you choose in favor of Donatus or Christ (and so the Catholic church)." Over the next nearly four decades the voice of Augustine the polemicist, controversialist, debater, God's lawyer and prosecutor will echo throughout the Mediterranean.

Letter 29—Some Cultural Insights

But if Augustine's voice took up the Catholic cause (*causa Catholicae* is the Latin expression that Augustine uses; "cause" has legal overtones: "a court case") against its opponents, he was equally determined to apply it internally. If Donatist opponents learned to shudder when Augustine began to speak, Catholic "backsliders" could expect no less. We get a taste of this in a letter written by Augustine the priest to his dear friend Alypius, now bishop of Augustine's hometown, Thagaste. In the letter Augustine recounts his efforts to put an end to a practice that accompanied the celebration of the festival of martyrs: a practice that might be likened to an "open bar." The feast had the name Thrill (*Laetitia*) and, at least as Augustine recounts it, the enjoyment was not very "religious."

Even though Augustine was only an assistant priest, he seems to have been able to persuade the bishop to ban the celebrations, a decision which was decidedly unpopular. He tells Alypius:

> After your departure it was reported to us that people were in an uproar and were saying that they could not tolerate the prohibition of that solemnity. In calling it "joy," they try in vain to hide the term "drunkenness," as was already reported even when you were present. By the hidden providence of almighty God it turned out opportunely for us that on the fourth day of the week this passage in the gospel was to be commented on in sequence, Do not give what is holy to dogs, and do not cast your pearls before swine (Mt. 7:6). I commented, therefore, on dogs and pigs in such a way that those arguing against the commandments of God with an obstinate barking and devoted to the filth of carnal pleasures were forced to be ashamed, and my sermon came to such a conclusion that they saw how wicked it is to do something in the name of religion within the walls of the church that, if they continued to do it in their homes, it would be necessary to exclude them from what is holy and from the pearls in the church. (*Letter* 29.2)

It seems that Augustine found before him in church an unhappy congregation, but he felt that he had won them over by the end of his sermon. Even so, that small crowd, once they had left church and reported the sermon to others, was then persuaded by the criticisms of those who were not there. The next day Augustine was again called upon to preach, now to a crowded church of decidedly unreceptive listeners.

> But after the day of Lent had dawned and a large crowd came for the hour of preaching, that passage in the gospel was read in which, after driving out the sellers of animals from the temple and after overturning the tables of the money changers, the Lord said that the house of his Father had become a den of thieves instead of a house of prayer. (*Letter* 29.3)

Augustine had carefully chosen the scriptural text for the day, Matt 21:12-13, the account of Jesus "cleansing the temple." He realized that he was not engaged in petty politics against a social custom, but preaching the Word of God; he used it, in fact, to good effect. If Jesus chased from the temple "buyers and sellers" would he do less in the face of "drunkenness."

> After having made them attentive by raising the question of drunkenness, I myself also read out that passage, and I added an argument to show with how much more anger and forcefulness our Lord would have expelled from the temple drunken banquets, which are shameful everywhere, since he expelled from there licit commerce. For they were selling things necessary for the sacrifices, which were licit at that time. I asked them whom they thought a den of thieves resembled more, those selling necessities or those drinking immoderately. (*Letter* 29.7)

Augustine offers Alypius (and other readers) a play-by-play account of his sermon. There was a crescendo of scriptural texts and commentary that eventually built up to a fair amount of fire and brimstone:

> I said, therefore, that I trusted in him that, if they scorned all these words that were read and spoken to them, he would visit them with the rod and scourge, but would not allow them to be condemned along with this world. In this appeal I acted as our protector and ruler gave me the energy and power for the magnitude of the problem and the danger. I did not evoke their tears with my tears, but when I said such things, I admit, I was caught up in their weeping and could not hold back my own. And when we had both equally wept, I brought my sermon to an end with the fullest hope of their correction. (*Letter* 29.7)

At the end, both the congregation and Augustine are in tears, but at the same time Augustine succeeded in uniting himself with the congregation in a common wail. And the desired effect endured: the next day they were all once again gathered together in church for a sober celebration of prayers, scripture readings, and commentary—and in the background Augustine, Valerius, and the subdued congregation could hear the boisterous celebration of the nearby Donatist church—apparently, they had no one the likes of Augustine to put an end to their *laetitia*.

> And since we could hear the customary banquets that were being celebrated by the heretics in their basilica, for they were still drinking at the very time when we were doing this, I said that the beauty of the day stands out in comparison with the night and that the color white is more pleasing by reason of its nearness to black. So too, our gathering with its spiritual celebration would perhaps have been less pleasing if the carnal binge did not stand in contrast with it, and I exhorted them constantly to desire such feasts as ours if they had tasted how sweet the Lord is. (*Letter* 29.11)

Augustine ends the letter with a fervent wish that these efforts may continue: "Pray that God may deign by our efforts to turn aside all scandals and all offenses." But he also mentions a somewhat ominous incident, one that portends future turmoil: "At Hasna where our brother, Argentius, is priest, the Circumcellions invaded the basilica and smashed our altar. The case is now being heard; we ask you to pray much that it may be settled peacefully and as is proper for the Catholic church in order to subdue the tongues of the restless heretics" (*Letter* 29.12). The Circumcellions were roving bands of thugs, always identified by Augustine with the Donatist movement, and frequent perpetrators of anti-Catholic violence. This will not be his last mention of them.

In *Letter* 29, written to Alypius sometime in 395 CE, Augustine appears as a forceful reforming voice for the Catholic church in Roman Africa. His offensive against "the opposition," in fact, was secondary to the other part of the story: the "restoration" of the Catholic church to real unity. He was most committed to raising the level of Catholic religious awareness and practice: a united and worthy clergy, an informed and committed laity. In this regard he formed a powerful team with the Catholic bishop of Carthage, Aurelius; together they had committed themselves to a vigorous campaign of clergy education and renewal combined with a strenuous effort to wipe out religious practices that were seen as inconsistent with Christian faith and which compromised its public witness. Aurelius was the brilliant organizer and Augustine the brilliant orator; their combined talents and efforts, indeed, reshaped the Catholic church in Roman Africa. That becomes clear when one steps back two years to what happened on October 8, 393 CE.

As Primate (or Head) of the Catholic church in Roman Africa, one of Aurelius' first steps toward reform was to call for annual meetings of the Catholic bishops in Carthage. Those meetings enabled the assembled bishops to collaborate more directly and to formulate mutually agreed upon policies in the face of the many challenges they faced. In October of 393 CE the bishops broke with precedent and met, not in Carthage, but in Hippo Regius. They also broke with precedent by having a priest deliver a formal address to the gathering; Augustine calls his address a *disputatio*; it was later published under the title Faith and Creed. Valerius had already innovated by having his priest preach in his presence, something quite unusual for Western Christianity. Now he did so again by having him preach to all the gathered bishops. Many scholars see Aurelius behind the choice of Hippo Regius (instead of Carthage) as the place for this council and of Augustine as speaker. Aurelius certainly saw in this new priest a capable partner and trustworthy ally to assist him in renewing the African Catholic church.

This *disputatio* is heavily scriptural and does not yet manifest the theological depth that will characterize the Augustine of the decades to follow. Clearly, he is not there to explain the Creed, the statement of faith recited by all Christians at the time of baptism. But he did give them a model for their own catechetical instructions and, in the process, invited them to raise the level of that catechesis when they returned to their respective dioceses. He began by explaining: "This is the Catholic faith known as the creed and committed to memory by believers, a vast subject contained in such few words." (1.1) Augustine thus called the bishops to challenge their listeners to a more thoughtful understanding of the Creed as an important way to restore Catholic faith and practice.

In that *disputatio*, Augustine engaged in something that scholars call *intellectus fidei*, searching into and understanding faith. That will become one of Augustine's hallmarks. He tells the bishops: "an explanation of the faith can help protect the creed" (1.1). Reason and understanding are not opposed to belief, on the contrary, they strengthen and deepen faith. This theme will echo throughout Augustine's writings until the end of his life.

Christian Classics

During these formative years as priest, as Valerius' co-bishop, and finally as sole bishop of Hippo Regius (August 28, 397 CE, is our first official evidence), Augustine's "pen and voice" show remarkable output. The Bible was the well-spring of his productivity, as Augustine devoted himself to its study and virtual memorization. The intention of this chapter was to show how the first decade of Augustine's formal ministry set the course for what the rest of his life. In short, Augustine's "biblical pen" stands out as a key to understanding his focus. Shortly after Augustine's ordination he began to put into writing an explanation of the psalms, *expositio* is the word he used to describe the effort. This effort will continue for most of the next three decades—he will finish his final *expositio* in the early 420s. What began as brief notes on the verses of the psalms will evolve into elaborate commentaries, more often than not carried out before the people in the form of homilies or sermons. Throughout his commentary on the psalms, Christ will be his concern and his focus, as can be seen in his *Exposition on Psalm* 1:

> He will be like a tree planted alongside the running waters. This may refer to Wisdom itself, who deigned to assume humanity for our salvation, so that it is the human Christ who is planted like a tree by the running waters; for what is said in another psalm, the river of God is brimming with water, can also be taken in this sense. . . . That tree, therefore, is our Lord, who draws those who are in the way from the running waters, that is, from the peoples who sin. By drawing them into the roots of his discipline he will bring forth fruit; that is, he will establish churches, but in due time, that is, after he has been glorified by his resurrection and ascension into heaven. Once the Holy Spirit had been sent to the apostles, and once they had been established in their faith in him and sent out to the peoples, he bore the churches as his fruit. His leaves will not fall off: this means that his word will not be ineffectual; although all flesh is but grass, and human glory like the flower of grass; the grass is dried up and the flower is fallen, yet the word of the Lord abides for ever. And whatever he does will prosper, namely, whatever the tree bears, its fruits and leaves, which stand for deeds and words (*exp. Ps.* 1, 3).

The depth of feeling in these words can be "sensed," and yet his concern is to recognize growth both in individuals and in Christianity. As he progresses through the psalms, the increasing depth that he kept discovering will tie them ever more fully to the Christ that they prefigure.

During this same period he preached and published a commentary on the *Sermon on the Mount*, attempted and then abandoned a commentary on Genesis (a book to which he returned several times). In a way that will forever mark Augustine and western tradition as well, he began a commentary on the writings of the apostle Paul. Four writings of this period are explicitly dedicated to Paul. Two of them explore Paul's Letter to the Romans. The first is a series of "propositions" or short commentaries on specific excerpts from Romans, and the second is an attempt at a complete commentary on Paul's Letter. But Augustine's second effort came to a quick end, since he never made it past Chapter 1, verse 7 of the Letter's 16 chapters and 433 verses). He then writes an integral commentary on the Letter to the Galatians—the only commentary on one of Paul's letters that he completed. The final Pauline work of this period was part of a longer group of responses to the questions on the Bible that his Milanese priest mentor, Simplicianus, posed to him. Those questions concerned verses in the *Book of Kings* and in Paul's *Letter to the Romans*.

His comments on the *Letter to the Romans* signaled a new depth of study and thought regarding the Apostle and pointed to issues that increasingly demanded his attention: the will, sin, the intersection of "God's freedom" and "human freedom," how to explain the present misery that seems to pervade the human heart and life, and most especially, what role God's grace or direct action plays in all of this. What all commentators note, with a panoply of interpretation and commentary, is how Augustine increasingly moved the focus of the question of salvation away from what any man or woman can do to what God alone can do. By the end of his reply to Simplicianus, it is clear that the only action free will can perform is to cry out for God's grace. Augustine has clearly reached a cross-road in his understanding of the teaching of Paul and the results that flow from his position will be played out over the course of the rest of his life.

The *Confessions* is the most remarkable and original work of the period, if not of all his writings. It begins and ends with the Bible. It is likewise no coincidence that the psalms, the letters of Paul, and Genesis all play a prominent role in that work. The first chapters of this present study of Augustine's life, thought, and writings have already drawn heavily upon the bibliographical wealth contained in Books I through IX of this work, but the *Confessions* as a work is much more than a biography. In the opening passage, the words in bold indicate significant themes that will be found throughout this work.

> Great are you, O Lord, and exceedingly worthy of **praise**, your power is immense, and your **wisdom** beyond reckoning (See Ps. 47:2; 95:4; 144:3; 146:5; 1 Cor. 1:24). And so we **humans**, who are a due part of your **creation**, long to **praise** you – we who carry our **mortality** about with us (see 2 Cor. 4:10), carry the evidence of our **sin** and with it the proof that you thwart the **proud** (see 1 Pt. 5:5). Yet these **humans**, due part of your **creation** as they are, still do long to **praise** you. You arouse us so that **praising** you may bring us **joy**, because you have made us and drawn us to yourself, and our **heart** is **unquiet** until it **rests** in you. (*conf.* I.1.1)

These opening lines of the *Confessions* are permeated with biblical quotes, phrases, allusions, paraphrases; the citations given could be expanded. Book X has Augustine speaking as a bishop at the time of the writing, and Books XI through XIII are a commentary on the creation story of Genesis. The term *confessio* in Latin has the primary meaning of praise; to profess faith and to acknowledge one's sin, after all, are actions which praise God. In the course of the narrative Augustine becomes, in many ways, more than Augustine; he is the human and his story embodies "the human story." Augustine's conversion begins with a quest for wisdom, but is interrupted by his own sin and the fallout from his inherited mortality; he is indeed the unquiet heart, yearning for rest in God, and yet all of this is a source of wonder and praise. Augustine is doing much more than talking about his life—he is doing theology, he is interpreting the Bible, he is outlining a path toward holiness, and he is probably even defending himself against Donatist critics, while also leaving no doubt that he is no longer a Manichee. Even more interestingly, Augustine did something never done previously: He used his own experience to explore the meaning of being human. But the "within" of his experience is a mystery that kept pushing him beyond his "self" to the one in whose image he was created. This work, therefore, united the human being to God in a way never seen before. That fascinating fact, at least in part, helps to explain why modern studies of the work continue to be written at a dizzying pace.

The *Confessions* is complemented by another original work, *On Christian Doctrine* (*De doctrina christiana*). The almost literal English translation of the original Latin title is perhaps misleading because of the narrow meaning that doctrine has for modern readers. In this context Augustine understood *doctrina* as all that the Christian Bible teaches about believing and living—and everything in between. He begins the work with these words:

> There are some rules for dealing with the scriptures, which I consider can be not inappropriately passed on to students, enabling them to make progress not only by reading others who have opened up the hidden secrets of the divine literature, but also by themselves opening them up to yet others again. I have undertaken to pass these rules on to those who are both willing and well qualified to learn, if our Lord and God does not deny me, as I write, the ideas he usually suggests to me in my reflections on the subject. (*On Christian Doctrine*, Preface 1)

He is offering rules (*praecepta* in Latin) for interpreting and understanding the scriptures as well as for communicating what the interpreter has learned to others. It is a pioneering work as the first formal book on biblical interpretation to have been written, at least in the Latin-speaking West. In its final form it consists of four books; he began to write it in about 396 CE and the first two-and-a-half books circulated before the work was finally completed in 426 CE. Augustine draws upon a Donatist theologian, Tyconius, as Book III draws to its conclusion—a fact that may indicate why its completion was delayed, that is, it may have been inappropriate to refer to a schismatic theologian at a time when the Donatist crisis was fully engaged. It would have been prudent to wait until later to make explicit reference to Tyconius' ideas.

Book IV lays out what might be called a "Christian rhetoric"—how to communicate effectively to others the product of one's biblical studies. On the one hand Augustine can reduce the entire Bible to one word love, on the other hand he can offer a sophisticated rhetorical analysis of a text from Paul. In the course of the four books, he both mines the richness of classical culture and subverts it with a constant emphasis on that most un-Roman and nonclassical virtue, humility. It became one of Augustine's most copied works in the Middle Ages and was looked upon as a virtual charter for the creation of a Christian classical culture, the wedding of ancient and Christian thought.

Looking back to that startling day in 391 CE when Augustine found himself unexpectedly drafted into the African Catholic clergy and thrust into a public and controversial role certainly generated anguish enough as evidenced by Augustine's Letter 21 to Valerius almost immediately afterward. The ten years that followed, however, show little anguish and much creativity and originality. His literary output is evidence of much that remains hidden and unavailable to us: his reading and studying, his discussions and debates; his trips to Carthage and elsewhere, some extending for many months; his day-in and day-out contact with the people of Hippo Regius and surroundings, not all of which were agreeable; his preaching in the presence of Valerius; his election to Valerius' episcopal chair. Memories flooded his mind and some of them are certainly reflected in his *Confessions*. If mortality had overtaken Augustine in 401 CE, we would still likely be reading him today—such would have been the impact of his initial writings as priest and bishop of Hippo Regius. But he continued to live and to contribute—and this first decade is only a warm-up for what will follow over the course of the next three decades.

Reading Augustine:

Augustine's sense of the challenge of being a minister did not diminish with the passing of years. In the following sermon, he looks back to the time when he was first charged with the ministry of priesthood and explains what it means to him to continue in that service.

Sermon 340.1 From the moment this burden, about which such a difficult account has to be rendered, was placed on my shoulders, anxiety about the honor shown me has always indeed been haunting me. But this sort of consideration troubles me much more when the anniversary brings back afresh the old memory of that day, and sets it before my very eyes in such a way, that I feel as though I were coming up today to receive what I have already received all that time ago. What, though, is to be dreaded in this office, if not that I may take more pleasure, which is so dangerous, in the honor shown me, than in what bears fruit in your salvation? Let me therefore have the assistance of your prayers, that the one who did not disdain to bear with me may also deign to bear my burden with me. When you pray like that, you are also praying for yourselves. This burden of mine, you see, about which I am now speaking, what else is it, after all, but you? Pray for strength for me, just as I pray that you may not be too heavy.

I mean, the Lord Jesus wouldn't have called his burden light, if he wasn't going to carry it together with its porter. But you too must all support me, so that according to the apostle's instructions we may carry one another's burdens, and in this way fulfill the law of Christ (Gal 6:2). If he doesn't carry it with us, we collapse; if he doesn't carry us, we keel over and die. Where I'm terrified by what I am for you, I am given comfort by what I am with you. For you I am a bishop, with you, after all, I am a Christian. The first is the name of an office undertaken, the second a name of grace; that one means danger, this one salvation. Finally, as if in the open sea, I am being tossed about by the stormy activity involved in that one; but as I recall by whose blood I have been redeemed, I enter a safe harbor in the tranquil recollection of this one; and thus while toiling away at my own proper office, I take my rest in the marvelous benefit conferred on all of us in common.

So I hope the fact that I have been bought together with you gives me more pleasure than my having been placed at your head; then, as the Lord has commanded, I will be more effectively your servant, and be preserved from ingratitude for the price by which I was bought to be, not too unworthily, your fellow servant. ...

3. So it is, my brothers and sisters, that commanding we implore you not to receive the grace of God in vain (2 Cor 6:1). Make my ministry fruitful. You are God's agriculture (1 Cor 3:9); from the outside receive the work of the planter and the waterer; from the inside, though, that of the one who makes you grow. The turbulent have to be corrected, the faint-hearted cheered up, the weak supported; the gospel's opponents need to be refuted, its insidious enemies guarded against; the unlearned need to be taught, the indolent stirred up, the argumentative checked; the proud must be put in their place, the desperate set on their feet, those engaged in quarrels reconciled; the needy have to be helped, the oppressed to be liberated, the good to be given your backing, the bad to be tolerated; all must be loved. In all the vast and varied activity involved in fulfilling such manifold responsibilities, please give me your help by both your prayers and your obedience. In this way I will find pleasure not so much in being in charge of you as in being of use to you.

4. Just as it is very proper for me to pray earnestly for God's mercy to bring you to salvation, so it is right that you too should be pouring out prayers to God for me. Nor should we judge this to be unsuitable, since we know that the apostle did it; so much indeed did he long to be recommended to God by their prayers, that he himself made his plea to every community with the words Pray for us (1 Th 5:25; 2 Th 3:1; Rom 15:30; Col 4:3). And that's why I should indeed be saying this, being able in this way both to encourage myself and instruct all of you. Just as I, you see, have to give thought with great fear and anxiety to how I may blamelessly carry out my duties as bishop; so you for your part must make a point of showing a humble and eager obedience to everything that is commanded you.

8

Augustine and the Donatist Challenge—Compelling Love

Religion in the ancient world was everyone's concern, a fact of public and of imperial life. It is not possible to comprehend the history that follows without some appreciation of that reality. This chapter (as well as Chapter 10) deals with intense, public religious conflict. In the West of today, in fact, questions of religious affiliation are rarely played out in the public forum. Faith issues are viewed as private and individual. That, however, was not the world of Late Antiquity, and certainly not the world of Augustine. In the Roman world of his experience and even beyond its frontiers, there was no clear dividing line between what today would be called "church" and "state." Everyone knew the difference between a law court and a temple, but that difference did not translate into a "wall of separation" between religious and secular matters. This was the case in each of the first centuries of Christianity, and it also explains why there were periodic persecutions against Christians and against other religious movements. Rome's behavior toward its gods was seen as directly impacting the gods' behavior toward Rome. It seemed perfectly natural for the emperor—as protector of the state and its future—to be involved in matters religious. When Augustine was still a young boy, the Emperor Julian (360–363 CE) publicly renounced Christianity and embraced "paganism." One of his first public acts was to prohibit Christians from teaching letters. Since the Greco-Roman culture was imparted through its literature, so Julian reasoned, it was also inseparable from the gods narrated in that literature. If one did not accept that religious world, one could not teach in the schools of the empire.

When Augustine became a priest in Hippo Regius in 390/391 CE he was already well-practiced in public religious controversy. As a young Manichaean adherent in Carthage, he had publicly debated Catholics with great success and won over several of his friends in the process. In his *Confessions*, he recounts how he watched from the sidelines as Bishop Ambrose of Milan, a Catholic Christian, engaged in hostile public confrontation with Justina, the Arian Christian empress-mother of young Valentinian II. After his conversion, Augustine published a series of works against Manichaeism; they were circulated and contributed to his reputation and thus gave him a public, though unofficial, voice. Hence he was known, and that was surely a factor in the choice of the people of Hippo to have him as their priest.

One of the first realities that Augustine encountered in Hippo Regius was that Catholic Christianity was the minority Christianity in that port city, as well as in most of Roman Africa. The vast majority of the city's Christians did not attend his church and were not under Bishop Valerius, but rather, under Bishop Proculeian. Augustine called those "other Christians" Donatists, distinguishing them from his own Catholic Christian community. The conflict over who could rightfully claim the name Catholic (with a host of implications) was what the Donatist Controversy, as scholars subsequently labeled it, was all about. It engaged Augustine directly and explicitly for more than two decades, although it hovered in the background for much longer.

There is no indication he had any real appreciation of the conflict until he came to Hippo Regius. It is never explicitly mentioned in his writings until he arrives there. But once he had a public role there, he was forced to learn quickly, both through firsthand experience and by reading about the affair and its history. The division between Christians was a daily reality, and it included a constant threat of violence from some members of the Donatist religious community. It has already been mentioned that one of first writings in Hippo Regius was an alphabetical Psalm against the Donatists, written in a popular format.

The Weight of History

Following upon the Council of Hippo of 393 CE, Augustine worked hard and long to inform his own as well as the Donatist community of what he saw as the real nature of this conflict. This sermon, preached by Augustine on January 1, 404 CE, is a typical example of his emphasis:

> My brothers and sisters, I am speaking to Catholics. The Donatists put Donatus in the place of Christ. If they hear some pagan disparaging Christ, they probably put up with it more patiently than if they hear him disparaging Donatus. You know what I'm talking about, and you are forced to experience this every day. They are so perverse in their love of Donatus that they put him before Christ. Not only, I mean, do they have nothing they can say, but they even know they have nothing they can say. Nothing, you see, holds them under the name of Christ but the name of Donatus; they have been seduced into accepting the name of a man against Christ. The reason they have conceived the most monstrous . . . hatred against us is that we cry out to them, "Do not place your hopes in a man, or you will be accursed" (see Jer. 17:5). They hate those who preach peace, and if they ever suffer anything for this colossal villainy of theirs--and not for Christ's sake, but for the sake of Donatus--they think they are martyrs. And because we say to them, "Don't puff out the baptism of Christ; love

peace, give yourself back to the whole wide world; Christ redeemed the whole; don't reduce the buyer of the whole to a mere part," that's why they hate us, and if they get the chance kill us at the hands of the Circumcellions. But because the Lord was at hand to help us, we escaped, giving thanks for the Lord's mercy, which is why we admonish and beg you to pray for us, that the Lord may always inspire us with the confidence to preach his peace, and that we may not be afraid of them, but may rather love them and rejoice that there is fulfilled in us what is written: With those who hate peace I was peaceful; when I spoke to them, they waged war on me for nothing (ps. 120:7). And if they cannot be cured in any other way, let them wage war on us, let them strike, let them slay, and still let them be cured. (*ser. Dolbeau* 26.45)

It is the longest sermon that Augustine left us, lasting perhaps three hours. This sermon is called against the Pagans and its length was meant to keep his people in church so as to keep them off the streets. Augustine is reacting against a public festival held in Hippo Regius on New Year's Day, a festival that was pagan both in its origin and in the way it was celebrated. So he held something like a preach-in. For a brief moment Augustine departs from the topic at hand to comment about the Donatist controversy; this is the passage cited above. What is particularly striking is his stark remark: we escaped! It is recounted elsewhere, by Possidius, his first biographer, that Augustine narrowly escaped an ambush by Donatist thugs, a group called the Circumcellions. Because Augustine happened to make a "wrong turn" on one of his travels, he avoided an ambush that had been set for him. Did they intend merely to intimidate and perhaps rough up the bishop of Hippo or something worse? What had Augustine done to provoke such a violent reaction? To answer such questions there is need for some brief historical background about the Catholic-Donatist division of Christianity.

During the latter part of the reign of the emperor Diocletian, in particular during the years 303 to 305 CE, Christian Roman Africa experienced a brief but violent outbreak of persecution. Many clergy, including bishops, succumbed to imperial pressure which demanded that the sacred books be handed over to the authorities. The Latin verb for "handing over" is *tradere* and its noun equivalent is *traditor* and it is the source of the English word traitor. Those who succumbed to imperial threats and handed over the books were looked upon and treated as betraying Christ. They stood in marked contrast with those who refused to give in, and paid the price with imprisonment, torture, and even martyrdom. Those who were not executed became known as *confessores*, those who publicly confessed their faith.

In 311 or 312 CE Mensurius, Catholic bishop of Carthage, died and Caecilian, one of his assistant priests, was hastily elected to take his place. The quickly arranged consecration did not include the senior bishop of the region, the primate of Numidia, thus nullifying his right to participate in the ordination of the bishop of Carthage. Even worse, one of the bishop consecrators was accused of being a *traditor*, and an accusation was made against Caecilian that he forcefully prevented Christians from bringing food to the confessors in prison.

A period of confusion and consternation followed for the church of Carthage, one that would only worsen over the next 100 years.

The primate of Numidia called a council of 70 bishops, deposed Caecilian, and consecrated Maiorinus. Maiorinus was the chaplain of a certain Lucilla, a wealthy Spanish matron, who had accused Caecilian of preventing her support of the confessors. Her personal involvement in the whole affair further muddied the waters. Caecilian, for his part, protested his innocence, affirmed the validity of his ordination as bishop, and refused to accept the deposition.

The number of bishops, priests, and laity who rallied around Donatus grew rapidly, so much so that a gathering of their bishops in 336 CE numbered 270: Almost all of Christian Africa seemed to be in the hands of Donatus, and his opponents named the movement after him: Donatists. There are two things that are striking about this turn of events: first, its popularity and success cover a wide spectrum of both geography and class in Roman Africa; second, it remained in virtual isolation from the rest of the Christian world. What was it about Donatus and his followers that made them so successful, becoming the majority church of Christian Roman Africa in the fourth century? It has been argued, for example, that Donatism was ultimately an anti-Roman movement; it has also been proposed that it was an ancient form of rural proletariat revolt, that is, that behind it all was economics or a revolt of the oppressed and ignored poor who tilled the soil; it has likewise been presented as an indigenous religious movement—a reaction against an overly universal, even imperial, Christianity, and thus Donatism sought to maintain traditional African Christianity, thus opposing Roman Christianity.

In the fall of 312 CE it was learned that Constantine wanted to restore churches and cemeteries to the Catholic Church, but, to do so, he had to know which of these two groups was "Catholic." A local dispute thus became a concern for the Empire. In the meantime, Maiorinus died and was succeeded by Donatus. An appeal was made to Rome to settle the matter. In October of 313 CE Constantine requested Pope Miltiades, bishop of Rome, to decide the matter in council. The council ruled in favor of Caecilian, declaring him innocent of the charges and placing blame for the divisions on Donatus. Donatus and his followers appealed that decision, and Constantine asked for another church council to be led by bishops from Gaul; a regional council was held in Arles in August of 314 CE. The Council of Arles also ruled in favor of Caecilian and against Donatus. But the divisions only hardened. Again, on November 10, 316 CE, Constantine responded to a new appeal personally, ruling again in favor of Caecilian. That decision was supported by an aggressive series laws intended to establish peace: property confiscation, exile, and the like. Accusations and counter-accusations about who had or had not remained faithful, about who was or was not a *traditor*. Finally, Constantine washed his hands of the entire affair, leaving African Christianity to work things out for itself. The division continued and its intensity made it difficult to remember what actually happened—thus allowing for continual reinterpretation by subsequent generations.

The difficulty with each of these theories is that no one of them has withstood rigorous analysis nor provided the explanation. It has been shown that Donatism comprised all social classes, from farmers to senators; that there were both rich and poor among their numbers; that, in terms of specific African Christian religious practices, there are few, if any, significant differences between the habits of Donatus and of Caecilian.

The heart of the controversy, at least at the outset, while clearly involving personality issues, seemed to be fueled by radically different theological understandings of the relationship between the holiness of the church and the holiness of its ministers, in this case, its bishops. The rallying point became the sacrament of baptism. If baptism is what made someone holy, and the administering bishop was a *traditor*—and so someone who lost his holiness, the baptism administered by him was invalid, worthless. Caecilianus and those loyal to him, so insisted Donatus and those loyal to him, could not baptize since they had betrayed their commitment to holiness. Donatus had not because he, along with his fellow clergy and faithful had been faithful to the true Christian Catholic church. The community of Donatus insisted on rebaptism for anyone coming from Caecilian's religious community. At that time, the accusations were hurled back and forth, doubting the worthiness of each community's respective bishops, each side seeking to prove that the others were *traditores*. By all estimations the disunion quickly became a fact of life. Imperial attempts at suppression only seemed to increase Donatist successes, and subsequently did seem to bring into the affair a certain anti-imperial strain—but it is hard to show that this was not a later development. A particularly ferocious attempt to restore unity by two imperial commissioners, Paulus and Macarius, during the mid-340s, had seemingly the exact opposite effect. Their harsh measures were met with a violent response, which in turn prompted even harsher imperial measures leading to the death of some members of the community of Donatus. Much was made of these martyrs as the Donatist church quickly self-identified as the church of the persecuted.

Throughout the remainder of the century, up until the early 390s, Donatism gained in strength, served in particular by the fiery leadership of Donatus' successor, Parmenianus. Imperial involvement fluctuated between intervention and abstention, and often enough local officials threw the weight of their support behind Donatist causes. Two significant events, however, were portends of the future. First, in 362 CE, with the accession of the anti-Christian emperor, Julian, the Donatists bishops appealed to the emperor to revoke the exile imposed upon a number of their bishops. He was more than willing to comply, anxious to divide Christianity, apparently so as to favor a return to a non-Christian State. Second, within Donatism itself conflict occurred, resulting in splinter communities that were condemned and. These dissidents, for their part, claimed that they were victims of persecution and established separate churches. Reconciliation was sometimes achieved and the dissidents allowed back—without rebaptism. Both of those events were part of the 'case' that Augustine developed against the Donatists.

When Augustine began to exercise his priestly ministry a de facto stalemate seemed to have been accepted. Even though there were some strong pockets of Catholicism scattered throughout Numidia (e.g., Thagaste), the Donatist church was dominant overall, and the Catholic church was indeed a minority in Hippo Regius. While Catholic Carthage seemed to have regained some strength, Donatism appeared secure as the Christian Church of Africa. Catholics, while protesting, appeared to be unwilling or unable to do anything other than bemoan and endure the situation. At about the same time as Augustine's ordination, Aurelius was consecrated Catholic bishop of Carthage. A man with strong leadership skills, he began to bring the Catholic bishops together to talk. In 393 CE, the Catholic bishops met in council in Hippo Regius, and that meeting seemed to rekindle a new sense of purpose. That very same year Africa saw a revolt, led by Count Gildo and supported by a prominent Donatist bishop, Optatus of Timgad.

In the 20 years, from 391 to 411 CE, there would be a complete reversal of the Catholic and the Donatist roles as Catholic Christians became more numerous than Donatist Christians. The alliance between Aurelius and Augustine was the primary reason for that turn-around. Aurelius used his authority to organize; Augustine was the voice. Writing in 407/408 CE, he recounts something of his own history of involvement with the conflict, and the dramatic change that took place in his thinking:

> For my opinion originally was that no one should be forced to the unity of Christ, but that we should act with words, fight with arguments, and conquer by reason. Otherwise, we might have as false Catholics those whom we had known to be obvious heretics. But this opinion of mine was defeated, not by the words of its opponents, but by examples of those who offered proof. (*Letter* 93.5.17)

"Act with words, fight with arguments, and conquer by reason"—Augustine probably began his involvement against the Donatists with individual conversations (see *Letter* 44). When those efforts failed to gain any traction he waged a campaign of letter writing, preaching, and "pamphleteering." These efforts continued for nearly three decades and, in the end, produced hundreds of thousands of words that today stand as a lasting testament to just how important this controversy and its outcome was to Augustine and to his Catholic colleagues. These writings provide historical witness to his own developing perception of the conflict and its remedy. From the outset, he had no doubt as to what was at stake and why he could not remain silent. In a letter dated 396 CE, he makes this clear, writing to Valerius' Donatist counterpart in Hippo Regius, the bishop Proculeian.

> For, when it happened by chance that you gathered in one house and a discussion emerged between you about our hope, that is, about the heritage of Christ, he [Evodius, Augustine's episcopal colleague] said that Your Grace said that you wanted to confer with us in the presence of good men. I am very happy that you have deigned to offer this to my lowly self, nor can I in any way ignore such a great opportunity afforded by your good will, namely that, to the extent that the Lord will deign to provide strength, I may seek with you and discuss the cause, the origin, and the reason for such a sad and deplorable division in the

Church of Christ, to which he said, "I give my peace to you; I leave my peace with you (Jn. 14:27)." (*Letter* 33.2)

"Division in the Church of Christ" was, in 396 CE, Augustine's great concern. Clear as well was his concern for "the unity of the Church of Christ." That goal, stated and restated in innumerable ways, was a constant refrain in all of Augustine's writings on the conflict. But underlying this refrain Augustine clearly saw an even more fundamental theological issue: belief in Christ as the sole mediator. Christian disunity compromised belief in the salvation that Christ alone offered; that was an important theological issue with practical consequences. Division within the Christian Church was a counter sign, offering an excuse to those who wanted to dismiss the claims of Christianity—and there was no lack of resistance to the dominance of Christianity, even though it may appear, to a present-day reader, that its state-supported status gave Christians an advantage at that time. But paganism was still active. The vigorous anti-Pagan legislation of the 390s did not come close to eradicating it.

The Christian Church could only benefit by becoming united. But, even though it is clear that Augustine saw unity principally as a theological necessity, reflected in his quoting to Proculeian from John's Gospel: I give my peace to you; I leave my peace with you (Jn 14:27), Augustine, in this same letter, found it necessary to remind his interlocutor that the issues are more than a matter of mere social unity:

> I beg you to remember what you graciously promised, namely, that in the presence of those whom you choose we would investigate in harmony *an issue so important and pertaining to the salvation of all* (italics added). Only let our words not be futilely carried off by the breeze, but rather set down in writing in order that we may hold our conference with more tranquility and orderliness, and if something we said should slip from our memory, it may be recalled by being read back to us. Or, if you prefer, let us first confer with each other without any intermediary either by letters or by conversation and reading, wherever you wish. Otherwise, some unrestrained listeners might prefer to see a battle, as it were, between us rather than to *ponder their own salvation* (italics mine) during our discussion. The people could be informed afterward by us of the conclusion we have come to. Or, if you prefer to use letters, let them be read out to our peoples in order that we may at some point say, not "peoples," but "one people." (*Letter* 33.4)

Augustine saw this conflict in terms of eternal salvation from the very beginning, noting that he needed to understand this matter as an "issue so important and pertaining to the salvation of all." The temptation to fail to "ponder their own salvation" was real. Neither side in the controversy would have seen the matter otherwise. The Donatists, by insisting on rebaptism, were saying that Catholic baptism was not valid; they baptized all who came to them, making rebaptism into their sign of salvation as members of a distinct group of Christians. Such an attitude was abhorrent to Catholics. In a letter from the same time period as the one to Proculeian, Augustine recounted his dismay to a local official. A young man who had physically threatened his mother and had been severely rebuked by Augustine "changed allegiances," and he was received into the Donatist church by accepting their baptism:

> God, who sees the secrets of the human heart, knows that, as much as I desire peace among Christians, I am troubled by the sacrilegious actions of those who persevere in its disruption in an unworthy and impious fashion. God knows that this attitude of my mind is directed toward peace and that I am not trying to force anyone involuntarily into the Catholic communion, but to reveal the plain truth to all who are in error. Then, once our ministry has made it evident with God's help, the very truth may be enough to persuade them to embrace and follow her.
>
> After all, what is more terrible, I ask you, than what has now happened – not to mention other things? A young man is rebuked by his bishop because in his madness he constantly beats his mother and does not, even on those days when the severity of the laws pardons even the most wicked, hold back his impious hands from the body from which he was born. He threatens the same mother that he will go over to the sect of Donatus and that he will kill her whom he is accustomed to beat with an incredible furor. He threatens her, goes over to the sect of Donatus, is rebaptized in his madness, and is clothed in white garments, while clamoring for his mother's blood. He is placed within the altar rail where he stands conspicuously, and the eyes of all the groaning faithful have set before them, as if he were reborn in Christ, a man plotting to kill his mother. (*Letter* 34.1-2)

Catholics accepted the validity of Donatist baptism, and did not rebaptize Donatist converts—a service of reconciliation was all that was needed. Rebaptism thus became Donatist rallying point and Catholic provocation. For the Donatist community it was a concrete, visible, public means to denigrate their adversaries—the notorious case Augustine refers to seemed perfectly suited to those purposes (though we could wish to have more information about the exact nature of this mother/son incident). It is clear that for Augustine such action only served to convince him that such practices should be countered in a public forum. He had to develop a response to the theology that was used to justify them.

> We deplore and grieve over the violated peace, the sundered unity, the repeated baptisms, and the abused sacraments, which are holy even in wicked persons. If they consider these of little importance, let them look at the examples that show how important God considers them. (*Letter* 43.8.24)

The excerpt from Letter 43, written to Donatist bishops during the same period, briefly alludes to what will become the cornerstone of much of his writings against the Donatists: Sacraments are not made holy by the minister but by Christ. Thus, they are even holy when administered by wicked persons. Interestingly, Augustine rarely exercises this argument without also reviewing the historical events leading to the beginning of the division, and the fact that Caecilian was not a wicked person. Augustine repeatedly affirmed that on numerous occasions he was exonerated of the charge of *traditor*. Throughout the letter Augustine insists that his efforts were only prompted by motives that were spiritual and peaceful:

> I said this in the beginning so that no one would think that I sent this letter to you with more impudence than prudence in that I wanted to deal with you in this way about the business of your soul, since you do not belong to our communion. And yet, if I wrote something to you about the business of a farm or of settling some other financial dispute, perhaps no one would find fault. This world is so dear to human beings, and they themselves have grown worthless in their own eyes! This letter, then, will be a witness for my defense in the judgment of God, who knows with what intention I acted and who said, Blessed are the peacemakers because they will be called the children of God (Mt. 5:9). (*Letter* 43.1.2)

All he asks for is a response from his Donatist colleague:

> There you are, go and consult; learn what can be said against these views of ours. If they produce papers, we produce papers; if they say that ours are false, let them not be angry that we say this of theirs. No one wipes out from heaven the decree of God; no one wipes out from the earth the Church of God. He promised the whole world; she has filled the whole world. And she contains both evil and good, but on earth she loses only the evil, while in heaven she admits only the good. But this discourse which we have drawn from the grace of God with a great love of peace and of you--as he knows--will be for you a source of correction, if you are willing, but a witness against you, if you are not. (*Letter* 43.8.27)

Augustine ends this letter on a stark note. Perhaps, there is already a gnawing awareness and growing frustration that his "acting with words, fighting with arguments, and conquering by reason" was being met by silence and closed doors on the part of his Donatist colleagues. His awareness of the intransigence of Donatist leaders will lead a changed attitude and approach as the years pass. When Donatist bishops refused to listen, Augustine sought an audience among the Donatist laity.

The active leadership of Aurelius in Carthage and the forceful voice and pen of Augustine in Hippo Regius was primarily interested in the restoration of Catholic faith and identity. It also had the obvious effect of encouraging the Catholic bishops and their communities. Results soon began to be evident on a variety of fronts. This revitalization of the Catholic community had two results. The Catholic bishops began to appeal to the local Roman administration to apply the imperial legislation against heretics—already on the books—against the Donatists. Initially, these appeals went unheeded. Tragically, the renewed efforts triggered violence against the Catholic community by a group that was more or less clearly the 'arm' of Donatist leadership: the Circumcellions.

The Circumcellions were briefly mentioned by Augustine in the early years of his priesthood, in a letter to a Donatist bishop who had baptized a member of Augustine's Catholic congregation in Hippo Regius—and not just any member, but one of the Catholic church's deacons. As found in all of these first attempts at Catholic-Donatist dialogue, Augustine tried to establish neutral ground for discussion, and so pleads with Maximinus:

> Let us remove from the center stage those empty objections that are often hurled at one another by ignorant parties. You should not raise as an objection the era of Macarius, nor should I do the same with the violence of the *Circumcellions*, if this latter problem does not apply to you, nor those earlier events to me. The threshing floor of the Lord has not yet been winnowed; it cannot be free from straw. Let us pray and do as much as we can that we may be the wheat. I cannot be silent about our deacon who was rebaptized, for I know how dangerous for me such silence is. (*Letter* 23.6)

If Donatists had claimed to be the "persecuted church" after the harsh measures of Macarius in the 340s, "the violence of the Circumcellions" in Augustine's own day moved in the opposite direction, against Catholics. Augustine proposed that the letters of both be read out to their respective congregations. As he concludes the letter, the subject of violence becomes a plea for a response by Maximinus:

> But if you do not accept this calmly, what shall I do, brother, even though you are unwilling, but read our letters to the Catholic people in order that they may be better instructed? But if you refuse to reply by letter, I have decided to read at least my letter in order that, when people recognize your lack of confidence, they may at least be ashamed to be rebaptized. And I will not do this when the army is present for fear that someone of yours might think that I wanted to do this with more violence than the cause of peace requires. I will do it after the departure of the army in order that all who hear us may understand that it is not part of my purpose that people be forced against their will into communion with anyone, but that the truth may become known to those who seek it most peacefully. Terror from temporal authorities will cease on our side; let there also cease on your side terror from bands of *Circumcellions*. Let us deal with the facts; let us deal with reason; let us deal with the authorities of the divine scriptures; as quiet and peaceful as we can be, let us ask; let us seek; let us knock that we may receive and find and have the door opened for us. For it may perhaps be possible that, with the Lord helping our single-hearted efforts and prayers, this great deformity and impiety may begin to be wiped out from our lands. If you do not believe that I want to do this after the departure of the soldiers, write back to me after the departure of the soldiers. For, if I choose to read my letter to the people when the army is present, you can produce my letter to prove that I violated my word. May the mercy of the Lord keep this from my conduct and from the aim with which he has deigned to inspire me through his yoke. . . . (*Letter* 23.7)

Two threats loom across the conflict: first is an official threat from the government against the Donatists; second, roving "bands of Circumcellions" seeking Catholic targets. Augustine calls for a mutual cessation of violence and a renewed commitment to dialogue.

To judge from Augustine's frequent remarks about them, the Circumcellions were something equivalent to adult gangs, who were prone to violence against Catholics. They entered Catholic churches and vandalized them, physically attacking and mutilating Catholic clergy and Donatist converts to Catholicism and even engaging in outright murder. Augustine's letters, written in outraged protest, offered a list of names and incidents that document such atrocities. Their exact relationship to Donatism is disputed. While it is clear that most Donatists, both bishops and laity, distanced themselves from them, little was done concretely to stop their attacks. It came close to home when Augustine himself narrowly escaped an ambush that had been set for him, and when his colleague Possidius suffered violence at their hands, barely escaping with his life. Augustine recounts the incident in a letter "to the Donatists," dated sometime after August 406 CE.

> What else were we trying to achieve [peaceful reconciliation] when one of us, Possidius, the bishop of Calama, went to the estate at Figli so that our people there, who were few in number, might be visited and that those who wanted might, once they heard the word of God, be converted to the unity of Christ? As he was traveling on the road, your people ambushed him like robbers, and because he was able to avoid their ambush, with open violence they almost burned him alive along with the house where he had fled on the estate at Liveti, except that the farm workers of the same estate extinguished the flames set to it the third time on account of the danger to their own safety. (*Letter* 105.2.4)

In fact, the violence of the Circumcellions only served to weaken the Donatist cause. Not only did they continue to lose ground to the Catholics, but it also awakened official governmental support for seeking to put an end to the conflict. In 403 CE, the Catholic bishops welcomed an imperial mandate for a conference to decide the question once and for all. Donatist refusal to participate prompted enforcement of long dormant legislation against them, including confiscation of property, exile, and other punishments, though always short of physical violence. As the tide turned, the violence of the Circumcellions increased, serving only to harden Catholic resolve—and government insistence. In the meantime, the Donatist community itself suffered a great deal of internal conflict, leading to schisms within. Augustine and his fellow Catholic bishops found in the violence of the Circumcellions and in the published accounts of Donatist internal disunity further ammunition for bringing an end to a conflict. Roman authorities, too, wanted social order and peace.

In the early years of the fifth century, we begin to see a change in Augustine's approach to the controversy. By now, he had lost all hope that union was possible through "acting with words, fighting with arguments, and conquering by reason." These efforts had been met by a Donatist wall of stoney silence. Further, he increasingly came to believe that many Donatist laity were themselves victims of fear, habit, or ignorance: They feared violence if they became Catholic, and, besides, they were habituated to the only church they had ever known, and ignorant of the real history behind the disunion. Augustine became convinced that there was only one possible solution: recourse to the intervention of civil government to stop the violence against Catholics and to outlaw the existence of this sectarian division.

> But what should I say against these whose pernicious perversity is either repressed by a fear of fines or is taught by exile how the Church is spread everywhere, as it was predicted that she would be, the Church that they prefer to attack rather than recognize? And if those things that they suffer through a most merciful discipline are compared to those deeds that they commit out of a mindless fury, who would not see which of us should rather be called the persecutors? After all, by the very fact that bad children live wicked lives, even if they do not lay their hands on their parents in violence, they persecute more grievously their loving parents than when a father or a mother compels them all the more to lead a good life without any pretense to the extent that they love them more. (*Letter* 89.2)

"Compel them": This term will become a last resort for Augustine, seen as the only way to bring about an end to the bitter and now often-bloody disunity of the Christian church in Africa. Every other means had been tried—with no diminishment in the violence. Writing to a splinter group of the Donatists in 407 to 408 CE he comments:

> But the Donatists are excessively restless, and I think that it is not useless that they be held in check and corrected by the authorities established by God. After all, we rejoice over the correction of many who so sincerely hold and defend the Catholic unity and are happy that they have been set free from their former error so that we look upon them with great satisfaction. Given the force of habit they would, nonetheless, by no means have been changed for the better, if they were not struck with this fear and turned their worried mind to a consideration of the truth. (*Letter* 93.1.1)

What Augustine continued to address throughout the letter was the salutary, medicinal effect that compulsion had already had on many former Donatists, now Catholic.

> Oh, if I could show you how many sincere Catholics we now have from the *Circumcellions*! They condemn their former life and wretched error, because of which they thought that they did for the Church of God whatever they did in their restless rashness! They would, nonetheless, not have been brought to this healthy position if they were not bound, like men out of their minds, by the chains of these laws that you find displeasing. (*Letter* 93.1.2)

"Bound by the chains of these laws, like men out of their minds": Provocatively, Augustine will comb the Bible looking for divine support for what has become for him, the "last resort": "compelling love."

> You think that no one ought to be forced into righteousness, though you read that the head of the household said to his servants, "Whomever you find, force them to come in" (Lk. 14:23), though you read that he who was first Saul and afterwards Paul was forced to come to know and to hold onto the truth by the great violence of Christ who compelled him, unless you perhaps think that money or any possession is dearer to human beings than this light that we perceive by these eyes. Laid low by the voice from heaven, he did not recover this light that he lost suddenly, except when he was incorporated into the holy Church. And you think that one should employ no force upon a man in order that he might be set free from the harmfulness of error, though you see that God himself, than whom no one loves us more to our benefit, does this in the most obvious examples and though you hear Christ saying, "No one comes to me unless the Father has drawn him" (Jn. 6:44). This takes place in the hearts of all who turn to him out of fear of God's wrath. And you know that at times a thief scatters grain to lead cattle away and that a shepherd at times calls wandering cattle back to the herd with a whip. (*Letter* 93.2.5)

Force them to come in: The gospel parable of the banquet whose guests are forced to attend and the example of St. Paul who suffered violence at the hands of God (struck blind by a light from heaven) provided Augustine with a divine sanction for "compelling love." He will also turn to ancient health care to support his argument. Medical practice in his day used surgery, without contemporary refinements, such as anesthesia: Patients had to be "restrained" in order to be cured. Augustine calls this "healing love" (*Letter* 93.2.6), and he repeatedly points out how successful this healing love had already been for numerous former Donatists. Imperial laws may be painful, but their intention is medicinal.

> The fright over these laws, in the promulgation of which kings serve the Lord in fear, benefited all these people so that some now say, "We already wanted this, but thanks be to God who gave us the opportunity of finally doing it and cut away time for delaying." And others say, "We already knew that this was true, but we were held back by some sort of habit. Thanks be to the Lord who has broken our chains and has brought us to the bond of peace." Still others say, "We did not know that the truth was here, nor did we want to learn of it, but fear made us concentrate on coming to know it. For we were afraid that we would suffer the loss of temporal goods without any gain of eternal ones. Thanks be to the Lord who shook us free of our negligence by the goad of fear in order that we at least might be worried and seek what we never cared to know in our security." Others say, "We were deterred from entering by false rumors, and we would not have known they were false if we did not enter, nor would we have entered if we were not forced. Thanks be to the Lord who removed our fearfulness by his scourge and has taught us by experience how vain and empty were the reports that deceitful rumors spread about his Church. For

this reason we now believe that those charges were also false that the authors of this heresy raised, since their successors have made up false charges and worse ones." Others say, "We, of course, thought that it made no difference where we professed faith in Christ, but thanks be to the Lord who has gathered us back from our schism and has shown us that it is fitting that the one God be worshiped in unity." (*Letter* 93.5.18)

Throughout the letter, Augustine rehearsed two points: initially, the Donatists had appealed to the intervention of the Emperor Constantine; should Catholics not do the same? Also, the Donatists had implored imperial officials to suppress their own dissidents; that is what Catholics sought too. He returns to this notion of the success of this "compelling love" time and again, noting its effect in Hippo Regius:

For the first argument against me was my own city. Though it was entirely in the Donatist sect, it was converted to the Catholic unity out of fear of the imperial laws, and we now see that it detests the destructiveness of this stubbornness of yours so that no one would believe that it was ever a part of it. And it was the same with many other cities, which were reported to me by name, so that I might recognize by the very facts that one could correctly understand the words of scripture as also applying to this case, "Give a wise man a chance, and he will become wiser" (Prv. 9:9). For how many, as we know for certain, already wanted to be Catholics, because they were convinced by the clearest truth, but because they feared offending their own people, they daily postponed doing so! How many were bound, not by the truth, in which you never had much confidence, but by the heavy chain of inveterate habit, so that those words of God were fulfilled in them, "A difficult servant will not be corrected by words, for, even if he understands, he will not obey" (Prv. 29:19)! How many thought that the true Church was the sect of Donatus because security made them uninterested, reluctant, and lazy to gain knowledge of the Catholic truth! (5.17)

The final outcome of this "compelling love" was the great Council of 411 that took place in Carthage, under the authority of an imperial commissioner, Marcellinus.

After decades of avoiding a showdown, now all-too-well-aware that the imperial government could no longer look the other way, 285 Donatist bishops and 286 Catholic bishops assembled to argue their case before an imperial judge who would pass sentence "once and for all." A rather substantial account of the proceedings survives, the product of official notaries who recorded them. These were supplemented by Augustine's own synopsis of the proceedings. Taken together, they offer a window into this remarkable event. Augustine's voice was clearly dominant on the Catholic side, met often enough by a barrage of Donatist slander. This was clearly intended to provoke Augustine into incautious speech—the conference had all the trappings of a "trial" and opposing bishops acted like lawyers trying to lead their adversaries into deadly traps. Augustine reports how the Donatist bishops unthinkingly undermined their own case. After demonstrating that Caecilianus was judicially exonerated of the charges made against him (and after retelling the past events of Donatist history), Augustine turned to the Donatist court cases involving their own dissident groups.

> After this case reached their ears, they were afraid and upset and, having forgotten how they earlier argued against us, they immediately said, "One case does not prejudice another, nor does one person prejudice another." And they supported with their own words what we said before about the Church . . . (*Letter* 141.6).

"One case does not prejudice another, nor does one person prejudice another" was precisely the legal opening Augustine needed to argue once and for all against the Donatist cause. It became a virtual refrain of Augustine, turning the Donatist's very own words against them—further enhanced by the introduction of incriminating documents:

> Who would believe that they read out these documents against themselves and in our favor, if the will of God almighty had not brought it about that the proceedings contained not only their words but also their handwritten names?" (*Letter* 141.11)

"Who would believe. . . .": Augustine marveled at the sudden turn of events and had no doubt that "the will of God had brought it about." Donatist self-incrimination hastily brought the proceedings to a conclusion as the imperial commissioner ruled in favor of the "Catholic cause" and imposed harsh civil measures that virtually suffocated the Donatist church through property confiscation, loss of legal recognition, exile, and the like. Tension and bitterness did not end, however—and in its losses the Donatists claimed impropriety on the part of Marcellinus.

> Let them, therefore, not tell you that we bribed the judge with money. What else, after all, are losers accustomed to say? Or, if we gave something to the judge in order that he would rule against them and for us, what did we give them in order that they would not only say but read out so much against themselves and for us? Or do they perhaps want us to thank them in your presence because, though they say that we bribed the judge with money, they offered to us gratuitously all those many things that they said and read out in our favor and in opposition to themselves? Or at least, if they say that they defeated us because they managed the case of Caecilian better than we did, clearly believe them on this. After all, we thought that it was enough to read two documents in his defense, but they produced four. . . . (*Letter* 141.12)

With irony, Augustine notes how it might have been claimed that the Catholics had bribed the Donatists to self-incriminate. But, despite the victory, Donatism did not die out—it continued on the periphery, produced some subversive activity, and as late as 418 CE Augustine was constrained to debate dissident Donatist bishops.

In fact, Donatism has not died out in scholarship either. Augustine has been accused of being the "father of the Inquisition," the "patron of intolerance," and much worse in accounts of the "Donatist controversy" and the role bishop of Hippo played in it. This chapter has tried to present it from the perspective of Augustine's own writings, even though readers of the twenty-first century might find his arguments and approaches both alien and disturbing. They are certainly unsettling for anyone accustomed to modern approaches to religious questions that sharply separate church and state, and prizes freedom of conscience and freedom of belief as inalienable rights. But Augustine was not operating in a modern context, and, if he had been a Donatist bishop, very little would have changed. For him questions of truth, love, unity, and salvation did not allow for indifference—and were never merely private. And the questions were always much bigger than Augustine. Both sides called themselves Catholic (despite the Donatist label used here for clarity sake); both sides looked upon "the other" as beyond the pale of salvation—eternally damned; both sides were willing to "use the government" when it served their advantage—and ignore or condemn it when it did not; both sides worked collectively to defeat their adversaries and secure the upper hand—Augustine never worked alone. But both sides did not have Augustine—and perhaps that is why the Donatist controversy is still being argued today.

Reading Augustine: Commentary on Psalm 10, 5–6

In this commentary on Psalm 10 from the time of Augustine as a priest, it is clear that he has already recognized the difficulty of Donatist practice and belief. Even though they describe themselves as Christians, their violence toward Catholics was hardly Christian; even worse, their leaders often presented themselves as the focus of their people's trust. Baptizing a second time denies that the one who baptizes is Christ; the Donatist priests, therefore, put themselves in the place of Christ.

> 5. *Trust in the Lord*, then. Those who put their trust in a fellow-human have good cause for alarm, and people who swear by a man's grey hairs cannot deny that they belong to a man's sect And when in conversation they are asked to whose communion they belong, unless they say they are of the party of Donatus, they cannot be identified. Tell me, what do they do when the countless daily sins and crimes of those with whom their community is full are recounted to them? Can they possibly say, *In the Lord I trust. How can you say to my soul, Go off into the mountains like a sparrow*? No, for those who say that sacraments are valid only when administered by holy persons fail to trust in the Lord. When they are asked who these holy people are, they are embarrassed to say, "We are." Or even if they are not embarrassed to say it, those who hear are embarrassed for them. Therefore these Donatists force those who receive the sacraments to place their hope in a mere human whose heart they are unable to see. And cursed is everyone who places his hope in someone human. For what does it mean to say, "What I give is holy," except "Place your hope in me"? But what if you are not holy? Show me your heart instead. If you cannot do that, how am I to see that you are holy? Or perhaps you will say that it is written, *By their works you will know them* (Mt 7:16)? Well then, I see some amazing works, the

daily acts of violence perpetrated by the Circumcellions under the leadership of bishops and priests, how their gangs roam around and call their terrifying cudgels Israels. These are things which the men and women who are alive now see and feel daily. . . . Why do you presume to rebaptize Christians coming from Mesopotamia who have not so much as heard the names of Caecilian and Donatus, and to deny that they are Christians? If the sins of other people about which they know nothing defile them, you yourself are condemned by whatever is committed every day by members of your party without your knowledge. You vainly hurl imperial edicts at Catholics when in your own camp the cudgels and firebrands of private citizens wreak such savagery."

Look how far they have fallen, those who, seeing sinners in the Catholic Church, have been unable to say, *I trust in the Lord*, and instead have placed their hope in a fellow human being. This is what they would say were not they themselves (or rather they too) just what they thought other people were—those others from whom, in their sacrilegious pride, they pretended to seek separation.

6. Therefore let the Catholic soul say, In the Lord I trust. How can you say to my soul, Off you go to the mountains like a sparrow? For see, sinners have bent their bows; they have their arrows ready in the quiver, to shoot those of honest heart when the moon is darkened; and let this soul turn from the Donatists and address the Lord, saying, They have destroyed what you made perfect. And let the Catholic soul say this not against them alone but against all heretics. For all, as much as in them lies, have destroyed the praise which God has made perfect from out of the mouths of babies and nurslings, disturbing little children with pointless and over-ingenious questions and refusing to allow them to be nourished on the milk of faith. It is as though such a soul were asked, "Why do they say to you, Go off into the mountains like a sparrow? Why do they frighten you with sinners who have bent their bow to shoot at those of honest heart when the moon is darkened?" It replies, "This is why they terrify me: because they have destroyed what God made perfect." . . . if Caecilian did you harm, what did Christ do to you? He said, My peace I give to you, my peace I leave with you (Jn 14:27), but you have besmirched that peace with your unspeakable schism. What did Christ do to you? It was Christ who endured his own betrayer with such patience that he gave him the first Eucharist consecrated with his own hands and blessed with words from his own lips, as he gave it to the other apostles. What did Christ do to you? It was Christ who sent his own betrayer with the other disciples to preach the kingdom of heaven, that same betrayer whom he called a devil, who even before his treason could not be trusted with the Lord's purse. And he sent him out to preach in order to show that the gifts of God come to those who receive with faith, even if those through whom they receive are like Judas.

9

Augustine, Bishop of Hippo Regius—Community-Building

An offhand remark by Augustine in one of his letters calls to mind the reluctant episcopal candidates who suffer virtual imprisonment until they accepted the office of bishop:

> Listen to what the apostle says, "He who desires the episcopacy desires a good work" (1 Tm. 3:1), and yet how many – that they might accept the episcopacy – are held against their will, led off, imprisoned, kept under guard, and suffer much that they dislike, until there is a willingness to take on that good work. (*Letter* 173.2)

Was that comment is self-referential? Did the people of Hippo Regius force him to say yes? That is possible, but here is no way to tell whom Augustine has in mind. Such a question does at least indicate why a sensitive, thoughtful person like Augustine might have looked with dismay at the prospect of being bishop. From what has been seen in the past chapters, however, it seems that Augustine never looked back. There is good reason to think that the pastoral burden never ceased to be anything but heavy for him, at least because of the kinds of questions he kept asking himself. How is one to act for the common good? How can one determine when correction is better than comfort or vice versa? How can anyone balance truth and love?

"Burden," in fact, is the word he often uses to refer to the demands of his office. The Latin word, *sarcina*, refers to the heavy backpack shouldered by the Roman soldier on marching campaigns. One day, as he was preaching a sermon on Psalm 36, he told the gathered congregation about the personal slurs that the Donatists were directing against him. He offered his listeners a way to respond to the mud-slinging:

> Say nothing to them except this: "Keep to the point, friends. Augustine is a bishop in the Catholic Church, he has his own burden (*sarcina*) to bear and he will have to render an account to God. I have known some good of him. If he is bad, he knows it himself, but if he is good, he is not the foundation of my hope

for all that. This above all I have learned in the Catholic Church, not to set my hope on any human being. It is understandable that you reproach us for the human faults among us, because you do set your hope on human beings." (*exp. ps.* 36.3.20)

"Augustine is a bishop in the Catholic church, he has his own burden (*sarcina*) to bear." Augustine did not look back to such things; the challenges of pastoral care, along with the constant demands made upon his own example and the consequences of his of his own actions, required his full attention.

One Bishop Among Many

The sheer volume of his writings suggests that he was primarily a thinker and writer—a scholar at his desk. In fact, he surely would have preferred giving his full attention to being a thinker and a writer; but that was never possible. Given the influence of his voice and of his pen, Augustine the bishop was a singular figure in the Roman African world of Late Antiquity, but he was also one bishop among many in a very crowded field.

In Roman Africa of the early fifth century, there were at least 286 Catholic bishops and 279 Donatist bishops. We know that because there was a roll call of those who participated in the Conference in Carthage in 411 CE. Marcellinus, the imperial commissioner, had the names called, one-by-one, and each bishop had to be acknowledged (often begrudgingly) or challenged (often bitterly) by a Catholic or a Donatist counterpart. That tedious process went on for hours, but, in the end, it gave history a list of all the bishops, indicating as well that there were about 120 Catholic bishops and about the same number of Donatist bishops who were not present.

In the Catholic roll-call, which was usually made according to seniority, Augustine's name is well down the list, one among many. The bishops were very protective of and sensitive to their order of seniority. We know from one of Augustine's letters that he was concerned that in a listing of bishops his name was called ahead of someone whose name should have preceded his own (see *Letter* 59.1). Augustine felt obliged to set the record straight, lest his colleagues be slighted. Despite the large number of Christian bishops and the careful attention to seniority, there is little doubt that there were enormous differences between episcopal sees as well as individual bishops. Aurelius was bishop of Carthage, the principal city of Roman Africa; his name began every Catholic bishops' list. On the other hand, some were bishops of small country towns and had little advanced education. Some bishops signed documents but the location of their episcopal see cannot be identified. Hippo Regius was an important port city, but it carried no special weight in the political sphere, and culturally it was unquestionably a backwater. It is no exaggeration to say that Augustine put Hippo Regius on the map.

The Life of a Bishop

What did it mean to be the Catholic bishop of Hippo Regius? Augustine repeatedly emphasizes how he saw his primary task and responsibility: caring for the good of all as a "steward of Word and Sacrament" (see, e.g., *ser.* 301A: *dispensator verbi et sacramenti*). This meant, above all, the daily celebration of the Eucharist, a worship service that was divided into two parts, a service with biblical readings and preaching, followed by an altar or table service (Augustine uses both Latin words, *altar* and *mensa* frequently) that commemorated Jesus' Last Supper and culminated in communion. There was, it seems, a porter at the door to screen those who entered (see *ser.* 46.31). The service of the Word was apparently open, but, to remain for the celebration of the sacrament of the altar, one had to be baptized. The African practice, predating Augustine, was the daily celebration of the Eucharist. So the ministry of Word and Sacrament defined Augustine as a bishop. "We're not bishops for ourselves, but for those for whom we minister the Lord's Word and Sacrament." (*Against Cresconius* 2.11.13)

Eucharist provided the fundamental rhythm of life for Augustine and for his local Christian community, and it provided abundant opportunity for preaching over the course of nearly four decades. Along with daily Eucharist there was a regular evening prayer service called the lucernarium (lucerna in Latin means "lamp"; the prayer service began with the lighting of the evening lamps). Here scriptural readings and psalm singing (see *Letter* 29.11; *ser.* 308A.7; 342; *City of God* 22.8) were accompanied by the second sermon of the day. Although such abundant preaching was common practice in Roman Africa and elsewhere in the West (Milan, for example, also had daily Eucharist), what was unique about Augustine's preaching is that more sermons have come down from him than any other ancient Christian figure. We have more than 900 sermons and even that is but a fraction of his actual preaching. These sermons provide a rich and important portal into Augustine's world: They reveal the man, his thinking, and the people and situations he encountered day in and day out. As the years of his episcopacy passed, his reputation spread. Stenographers were often sent by interested parties to record his sermons, and we know that the church of Hippo Regius had its own secretariat. It is the work of these stenographers that allowed so many of his sermons to be preserved.

Augustine preached without a text in hand (though he did at times hold a biblical codex; see, e.g., *ser. Dolbeau* 23.20; 25.20), but this did not mean without preparation. He studied the biblical texts before hand, collected his thoughts, and then engaged in what scholars have called "dialogues with the faithful." From off-hand remarks scattered throughout his preaching we know that the people were not passive listeners; they shouted, groaned, moaned, beat their breasts, and cried; they were often distracted, bored, inattentive, tired, and even resistant. On more than one occasion, we can hear him pleading: "Hang in there (*attendite*), I beg you. We are near the end" (*ser.* 37.27).

"*Attendite*—pay attention! Hang in there!" This particular plea occurs hundreds of times in his preaching; the one just cited comes at the end of a very long sermon. Augustine was not thinking of a merely mental effort. Unlike present day practice, the churches of Africa were without seating for the people. Hence, the people were standing as they listened to the bishop who was seated on the *cathedra*—a seat for the bishop, raised slightly and located in the apse of the church in Hippo Regius; archeological remains still show its position today. One can thus often hear a veritable apology from Augustine for the sheer physical effort demanded of his people, especially if his preaching was lengthy. Preaching one day on the martyrs, and perhaps with a smile, he remarks: "We know that you have been listening patiently, and by your standing and listening for so long you have been suffering in sympathy with the martyrs." (*ser.* 274)

The preaching was usually based upon the biblical texts of the day. Since most people did not have any other access to the biblical text, that was necessary. On some occasions, however, there were readings from the Acts of the Martyrs. Evening prayer services also included sermons based on the psalms that were sung or on the biblical reading. Biblical readings were sometimes chosen for the occasion by Augustine himself. On at least one occasion, he was caught by surprise when the reader read the wrong passage—or at least from a reading that was different from the one Augustine had prepared:

> The reading from the gospel which we have just heard, dearly beloved, was not arranged by me, as usually happens. But all the same, thanks to the good management of the Lord, who controls all our activities, it fits extremely well with the psalm on which I had decided to speak to your graces. (*ser. Dolbeau* 5.1)

Augustine saw this mistake as an invitation from God and preached on the text that had been read.

A Bishop of the People

Much of Augustine's world is revealed in his preaching; in his sermons, he constantly drew upon the daily life experience of his listeners. Doctors, for example, prescribed cold liquids for fevers: "You are not to drink cool drinks, the doctor tells you, the enemy of your fever." (*ser.* 229E.3) Lawsuits against ship owners were common (perhaps because transportation of goods by ships was at the very heart of that society's economy, a fact which explains why Augustine refused a donation in this way: "I don't want the church of Christ to be a shipping company."—*ser.* 355.5) Food on the table was typically Mediterranean: "Fish, eggs, bread, apples, wheat. . . ." (*piscis, ouum, panis, pomum, frumentum*—*ser.* 61.2) Examples such as these are plentiful. Even if Augustine did not set out to teach us about his world, its likes and dislikes, pleasures and discomforts, opportunities and obstacles, his preaching opens a window into the daily life in Hippo Regius. He was, in fact, attentive to all that his world offered because he wanted to help his listeners consider what another world had to offer:

> How many people go to sleep rich, and with bandits coming and taking
> everything away, wake up poor? (*ser.* 61.10.11)

> When people want to place in complete safety what they love most on
> earth, they hire themselves the securest possible places, and take all the steps
> they can to keep a place for themselves which thieves cannot get at. And while
> that is what they want and what they try to keep safe, one can ask when can this
> ever really be done on earth? Perhaps the guard himself will be a thief. (*ser.*
> 390.1)

Comments such as these make it clear that life was fragile for all, rich and
poor alike.

Of course, his primary purpose in preaching was religious and spiritual; in
fact, his determined effort to bring the spiritual and secular "worlds" together
was what allowed his readers to learn about the day-to-day experience of his
city. But he was not always successful in uniting the everyday with the lofty.
From the newly discovered Dolbeau Sermons, we learn that, on at least one occasion, the time of preaching could be filled with tension and conflict. On January 22, 404 CE, preaching in Carthage, Augustine abruptly left the pulpit in
response to what he considered an unruly and disrespectful congregation. Was
Augustine angry? Did he have a temper? On the following day, an apologetic
Augustine talked about obedience to the same crowd, while he acknowledged
his own need for their forgiveness.

> Yesterday's disturbance, for which I was as much to blame as you, more
> in fact because of my responsibility to you, would properly, I admit, be calling
> for silence today. But because charity, whose slave one has of necessity to be,
> has brought an order from our master and brother [Bishop Aurelius of Car-
> thage] – though there is also evident in you an avid desire for hearing some-
> thing, which we confidently hope God will be good enough to make fruitful in
> your good behavior and your obedience – I am going to be your slave in the
> name of Christ, since I am the slave of Christ whose members you are. (*ser.*
> *Dolbeau* 2.1)

The discourse that follows manifests a contrite bishop who knew how to balance—deftly—both his authority and the dignity of his congregation.

As important as the preaching was, what followed was an even-more-
preeminent and sacred moment. After the sermon, those who were not baptized
were dismissed, and "the sacrament of the Lord's table" (*ser.* 227) followed. It
has already been mentioned that scholars often talk of early Christianity's practice of the *disciplina arcani*, the practice of not talking openly about Christianity's sacramental rites. This meant, for example, that those not yet baptized (and
this included those preparing for baptism) had never experienced nor witnessed
"the sacrament of the Lord's table." Augustine made a passing comment about
that fact in his *Homilies on John's Gospel*, saying that, if one were to ask a catechumen preparing for baptism about the Eucharist, "he would not know what
we were talking about, since Jesus has not yet made it known to him" (*On
John's Gospel* 11.3). What has come down in a number of sermons preached by

Augustine to the newly baptized is his instruction to them about what takes place at the altar:

> I haven't forgotten my promise. I had promised those of you who have just been baptized a sermon to explain the sacrament of the Lord's table, which you can see right now, and which you shared in last night. You ought to know what you have received, what you are about to receive, what you ought to receive every day. (*ser.* 227)

The sermon is very brief, typical of Easter Sunday preaching after an all-night vigil culminating in baptism and Eucharist. What it does offer is a unique window into what Augustine's Catholic Christian community saw as a most sacred moment:

> That bread which you can see on the altar, sanctified by the word of God, is the body of Christ. That cup, or rather what the cup contains, sanctified by the word of God, is the blood of Christ . . . In this loaf of bread you are clearly to understand how much you should love unity. . . . (*ser.* 227)

He continues to explain the unfolding of the ritual:

> First, after the prayer, you are urged to Lift up your hearts . . . after [those words] you reply, We have lifted them up the Lord . . . then, after the consecration is accomplished, we say the Lord's prayer . . . After that comes the greeting, Peace be with you, and Christians kiss one another with a holy kiss. It's a sign of peace; what is indicated by the lips should happen in the conscience; that is, just as your lips approach the lips of your brothers and sisters, so your heart should not be withdrawn from theirs. (*ser.* 227)

As he draws the brief sermon to a close he reminds his newly baptized and all the faithful of the seriousness and sacredness of the ritual:

> So these are great sacraments and signs, really serious and important sacraments . . . So receive the sacrament in such a way that you think about yourselves, that you retain unity in your hearts, that you always fix your hearts up above. Don't let your hope be placed on earth, but in heaven. Let you faith be firm in God, let it be acceptable to God. Because what you don't see now, but believe, you are going to see there, where you will have joy without end. (*ser.* 227)

He ends on a note of joy, highlighting the promise of life that is to come.

If Augustine saw his primary task as ministry to Word and Sacrament, this responsibility was often, much to his dismay, made more difficult by a host of other responsibilities. He often spoke of his "curarum ecclesiasticarum sarcina—the burden of cares about the Church" (*Letter* 101.3), and they often kept him out of the church proper and even out of Hippo Regius for extended periods of time. The journeys of Augustine were not infrequent, and during his absence the people complained and he worried, as reflected in a letter addressed to his own people in 410 CE from Carthage, as the Donatist question finally reached a boiling point:

> First of all, I beg Your Charity and I beseech you by Christ that my bodily absence not cause you to be sad. For I think that you have no doubt that I could in no way depart from you in the spirit and in the affection of my heart, though it saddens me perhaps more than you that my weakness cannot suffice to meet all the concerns that are demanded of me by the members of Christ, whom his fear and love compel me to serve. After all, Your Charity knows that I am never absent because of a capricious freedom but because of necessary services, which have often compelled my holy brothers and colleagues to endure labors, even at sea and across the sea. I have always been excused from these, not by a lack of concern of my mind but by the less suitable health of my body. (*Letter* 122.1)

The capital city (a distance of some 200 miles requiring several days of difficult travel), although a frequent destination for church councils, was only one of many settings that required his presence for a variety of reasons. He often traveled throughout his diocese to visit the various local churches under his care (*Letter* 56.1). He traveled to ordinations of bishops (*Letter* 126), to church trials (clergy charged with misconduct were tried ecclesiastically), in response to invitations to preach, and on special missions to the furthest corners of Roman Africa (see *Letter* 193). As burdensome as these travels were, Augustine endured them as a necessary part of his office—a necessary consequence of following the example of the Good Shepherd, he insisted (see esp. *sers.* 46 & 47).

A Bishop's Secular Reality

But if Augustine found spiritual purpose and strength to endure the burdens and challenges of his pastoral responsibilities, the same could not be said for the secular responsibilities thrust upon him. "When men need us because they want to settle their lawsuits over worldly matters before us, they call us holy men and servants of God so that they may accomplish their earthly business." (*Letter* 33.5)

This passing comment in a letter from his early days of ministry sheds light on a legal/civic obligation thrust upon bishops in late antiquity, the *audientia episcopalis*. The expression refers to a bishop's court. Beginning with legislation under Constantine, and subsequently refined by his successors, Christian bishops were given legal authority to act as judge in certain civil cases. While the initial Constantinian legislation gave bishops broad jurisdiction in a variety of matters, there was a concerted imperial effort under Gratian in 376 CE, Acradius in 398 CE, and Honorius in 408 CE to restrict episcopal jurisdiction. We get little evidence from Augustine that this in any way reduced the demands placed upon him. In Possidius' *Life of Augustine*, readers are told that he would have a morning "court session," with a long line of people, not all of whom were from his congregation. The sessions often extended well into the afternoon, leaving no time even to pause for the midday meal. In one of his composed homilies, thus deliberate and not spontaneous, he offered a comment about the bishop's court as less than pleasant business for him:

But what can the next verse mean? Go away from me, you spiteful people, and then I will thoroughly explore the commandments of my God. Observe that the speaker does not say, "And then I will carry out the commandments," but I will thoroughly explore them. He wants spiteful people to leave him alone, and he even drives them away by force, so that he may come to know God's commandments perfectly in a spirit of love. Malevolent persons give us plenty of practice in carrying out the commandments but distract us from any deep study of them. This happens not only when the ill-disposed persecute us and try to take us to court but also when they are compliant and flattering yet insistently demand that we engage in furthering their vicious, greedy business and spend our time on them. Or again, they harass weak people and force the victims to bring their cases to us. Yet we dare not say to such plaintiffs, Tell me, fellow, who appointed me a judge or arbiter between you? (Lk. 12:14) for the apostle appointed ecclesiastical assessors to hear such cases and forbade Christians to litigate in the civil courts. Even when those who appeal to us are not out to get their hands on other people's property but are seeking greedily to recover their own, we do not say to them, "Be on your guard against any kind of acquisitiveness"; we hesitate to remind them of the man to whom the Lord said, You fool: your life will be taken from you this very night; and then who will own what you have amassed? (Lk. 12:20) Even if we do say something like this, they do not go away and leave us alone; they insist and crowd in on us and plead and rant and pester, so that we are taken up with the things that matter to them rather than with exploring God's commandments, which matters to us. What weariness with the hordes of importunate people and what intense longing for the divine words wrung this cry from the psalmist, Go away from me, you spiteful people, and then I will thoroughly explore the commandments of my God! We are not speaking here about the obedient faithful who rarely trouble us with their secular disputes and willingly acquiesce in our decisions. May all these forgive our remarks, for they do not wear us out with their litigation; rather do they console us by their obedience. But with the other sort in mind, the ones who quarrel among themselves, who when they have plagued innocent people reject our ruling, who oblige us to waste time that ought to be spent on the things of God--with all these in mind, I say, we too must be allowed to cry out in words uttered by Christ's body, Go away from me, you spiteful people, and then I will thoroughly explore the commandments of my God. (exp. ps. 118.24.3)

Augustine preferred to study God's Word over trying to mediate business disputes, arguments over inheritances and properties. His task was the just application of Roman law. And while crowds flocked to Augustine, the Judge, because he had a reputation for honesty and fairness, this did not mean they always accepted his judgment. We get a sense of this, once again, in a passing comment from another sermon:

Now it may be that this judgment cannot be overturned, because it is upheld by the law, not Church law perhaps, but that of secular rulers who have conceded to the Church that anything decided in an ecclesiastical court cannot be undone. If the judge's decision cannot be overturned, then, the unsuccessful party is now unwilling to look honestly at himself; instead he regards the judge with a jaundiced eye and does his best to slander him. "He wanted to please the other fellow," he alleges. "He was prejudiced in favor of a rich man, or he received something from him, or he was afraid to antagonize him." So he accuses the judge of taking bribes. But suppose a poor person had a case against a rich person, and judgment was given in the poor person's favor, the rich party would still say, "The judge was bribed." What bribe could a poor person offer? "Well," replies the aggrieved party, "he saw that the person in question was poor, and to avoid getting a bad name for deciding against a poor defendant he suppressed justice, and gave his decision in contravention of the truth." One way or another, this is bound to be alleged, so you see that it is only in the presence of God, who alone sees who is accepting bribes, and who is not, that anyone who does not take them can say, "I have walked in my innocence. . ." (*exp. ps.* 25.2.13)

Despite some who resented a judgment against them, the vast majority, both Catholic Christians and others, expected to find in Augustine's court rulings marked by fairness and justice.

Yet you see Christ's Church so highly respected in his name that all those who do not yet believe lie under the feet of Christians. What crowds of people, not yet Christians themselves, come running to the Church and begging the Church to help them! They want temporal assistance from us, even if they are still unwilling to reign eternally with us. (exp. ps. 46.5)

As onerous as the task was, it gave Augustine an important source of knowledge quite distinct from what he acquired in his bishop's study, and the integrity of his decisions enhanced the perception of the church's integrity, something that Augustine valued highly.

If Augustine regularly found himself on the judging side of the bench, it was not unusual for him to have been on the opposite side, pleading with officials on behalf of his own congregation and of individual citizens of Hippo Regius. There he discovered how little authority a bishop really had. A remarkable sermon has come down to us, preached in the context of a civic riot that led to a mob lynching. The man who was lynched was a minor military official involved in shady business dealings that had economically devastated the lives of many. Those who gathered in church with Augustine seemed not to have been the actual perpetrators, but, the bishop asked them, were they really without guilt?

What am I to say to you, my brothers and sisters, what am I to say to you? Don't give such people your approval. But am I really to think this of you, that you do approve of such people? Far be it from me to think that of you. But it isn't enough for you to disapprove of such people, not nearly enough; there is something more required of you. None of you should say, "God knows I didn't do it, God knows I didn't do it, and God also knows I didn't want it to happen."

There you have two things you said: both "I didn't do it," and "I didn't want it to happen." It's still not enough. No, it's certainly not enough, if you didn't want it to happen, if you didn't also forbid it. . . . (*ser.* 302.11)

He voices publicly what everyone is saying under their breath:

But that bad man did so many things, oppressed so many people, reduced so many to beggary and penury (*ser.* 302.13)

Augustine answers himself:

There are judges to deal with him, there are the authorities to deal with him. The state is well ordered; for the authorities that exist have been ordained by God (Rom. 13:1). What business is it of yours to vent your rage like that? What authority have you received – except that this isn't a case of public punishment, but of open brigandage? (*ser.* 302.13)

As the sermon proceeds, it seems clear that local judges had looked the other way in the face of the victim's misdeeds, at least until mob justice took action.

"But that soldier did such dreadful things to me." (*ser.* 302.15)

"He oppressed me, when I was engaged in business." (*ser.* 302.16)

These justifications also point an accusing finger at Augustine, suggesting that he may not have intervened with the public officials as he could and should have. In exasperation, Augustine "vents," revealing another side of his office as bishop.

It is often said about me, "Why does he go to that authority?" and "What's the bishop looking for with that authority?" And yet you all know that it's your needs which compel me to go where I would much rather not; to calculate the appropriate moment, to stand outside the door, to wait while the worthy and the unworthy go in, to be announced, to be scarcely admitted sometimes, to put up with little humiliations, to beg, sometimes to obtain a favor, sometimes to depart in sadness. Who would want to endure such things, unless I was forced to? Let me be, let me not have to endure all that, don't let anybody force me to. Look, as a little concession to me, give me a holiday from this business. I beg you, I beseech you, don't let anybody force me to it; I don't want to have to deal with the authorities. God knows, I'm forced to do so. And I behave with the authorities as I ought to behave with Christians, if I find Christians in that authority; and with pagans as I ought to behave with pagans; wishing them all well . . . All the same, my brothers and sisters, excuse me, but you can say to me about the authorities, "He could admonish him, and he would do good.' And I will answer, "I did admonish him, but he didn't listen to me." And I admonished him where you weren't there to hear. Who could ever take the people aside to admonish them? At least we have been able to admonish one man on the side, and say, "Act like this, or act like that," where no one else was present. Who could ever take the people aside, and admonish the people with nobody else knowing?

It is this emergency that compels me to speak to you like this, or I will have a bad account to render for you to God; or else he will say to me, "You should warn, you should hand out, I will handle the accounting." So then distance yourselves, so distance yourselves totally from these bloody deeds. Your only concern, when you see or hear about such things, should be to feel pity.

"But it was a bad man that died!"

He is to be mourned twice over, because he died twice over; both in time, and for eternity. I mean, if a good man had died, we would grieve out of human feelings, because he had left us, because we wanted him to go on living with us. Bad people are to be mourned much more, because after this life they are caught in the clutches of eternal pains. So let it be your business, my brothers and sisters, to grieve, let it be your concern to grieve, not to vent your rage." (*ser.* 302.17–18)

Clearly, events in Hippo Regius are tense, and Augustine is pleading with his own people to do what they can to help restore order.

One thing I do know, and everyone else knows it together with me, that you will find many households in this city in which there is not a single pagan; while there is no household to be found in which there are no Christians. And if you were to examine the matter carefully, there is no household to be found in which there aren't more Christians than pagans. It's true, you all agree. So you can see that these bad events wouldn't have occurred, if Christians hadn't wanted them to. You haven't got an answer to that. Bad things can be done secretly, but they cannot be done publicly if Christians forbid them and refuse to take part; because each one of you would restrain his slave, each one restrain his son; youth would be cowed by the severity of a father, the severity of an uncle, the severity of a teacher, the severity of a good neighbor, the severity of greater corporal punishment. If this sort of thing had been done, we wouldn't have been so saddened by these evil occurrences. (*ser.* 302.19)

The anonymity of the crowd is no guarantee of escaping punishment, but there is a judge who sees all.

How readily it's said, "What the people has done, it has done; who is there who can punish the people?" Really so, who is there? Not even God? (*ser.* 302.20)

Augustine ends with a final plea for peace.

So let us at last wind up this sermon. My brothers and sisters, I urge you, I beseech you by the Lord and his gentleness, be gentle in your lives, be peaceful in your lives. Peacefully permit the authorities to do what pertains to them, of which they will have to render an account to God and to their superiors. As often as you have to petition them, make your petitions in an honorable and quiet manner. Don't mix with those who do evil and rampage in a rough and disorderly manner; don't desire to be present at such goings on even as spectators. But as far as you can, let each of you in his own house and his own neighborhood deal with the one with whom you have ties of kinship and charity, by warning, persuading, teaching, correcting; also by restraining him from such seriously evil activities by any kind of threats, so that God may eventually have mercy, and put an end to human evils. . . . (*ser.* 302.21)

Curiously, there is an addendum to the sermon where Augustine addressed the law of sanctuary which allowed people pursued by the law to seek safe refuge in the church. It is not clear that this addendum belongs with the sermon, but if it does, it suggests that some members of the lynch mob had sought sanctuary in the church and were making everyone else afraid.

But if we wanted to sort them out, so that evildoers could be removed from the Church, there would be nowhere for those who do good to hide themselves; if we wished to allow noxious criminals to be removed from here, there would be nowhere for the innocent to flee to. So it's better that noxious criminals too should be protected by the Church, than that the innocent should be snatched from the Church. Bear these things in mind, so that, as I said, it is your presence in strength, not your savagery, that may inspire fear. (*ser.* 302.22)

Augustine was a bishop in a harsh and dangerous world, one where health, shelter, security, and legal recourse were often sought after and always remained precarious. Newly discovered *Letters* from and to Augustine make this even more apparent. We read there of a husband selling his wife, parents selling their children, kidnappings. The breakdown of social order prompted desperate letters of pleading to public officials to take action. The sarcina never seemed to get lighter.

Episcopal Writing

If there was one place where Augustine the Bishop did find occasional refuge from tumult and turmoil, it was at his desk; he would work well into the night. With all of the commitments and responsibilities that took him away from Hippo Regius, it is remarkable that he could have written so much. In one of the newly discovered letters, we learn firsthand how good he was at composition. He wrote to his dear friend and fellow-bishop Possidius, the year is 419 CE:

I do not know which of our works we were dictating when you left. Hence I mention everything I have dictated since we left Carthage. I wrote to Optatus, the Spanish bishop, again on the question of the origin of the soul. I wrote to Gaudentius, the Donatist bishop of Thamugadi, who more or less replied to the replies I sent him earlier. I dictated something against the Arians, in reply to what our Dionysius from Vicus Juliani sent me, and three sermons to be sent to Carthage. When in the midst of these I was preparing to return to the books on The City of God, I suddenly received a letter from the holy Renatus from Caesarea, who sent me two books of some Victor or other, who was a former disciple of that Vincent to whom I had replied in the past and who has become a Catholic from being a Donatist . . . And he wanted me to write about the soul, reprimanding our hesitation, because I did not dare to state definitively whether it came by propagation or was infused as entirely new in each person who is born, and he himself declared that the soul is not derived from propagation but is given to us. In his two books he said very many incorrect and absurd ideas and ones opposed to the Catholic faith. And because our friend whom I mentioned above earnestly asked me to refute those ideas, since some of them would mislead many people because of their charming style, I wrote one book on this for the same very dear friend of ours, and I want to write to Victor himself, since it is very important. And, to finish as well what remains of the Gospel of John, I have already begun to dictate some popular and not very long homilies to be sent to Carthage on the condition that, if the same primate of ours wishes that the rest be sent to him, he should say so and not delay in publishing them when he says so. I have already dictated six; for I have devoted the nights of Saturday and Sunday exclusively to them. And so, since I arrived, that is, from the third day of the Ides of September up to the Calends of December, I have dictated approximately six thousand lines. (*Letter* 23*.3)

Six thousand lines over the course of a few months; Augustine the pastor never ceased to be Augustine the writer. And what he recounts in this letter is typical of his entire episcopal career: long-term writing projects, such as City of God; numerous occasional pieces, prompted by unexpected requests. And it is precisely during this same period when he writes Possidius, explaining that he has finally finished *The Trinity*, a work begun in 399 CE. That project took him 20 years.

The Trinity is perhaps Augustine's most important and profound doctrinal work. It is an exploration and explanation of the Christian doctrine of God, comprising fifteen books. In many ways, it is emblematic of the paradoxes of Augustine the Bishop. Day in and day out he dealt with petty lawsuits and business haggling in the bishop's court, he preached to the ordinary folk of Hippo Regius, he encountered public officials and disgruntled adversaries, and at night, he read, thought, prayed, and wrote. In the case of *The Trinity*, it meant writing in spurts in the midst of being forced to attend to other matters. At one point an unedited and unfinished manuscript of the work was circulated, certainly by someone within his own household, someone with access to his study. In an introductory letter to the work, addressed to Bishop Aurelius in Carthage when it was finally completed, we are provided once again with an insight into Augustine's mind and world:

I was a young man when I began these books on the Trinity which the one true God is, and I am now an old man as I publish them. I stopped working on the project when I discovered they had been lifted from my possession, and prematurely at that since I had not completed them, nor revised and polished them as I had planned to do. It had been my intention to publish them all together and not one by one, because the inquiry proceeds in a closely-knit development from the first of them to the last. So when those people managed to get at some of them before I was ready, and thus made it impossible for me to carry out my plans, I did not resume the work of dictation that other preoccupations had interrupted; instead, I was seriously thinking of complaining about the matter in a special pamphlet, to make it as widely known as possible that those books had not been published by me but had been pirated before I considered them ready for publication. However, at the urgent request of many of the brethren, and above all at your command, I have felt obliged to attend with the Lord's assistance to the completion of this laborious task. I have corrected the books as best I could, though hardly as I would or they might have varied too widely from the pirated copies that were already in people's hands. I now send them to your reverence by our dear son and fellow deacon, and give permission for anyone to listen to them, read them, or have them copied. (*Trin.* Preface, Letter)

The work did not turn out as originally planned, thanks to intervening circumstances beyond Augustine's control, nonetheless, it became a classic of Christian theology, and like all of Augustine's writings generated volumes of commentary and controversy.

The Trinity is a complex and challenging work, something that Augustine himself acknowledges, not intended for easy reading nor quick study. Up until this point in Christian theology, major efforts to "give an account of the Christian doctrine of God" had been written in Greek and were the product of a long-standing Greek tradition of thinking and writing, with a specific vocabulary and methodology. Augustine's *The Trinity* gave Western Latin theology its own theological voice and, in the centuries following him, it came to be accepted as the standard and rule for discussing and explaining the Christian doctrine of God. Perhaps what it best exemplifies is how Augustine pursued the task of theology (a term he does not use, for it still had pagan overtones). Scripture, the well-spring of Christian theology, and scriptural interpretation pervades the tome. He quoted a Scriptural text that perfectly described the theological task. It comes from his Greek version of the prophet Isaiah: "Unless you believe, you will not understand" (*Is.* 7:9, LXX).

> Faith seeks, understanding finds; which is why the prophet says, "Unless you believe you shall not understand." (*Trin.* 15.2)

One of the hallmarks of not just *The Trinity* but all of Augustine's writings is an approach to faith that pairs reason and faith rather than opposing them to one another. He states his position provocatively in one of his sermons: "understand, in order to believe; believe, in order to understand" and then goes on to explain:

> Understand, in order to believe my word; believe, in order to understand the word of God. (*ser.* 43.9)

What he means here becomes apparent from comments throughout his writings that encourage belief and understanding, understanding and belief. While he never denied that, in the case of Christian belief in a Trinitarian God, an essential and necessary first step is belief, he did not see it as the sole step. Seeking to understand was an important, even necessary, aspect of growing in faith, knowing at the same time that, when it came to the mystery of God, human efforts were limited. Augustine recognized that he made progress by writing (cf. *Letter* 143.2), and that may explain why he wrote so. Giving expression to his efforts was a way to encourage faith, not a replacement for faith nor a threat to faith. Such efforts had a lasting impact in the West—generating a long-standing tradition of high quality intellectual theological activity. The letter that introduces *The Trinity* concludes in this way:

> If I had been able to keep to my plans, the contents would indeed have been much the same, but their expression would have been much less knotty and much more lucid, as far as the difficulty of elucidating such deep matters and our own capacities would allow. Some people have the first four books, or rather five, without their prologues, and the twelfth without its considerable concluding section; but if they manage to learn about this edition, they will be able to correct their copies – if they want to and can afford it. May I ask you to give instructions that this letter be placed at the head of these books, though of course separately? Pray for me.

"If I had been able to keep to my plans"—the expression is emblematic of much of Augustine's career as bishop. Perhaps it was precisely the unpredictably, and especially his response to it, that best defines the life of Augustine the Bishop.

10

Augustine and God's Freedom—Against All Odds

The Conference in Carthage in 411 CE sought to reconcile the Catholic-Donatist division; it did, at least, represent the culmination of Augustine's efforts to end that crisis. Not long before that conference, in the summer of 410 CE, news of the Sack of Rome by Alaric both raised the level of fear throughout the empire, and signaled the beginning of a new polemic against Christians. Since the leadership of the empire was now Christian, they were blamed for the misfortune that had befallen Rome: Where was their God when Rome was most in need? In response, Augustine would write a massive work entitled the *City of God*, a work that cost him a decade and a half of labor (413–427 CE). He will later describe it provocatively as immense (*magnum*) and demanding (*arduum*).

Roman Africa witnessed a wave of refugees from the continent, including prominent families escaping to their vast and secure African estates. In the company of these refugees was a highly revered ascetical/spiritual guide named Pelagius and a disciple of his named Caelestius. These two began a preaching campaign in Carthage that was to have lasting repercussions. Their preaching gave birth to a conflict that haunted Augustine until his dying breath (412–430 CE), a phenomenon conveniently labeled by scholars as the Pelagian Controversy. This chapter explores that controversy; the following chapter will deal with the *City of God*.

Events in Augustine's life resist tidy compartmentalization; they intersect, overflow, and interpenetrate in unexpected ways. Yet, those unforeseen events also provided the impetus for Augustine's major writings. That means that the majority of his works were not the product of abstract ideas or theoretical questions, but responses to actual events. Such is the case for Augustine's development of a theology of grace. His response to Pelagian exaggerations and errors led him to reflect on the role of grace in Christian life, framing the questions that have occupied theologians ever since.

The Enemies of Grace

Augustine's first anti-Pelagian writing is from the winter of 411 to 412 CE. He writes in response to a request from Count Marcellinus, Imperial Tribune in Carthage, who asked him to respond to some "opinions" that were circulating in Carthage at the time. Marcellinus asks Augustine four questions:

1. Was Adam by nature mortal?

2. Was Adam's sin hereditary?

3. Why are babies baptized?

4. Can someone in this life live without sin?

The progression of these questions says much about the religious climate in the West during this period. Marcellinus' questions led to Augustine's first formal writing against Pelagian ideas: *On the Punishment and Forgiveness of Sins and the Baptism of Infants*. The title is a reminder that the controversy was complex, both in its history and in the theological issues it raised. Augustine explained what led him to write this work when writing his *Revisions* (*Retractationes*), a book in which he looked back over his writings with a critical eye a few years before his death.

> An urgent concern arose which forced me to write against the new Pelagian heresy. Earlier we were opposing it, when there was need, not in writing, but by sermons and conferences . . . After some questions of theirs had been sent to me from Carthage, asking me to resolve by a written reply, I first wrote three books. . . .
>
> In them the discussion focused principally on the baptism of little ones on account of original sin and on the grace of God by which we are justified, that is, become righteous . . . With views opposed to all of these, they founded a new heresy.
>
> In these books I still thought that I should not mention their names, in the hope that they could be more easily corrected. In fact, in the third book, which is a letter, but included among my books on account of the two to which I thought it should be joined, I mentioned the name of Pelagius with a certain amount of praise, because many spoke well of his life, and I refuted those statements which he did not set forth in his writings in his own name, but which he presented as what others were saying. Yet later, when he had become a heretic, he defended these ideas with a strong streak of stubbornness. . . . (*Revisions* II, 33, 60)

Marcellinus had been the one to write and Augustine acknowledges that he now found it imperative (he uses the word *necessitas*) to be more explicit in his reaction to these ideas: He took up the pen to write against this "new Pelagian heresy."

In his *Revisions*, Augustine was looking back to a time when the Donatist crisis was still his primary concern and when it had just been addressed by the

Council of Carthage (411 CE); a successful implementation of that council's decisions would mean the restoration of unity and peace to the Christian community of North Africa. Augustine made it clear that, wearied and distressed by the turmoil surrounding the Donatist question, he did not really want to deal with the questions posed. However, silence was not an option since his silence would imply that he approved of these "novel ideas." From winter of 411 CE to summer of 430 CE, Augustine was not able to put down his pen. Each hint of resolution and each pause in the controversy only led to new twists in the arguments or to new proponents of already-known arguments. Over the course of the controversy, both the emperor and more-than-one bishop of Rome were forced to intervene, one more reminder of the central place of "matters religious" in the world in which Augustine lived. In such religious debates or controversy, no one could imagine that silence or retreat was a viable response.

On the "Pelagian side" three names dominate the controversy: Pelagius, an ascetic from the British Isles who had made his way to Rome where he established a reputation as a spiritual director to elite aristocratic Christians; Caelestius, a disciple of Pelagius who served as the first public voice for the cause, although it is not clear whether he did so with Pelagius' consent; and, later, Julian of Eclanum, an articulate and able debater and polemicist, remarkably adept at getting under Augustine's skin. Some even claim that he actually won the argument. In a sense, the "Pelagian Controversy" could be seen as three separate controversies: Against Caelestius, Against Pelagius, and Against Julian; their "theologies" do not exactly match, even though they shared a common belief in the capacity of a human being to do good on one's own; they believed in full human freedom before God.

Let it be noted that the issues in the Pelagian controversy can be categorized under the heading of "grace." A simple "word count" of the terms used in the debates would show clearly the dominance of this word. Augustine came to call his opponents the *"enemies of grace,"* an epithet surely intended to provoke. However, by stepping back from the often-inflammatory discourse and paying attention to the direction of Augustine's arguments, it is clear that he saw himself as defending the core of Christian faith: What does it mean to speak about salvation in Jesus Christ?

> So now at last let us return to him [Adam], humbled and thrown out [of paradise] for being proud. The whole cause of our mortality, the whole cause of our feebleness, the whole cause of all the torments, all the difficulties, all the miseries which the human race suffers in this age, is nothing but pride. You have the text of scripture saying, The beginning of all sin is pride. And what does it say in the same place? *The beginning of man's pride is to apostatize from God* (Sir. 10:13.12). . . . Pride made man apostatize from God. So because this is the fountainhead of all our ills, that is why we are sick in this life. It is like when an experienced doctor sees someone ailing from a variety of disorders, he doesn't attend to the immediate causes and neglect the origin of all the causes; if he cures the immediate causes . . . and thus seems to have provided a remedy for a time, he is not curing the patient deep down. No, the really experi-

enced doctor is found to be the one who thoroughly ties up all the causes of all the disorders, and on finding the first of them from which all the rest seem to stem like branches, he cuts out the root, and the whole thicket of aches and pains is chopped down. That is how our Lord Jesus Christ did all these things, and because he could see that pride was the root cause of all our disorders, he cured us with his own humility – that is why he is called "Savior" (*salvator*), and why the one who said, It's not the healthy who need the doctor, but those who are ill (Mt. 9:12), came to the sick, because the sick couldn't go to him; he sought those who were not seeking him, he turned to the weak and feeble, he suffered many things, he allowed himself to be slain by the blind and used his death to heal their eyes. (*ser. Dolbeau* 21.11)

This sermon was preached before the Pelagian controversy began; it is dated rather precisely by scholars to February 404 CE. The pride of Adam who acted on his own is set in contrast with the humility of Jesus Christ who acted in full union with the Father. That humility is fully a part of what makes Jesus Christ Savior. A few years later, Augustine recognized that the role of the Savior, as well as his title, Savior, were jeopardized by the claims of Pelagius and his followers.

Dominating this particular controversy throughout, but most especially in its final stages, was an argumentative attitude, similar to something still heard in contemporary political debate. The boundaries drawn between positions almost always took the form of an either/or, removing the possibility of a middle ground; the adversaries almost always charged one another with "bad faith" or simple "stupidity"; epithet and insult regularly punctuated the exchanges, heightening their confrontational nature; There was an effort to *isolate*, to *provoke*, even to *offend*. It is not always obvious how such an approach was meant to be taken in Augustine's world. His anti-Pelagian works were occasional writings or responses to events as they happened, they were composed by dictation (spoken aloud to a secretary) and intended to be heard by being read aloud. They often take the form of simulated debates, with Augustine quoting at length from his opponents (he thus helped to preserve their writings). These "debates" need to be viewed within a specific rhetorical-oral culture with its accepted procedures and standardized modes of discourse: They do not automatically translate into modern dynamics and expectations. But, if one steps back from the fiery discourse and begins to note themes repeated over and over again in a variety of ways, what emerges is a series of fundamental concerns. Although these concerns are often implicit rather than spoken, the radical character of each side's position meant that there was little hope for any mutual give-and-take and even less for a real resolution.

Augustine's concern was deeply theological and apparently abstract; since he was speaking about the operation of God's grace, direct observation and concrete verification were not part of the discussion. Pelagius' concerns appeared to be much more concrete, that is, about the practice of a good Christian life. His concern with Christian discipline or Christian asceticism was framed in general terms; his "spirituality" (a word that entered the Christian lexicon at a later date) was fully centered on the capability of the Christian, paying little attention to God's role. Yet, neither Augustine nor Pelagius were able to define, demarcate and mutually agree upon the real range and domain of the controversy. "It all depends upon God," was Augustine's implicit operating principle. "It is up to you, you lazy Christian" was that of Pelagius.

At some time in the early 380s Pelagius arrived in Rome from Britain. We know virtually nothing about his life before that time, and even his final years are shrouded in mystery. He was well-educated, well-known, and well-respected for his holiness and asceticism. His brand of asceticism was serious but moderate to the extent that he did not "withdraw" from the cities to some deserted spot. In Rome he was actively involved in spiritual direction and guiding groups of Christians of a more serious bent, even though he was not ordained. Specifically, he was involved with groups of aristocratic Christians, helping to set up ascetical circles in their homes. Contemporaries described him as an imposing figure; one called him a "Goliath." St. Jerome, an eventual opponent, mocked him as "a huge brute weighty with Scottish porridge." This was a time when large numbers converted to Christianity and many serious-minded Christians were dismayed by the "lowering of standards" that was apparently underway. Both Pelagius and Augustine were reformers, but the focus of their theologies, as well as their ways to motivate went in opposite directions.

One of Pelagius' teaching tasks involved the study of the Scriptures and, during this sojourn in Rome, he began a series of commentaries on Paul's letters. This was one way of providing necessary, but substantial sustenance to his "directees" and fit well into a much larger renewal that was underway in Rome. It was in the course of such activities that Pelagius first came across the bishop of Hippo's writings, as Augustine reported later:

> But which of my works could have been more widely known and more favorably received than the books of my *Confessions*? Though I published them also before the Pelagian heresy emerged, I certainly spoke in them to our God and often said, "Give what you command, and command what you will." When these words of mine were cited at Rome by some brother and fellow bishop of mine in Pelagius' presence, he could not tolerate them and, attacking them somewhat emotionally, he almost came to blows with the one who had cited them. But what does God command first of all and most of all but that we believe in him? And he himself, then, gives us this faith if it is right to say to him, "Give what you command." (*The Gift of Perseverance* 20.53)

"He almost came to blows with the one who had cited them." Religious conviction was anything but lukewarm in these times. Further, one of the concerns in Rome at the time of Pelagius' sojourn was Manichaeism. It has been suggested that Pelagius' "positive spirituality" was formulated in reaction to negative Manichaeism dualism and its materialistic pessimism. The "Pelagians" even accused Augustine of being a "crypto-Manichaean." Pelagius' teaching enthusiastically affirmed the goodness of creation and the inherent capacity of human beings to choose correctly between good and evil. If Augustine said to God:

"Give what you command," Pelagius said to God: "I'll do what you command." Their respective spiritual frameworks were thus worlds apart. Conflict was perhaps inevitable.

Rather than pursue step-by-step the more than 20 challenging works and lengthy letters that flow from the debate, it will be useful to explore the arguments and issues and, then, highlight the chronology of the important events. After the arrival of Pelagius and Caelestius in Carthage in the autumn of 410 CE, they began to preach and teach their fellow-refugees and some of the Carthaginians as well. Pelagius then moved on to Jerusalem, but Caelestius remained in Carthage and, at some point, requested ordination. In the course of the necessary investigations of the candidate's faith and intentions, Paulinus of Milan, who happened to be in Carthage at that time, denounced the teachings of Caelestius, prompting an ecclesiastical inquiry. After investigation, his teaching was condemned and ordination refused. The condemnation listed six statements of Caelestius and they are a rather good guide to what will be the grist of the controversy in the following years. Augustine states these six points in his work, *The Deeds of Pelagius*, 11.23.

1. Adam was created mortal and would have died even if he had not sinned.

2. Adam's sin only had an effect on himself (and Eve), not on the whole human race.

3. The Law—and not just the Gospel—offers entrance to the kingdom of heaven.

4. Even before the coming of Christ, there were human beings without sin.

5. Children are born into the same state as that of Adam before he sinned.

6. The human race doesn't die corporately with Adam nor rise corporately with Christ.

It ought to be obvious that all of the statements are theological and might strike the modern reader as esoteric, but that was far from true for the parties involved. These affirmations emphasize human ability to live a morally upright life, both before and after the coming of Christ. Underlying them is a clear denial of a teaching of Augustine that, over the previous decade, had emerged with more clarity: an understanding of original sin. As the Pelagian controversy develops, that doctrine will take center stage. While many (though not all) scholars propose that Augustine drew upon an already existing theological tradition, they agree that he coined the term 'original sin' and consolidated and specified its meaning in a way that had not been previously known. The term 'original sin' first occurs well before the Pelagian controversy: in a writing virtually contemporary with the *Confessions*, his answers to some questions from Simplicanus, the priest who instructed him in Milan and subsequently succeeded Ambrose as bishop there. Simplicianus had queried his former pupil about the meaning of certain biblical texts, including certain statements from St. Paul. This is Augustine's reply:

> I know, in fact, that in me, that is, in my flesh, good does not dwell (Rom. 7:18). Regarding knowledge, I am in agreement with the law; regarding my action, I am under sin. If someone were to ask how is it that in my flesh good does not dwell but rather sin: where else does it come from if not from the root of mortality and the persistence of sensuality? The one is the penalty of original sin, the other the penalty of repeated sin. With the first we enter this life, the latter is accumulated by the way we live. United together, nature and habit render concupiscence most forceful and invincible, which he [Paul] calls sin and says that it dwells in his flesh, and so it possesses a kind of dominance and tyranny. . . . (*To Simplicianus* 1.1.10)

As he continues with this particular comment he notes the power of grace as remedy, and the fact that this original sin damages nature without taking away free will. The Latin term for free will, *liberum arbitrium*, will become one of the most disputed terms in the theological conflict with "the Pelagians." He makes clear in this early writing, dating from 396 CE—and thus well in advance of this conflict—that, as a result of Adam's sin, all humanity must confront two very different kinds of sin: One is called original because it is inherited as penalty from the first parents; the other was "added" (he uses *addimus*—we add this sin) because it refers to the sins that each one commits. Augustine insisted ever after that the idea behind the notion of original sin did not come from him but from St. Paul.

Let me now return to the six statements about Pelagius' views. Augustine saw them as at the heart of Christianity's basic faith claim: Jesus Christ, God become human. If these six statements were true, would Christ matter? Would he not seem unnecessary? If there was no problem, why was his horrific death by crucifixion the only answer to the plight of humanity? As the Pelagian controversy developed, there was an ever-clearer explanation of the implications of an absolute need for the grace of Christ, first on the level of initial forgiveness and healing, then in terms of the actual and on-going living of the Christian life. That need extended to our knowledge of how God works and culminates in our ability to love, and in the final confirmation of faithful perseverance until death. All of these are dimensions of the workings of the grace of Christ, and all are God's sovereign gifts.

Free will (*liberum arbitrium*) in particular emerged as a test case for understanding and accepting the workings of grace. For Augustine, the problem of free will revealed the presence and consequences of original sin. Those consequences were experienced as human *ignorance* (not knowing what to do) and as *human weakness* (no strength to do what is known as right). Mere freedom of will cannot restore humanity to the path of goodness and happiness because free will lacks knowledge and strength; it is impaired. Some intervention, that is, grace, is needed so that "free will" can begin to be healed or freed. A constant theme in Augustine's writings throughout the controversy is that God's intervention was not to be viewed as a diminution of or a threat to our free will. Grace, rather, actualizes and reempowers free will—and Augustine highlighted the paradoxical nature of that reality. True freedom, for Augustine, was to do God's will. That is, once again, a reminder that these battles were about Christian living from a deeply theological point of view.

Such issues took Augustine into questions that taxed both conceptual and terminological limits in his time. How was one to comprehend—humanly speaking—the workings of God's "salvific" and "sovereign" will? Augustine's line of argumentation required a delicate balancing of three assertions that may not—at first glance—appear to be compatible:

1. God's sovereignty: God must be free to be God, which means, theologically speaking, that one has to deal with the reality of "predestination";

2. Christ's necessity: To deny the existence of "original sin" is to deny the need for Christ;

3. Human freedom: "Just condemnation" is only thinkable if human beings are free; original sin does not deny human freedom.

Each of these affirmations was the tip of a theological iceberg that demanded volumes from Augustine. To explore each of them, he will turn to key texts from St. Paul for support. For the first, God's sovereignty, he repeatedly cites a Pauline text from the Letter to the Romans: "How rich are the depths of God—how deep his wisdom and knowledge—and how impossible to penetrate his motives or understand his methods!" (Rom. 11:33)

For Christ's necessity a text from 1 Corinthians echoes like a refrain throughout the controversy: "Just as all die in Adam, so all will be brought to life in Christ." (1 Cor. 15.22)

For the problematic of human freedom, Chapter 7 of Paul's letter to the Romans will provide Augustine's chief laboratory: "I cannot understand my own behavior. I fail to carry out the things I want to do, and I find myself doing the very things I hate. . . ." (Rom. 7:15)

To these Augustine added a host of other supporting biblical texts, always insisting that the arguments and issues of the debate were, before all else, rooted in the Scriptures. As the controversy proceeded, he found himself forced to tackle the ever-more-complicated challenges of his opponents. Their charges are the logical consequence of their perception that Augustine had read St. Paul in distorted fashion. Their questions concerned: the fate of unbaptized babies; the "reasons behind" God's election or nonelection; and the way that original sin was transmitted. This final point dragged Augustine deeply into what today are called sexual matters.

Pelagius emphasized freedom and responsibility; hence, he saw Augustine's theological vision as fueling the excuses of lazy Christians, and he had no interest in Augustine's theological concerns. He insisted that anyone can change because grace is already always present. To fail to will the good is a matter of unwillingness, laziness or "ill will," not because of a damaged will.

In that way, Pelagius and Augustine both sought to provide a diagnosis of human experience. Sin and evil were more subtle, seductive, insidious, and omnipresent for Augustine than for Pelagius. Augustine was also more aware of the "communal" dimension of sin and evil, insisting that "personal" evil intersects with "an already-established network of evil." For Pelagius, those issues were always more centered on the individual: "It is up to each of you." That meant that the choice was practical for Pelagius: Show some strength of will! What was at stake for Augustine is a correct understanding of how to live the mystery of Christ. He stated this clearly a number of times in his first formal writing against Pelagius:

> Every human being is separated from God and remains so unless reconciled by Christ the Mediator . . . reconciliation only takes place by means of the one grace of our most merciful Savior, only by means of the one victim of the only true Priest. (*Punishment and Forgiveness of Sins* I.28.56)

Augustine often painted his conflict with Pelagius starkly as a choice between Adam or Christ: to choose to follow Adam's example was to rely upon one's own willing and strength; to choose to follow Christ was to rely upon God. "In considering the question of these two human beings [Adam / Christ] the very essence of the Christian faith is at stake" (*Punishment and Forgiveness of Sins* II.24.28). Augustine thus made it clear that from his vantage point, the disagreement was not a matter of pastoral effort or of spiritual advice; it was a matter of faith and not about lukewarm or fervent effort. Hence, "the very essence of the Christian faith is at stake."

The events of the controversy and the progression and volume of writings that chronologically mark its unfolding are complex; hence, it is easy to lose sight of the principles and concerns that underpin the differences. Augustine's entry into the controversy was at first reluctant. The imperial official and close friend, Marcellinus, who asked him about these issues, also thrust him into the forefront as he became the major protagonist. These concerns, however, were shared by Aurelius of Carthage, Alypius of Thagaste, and the African conference of bishops as well. Augustine did not fight alone; on the contrary, these issues touched something deep within the episcopal leadership of Roman Africa.

The importance of these matters, however, was not immediately understood by others at the beginning. History recorded this dispute as Augustine's controversy—in part because Augustine was the most recognizable voice, both at the beginning and throughout the conflict, and perhaps in part because he had to work so hard to explain the many nuances and sub-texts of the problem (e.g., as it related to human freedom and predestination).

A first phase, lasting from 411 to 418 CE, started with the work already cited, the Punishment and Forgiveness of Sins and the Baptism of Little Ones. In 418 CE, an African Council condemned the teachings of Pelagius and that decision was supported by imperial and Roman decrees. Pelagius and Caelestius were exiled. That rather drastic conclusion was probably prompted by the decision of a Council in Jerusalem and nearby Diospolis (today Lydda in Israel) in 415 CE, which exonerated Pelagius, accepting his explanation of his theological stance. That decision alarmed the African bishops when they heard about it. In their outrage and dismay, they saw it as an affront to the African episcopacy. Augustine's response is clear from a few words from the middle of one of his sermons:

> . . . brothers and sisters, let me speak to you more plainly, because it is not something we should cover up; there is a new heresy lurking about and secretly spreading its tentacles far and wide. Until it broke out into the open, we tolerated it in silence as best we could, though we were always refuting the actual error. But to give the people concerned a chance to correct themselves, we kept quiet about their names. Nothing, you see, would have been better, nothing we would have liked more, than that when they heard what was being preached by us according to the Church's most ancient and fundamental tradition, they would be afraid to preach their errors, and would be cured of them in private, turning to the one who cures all that call upon his name (Jl. 2:32; Rom. 10:13).
>
> For a long time this was the course I preferred. I mean, I did write a number of things against this kind of impiety, and they came into the hands of readers; however, not all the works of the people whose ideas I had written about had yet been brought to my attention. There were some of these people here, and quite a few of them corrected their errors, over whose salvation we rejoice in the name of the Lord and in his mercy. In fact, some of these who were converted from that error have begged me insistently to publish letters too about the erroneous doctrine itself.
>
> Now, however, we have just heard that this very man, who is the chief author of this pernicious opinion, was absolved and declared to be Catholic by a synod of bishops in the East. This was because he denied that the things objected to in his teachings were his own, but seemed to have been intruded there by others; he not only denied that he held those views, but he even anathematized them. The acts of the synod have indeed not yet reached us here. (*ser. Dolbeau* 30. 5–6)

Augustine continued by noting that he had requested the official acts so as to verify this distressing news. Neither he nor his episcopal colleagues would have believed it possible—as he indicates clearly in the same sermon:

> . . . just a few days ago now, there came to us from those parts our fellow citizen of Hippo, the deacon Palatinus, son of Gattus. Many of you know him, even more know his name. His father is present here; he is here himself, standing there among the deacons, listening to me. This man, you see, has brought me a short pamphlet by Pelagius himself in answer to the objections made to his teaching. It doesn't seem to be a part of the acts of the synod hearing, but the defense he made and put into writing, recording perhaps how he had defended himself too at the hearing by the bishops, the record of which, as I said earlier, has not yet managed to find its way into my hands. And he instructed the deacon to give me this defense of his to read; he didn't, however, send me a cover-

ing letter. This makes me anxious that he may later on deny that he even sent me this pamphlet. So I have been reluctant to discuss any of it until we have read the official record, which can be seen to carry the authority of the Church and the bishops.

But why have I wanted to bring all this to the attention of your faithful ears? Because there has been heaven knows how terrible a disturbance in Jerusalem, and the very sad event has also been reported to us, that the rioting populace is said to have burned down two monasteries in Bethlehem. There would have been no need for me to mention this if I didn't know that the news has already reached some of you. So it's better that you should hear the whole story from me, rather than be hurt by rumors circulating stealthily. (*ser. Dolbeau* 30. 7)

He then entered into details:

So now let me tell you briefly what's wrong with this heresy, so that you may be on your guard against it, and not conceal from me the names of anyone you may hear whispering such things privately or noising them abroad in public conferences. I'm afraid, you see, of the canker spreading when it's ignored, and of our suddenly finding many such people, so many that we could hardly restore them to health, if ever. So listen then to what's wrong with this heresy. (*ser. Dolbeau* 30. 8)

Augustine's efforts were thus those of the community; they will involve both policing and rehabilitation. He then offered his understanding of the teaching of Pelagius:

A few minutes ago I was talking about and commending to you the grace of God through Jesus Christ our Lord (Rom. 7:25); well, this is the grace which that pestiferous heresy attacks with its conferences and in its arguments. You ask how? They say that human nature is capable of so much, we by the free decision of our will are capable of so much, that just as we became sinners by ourselves, so too we can be justified by ourselves. And since it's better being a just man than just being a man--the word "man," after all signifies a nature, the word "justice" points to happiness and blessedness; so since being a just man is better than just being a man, they say that God made man, but that man himself makes himself just, so that man seems to give himself more than God gave him in the first place.

. . . You see, when people say to you, "You're capable on your own of acting justly; if you want to, you can do it; you don't need any help from God for carrying out whatever it may be, because there is no other grace of God except that by which he made you with free will"--so when they say things like that, they are referring to the grace of God by which we were made, a grace we have in common even with the pagans. It's not the case, after all, that we were created and they weren't, or that we have issued from the workshop of another craftsman than they. Both we and they have the one God for our author, one maker, one creator, who makes his sun rise upon the good and the bad, and sends rain upon the just and the unjust (Mt. 5:45). That's what these people call the grace of God; they refuse to consider another kind, not by which we are human beings together with pagans, but by which we are Christians. (*ser. Dolbeau* 30. 8-9)

As Augustine continued he explored in greater depth his understanding of a Pelagian denial of the grace of Christ and the theological implications of his teaching. He concluded this lengthy sermon promising to report back to the people what he has discovered.

> As for that man, nobody should say he was absolved by the bishops. What was absolved was his confession, a kind of correction was absolved, because what he said before the bishops seemed to be Catholic, but the bishops who absolved him were unaware of what he has written in his books. And perhaps he really did correct his errors. We ought not, after all, to despair about the man, who possibly did decide to attach himself to the Catholic faith, and to take refuge in his grace and help. Perhaps this did happen. All the same, it's not the heresy that was absolved, but the man denying the heresy. But when I have read the official record, when it has come into my hands, I will have the duty of telling your graces, with the Lord's help, whatever further details I learn about this sorry business, and perhaps about his repudiating his errors. (*ser. Dolbeau* 30.14)

Two things are to be noted about this particular sermon. Augustine "brings it to the people" since it is not simply a matter for bishops. Secondly, commentators note that this marks a turning point in the controversy. Augustine is convinced Pelagius and his companions have broken faith, seeking to undermine true faith by stealth, by 'putting a good face' on their practice and belief. His response will thus become all the more aggressive and unrelenting.

Augustine and his fellow bishops immediately set about putting in writing their understanding of the controversy and sent a dossier to the bishop of Rome, Pope Innocent, asking him to confirm their findings that Pelagius and his followers were worthy of condemnation. At the very same time Jerome in Bethlehem sent to the imperial court in Ravenna a dossier of the "new heresy," asking for imperial intervention. Jerome himself had been the victim of violence, when a number of his monastic establishments in Bethlehem were set ablaze. He attributed this violence to the hostility of Pelagius' followers. On January 27, 417 CE, the African bishops received three letters confirming their findings and pronouncing Pelagius and Caelestius excommunicated. We have a sermon preached by Augustine precisely during this period, on Sunday, September 23, 417 CE. It is a lively sermon since it is punctuated by "holy shouting" from the congregation:

> My brothers and sisters, please share my anxiety and concern. Wherever you find such people, don't keep quiet about them, don't be perversely softhearted. No question about it, wherever you find such people, don't keep quiet about them. Argue with them when they speak against grace, and if they persist, bring them to us. You see, there have already been two councils about this matter, and their decisions sent to the Apostolic See; from there rescripts have been

sent back here. The case is finished; if only the error were finished too, some-time! So let us all warn them to take notice of this, teach them to learn the lesson of it, pray for them to change their ideas. (*ser.* 131.10)

"The case is finished—*causa finita est.*" That would be what a Roman lawyer would say at the end of a successfully defended court case. But the sigh of relief from Augustine and his fellow bishops was short lived. Innocent died after the letters were received and his successor, Zozimus, reopened the case and absolved Pelagius and Caelestius. Zozimus listened to their protests of innocence and of true faith, accepted their sincerity, and reported his decision to the African bishops. What followed was a series of initiatives on the part of the African bishops that showed their united front on the matter: their deeply felt collective-authority was not to be dismissed by Zozimus; so, with diplomatic and legal acumen, they challenged the decision of the bishop of Rome. In less than six months time, in March of 418 CE, they received word that Zozimus had done an "about face." He endorsed the African bishops' authority in the matter and confirmed what he had previously rescinded. In May, he sent an official letter "to all the Churches" requiring signatures of endorsement on the part of bishops for the decision against Pelagius and Caelestius. This letter also drew upon the authority of an imperial rescript dated April 30, 418 CE, in which the Emperor Honorius condemned the pair. Only then could Augustine truly believe *causa finita est.*

Clealy, the "Pelagian controversy" unfolded on a variety of fronts, and that along with specific theological issues it raised sensitive questions regarding jurisdiction between bishops and synods, questions regarding "East" and "West" (Carthage/Jerusalem), and even the nature of the authority of the bishop of Rome. The African bishops had no difficulty challenging Rome when they felt their own authority was being ignored. Added to this was the involvement of imperial authority. These elements of the controversy, along with the theological ones, have generated and continue to generate a variety of interpretations and positions. But even the disagreements among present-day scholars show that everyone agrees: Something momentous was underway.

In fact, even after Zozimus' letter and an imperial rescript, the "causa" was not finished. Some bishops in Italy reacted to Zozimus' condemnation of Pelagius and Caelestius. Emerging as the leader of the resistance and, certainly in Augustine's eyes, taking up Pelagius' mantle was a young and aristocratic bishop, Julian of Eclanum. Beginning in 419 CE and continuing until Augustine's death, these two bishops waged a war of words with great intensity. Interestingly and ironically, most everything known about Julian, especially about his "thinking and theology," is due to Augustine. In the four works he wrote "against Julian," Augustine cites Julian's own words against him repeatedly; two of Augustine's works are written as if there were an actual debate going on, thus providing us with statements that would come directly from their exchanges. It was as if Julian shouted arguments at Augustine, and Augustine countered in kind. Ironically, without Augustine's record of these debates,

Julian's writings would not be known. Although Julian was condemned, exiled, and eventually disappeared from history, Augustine preserved his voice.

Julian was the opposite of Augustine in several ways. He was a Catholic Christian, the son of a bishop. His family was apparently aristocratic, and Julian presented himself in a patrician-like way. Unlike Augustine, he had been married, but, once he was ordained, he appears to have embraced celibacy. If Augustine was the "restless heart" (*conf.* I.1.1.), Julian seems to be the "cool mind." Nonetheless, this cool mind's first manifest involvement in controversy took the form of attack and slander—at least that is how Augustine took it. The tone for each of their subsequent debates was, as it were, set. Julian's refrain throughout their 12-year-long verbal contest, a refrain that he repeated at every possible opportunity, was that Augustine was still a Manichee! Augustine's insistence on original sin, on the damage it did to human freedom, and on its mysterious transmission to procreation provided the fodder for Julian's verbal barrages. Augustine quoted Julian who addressed a certain Turbantius:

> Teachers of our time, my blessed brother, instigators of a rebellion that is still raging, have resolved to obtain through the ruin of the whole Church the dishonor and death of those persons whose holy aspirations are causing them pain. They [Augustine et al.] do not understand the great honor they bestowed upon those persons in showing that they could not destroy their glory without destroying the Catholic religion. For, if any say that there is free choice in human beings or that God is the creator of the newborn, they are called Pelagians or Caelestians. And so, to avoid being called heretics, they become Manichees, and out of fear of a false bad reputation, they rush into a true crime, like beasts surrounded with fans of feathers so that they are driven into the nets. Because they lack reason, they are driven to true destruction out of an empty fear. (*Marriage and Desire* 2.3.7)

"They become Manichees." The "they" is, in fact, Augustine and his colleagues. Julian knew from the outset that it was the one epithet that would irritate Augustine the most and make it difficult for him to respond. One of the realities that marked this controversy was that Augustine left no such epithet unanswered:

> Why do you deceitfully spread a veil over this common teaching in order to hide your own crime for which you have earned your name? In order to frighten the uneducated with a detestable name, you say, "And so, to avoid being called heretics, they become Manichees." (*Marriage and Desire* 2.3.8)

Augustine followed with a calm and succinct description of what is at stake and who, in fact, really deserved what label:

> Listen, then, for a few moments to what is at stake in this question. Catholics say that human nature was created good by the good God the creator, but that, having been wounded by sin, it needs Christ the physician. The Manichees say that human nature was not created good by God and wounded by sin,

but that human beings were created by the prince of eternal darkness out of the mixture of the two natures which always existed, the one good and the other evil. The Pelagians and Caelestians say that human nature was created good by the good God, but that in newborn little ones it is so healthy that they have no need at that age of the medicine of Christ. Acknowledge, then, in your doctrine the name that belongs to you, and stop raising as an objection to Catholics who refute you a doctrine and a name that does not belong to them. (*Marriage and Desire* 2.3.9)

These excerpts from Marriage and Desire will set the stage for all of the following verbal battles between Augustine and Julian. Augustine attempted throughout the subsequent exchanges—often marked by insult and overstatement on both sides—to walk a challenging tightrope: to affirm the goodness of marriage and, at the same time, the challenge of living with the effects of an original sin. Likewise, he affirmed human freedom and, at the same time, named its present impairment. He stated this clear intention in his opening lines of *Marriage and Desire*:

The aim, then, of this book is to distinguish, insofar as the Lord grants us his help, the goodness of marriage from the evil of carnal desire on account of which a human being who is born through it contracts original sin. After all, this shameful desire, which the impudent impudently praise, would not exist at all, if human beings had not sinned, but marriage would have existed, even if no one had sinned. Children would have been conceived without this disease in the body of that former life, though they cannot now be conceived without it in the body of this death. (*Marriage and Desire* 1.1.1.)

Note the phrases: "The evil of carnal desire," "shameful desire," "conception in a diseased body." One of Augustine's unrelenting arguments against Julian was that the present, disruptive nature of human sexual experience is proof positive that it is no longer operating as originally intended by God the creator. Augustine envisions a paradisiacal sexual practice, before the sin, that is tranquil, rational, and tensionless—the opposite of present sexual experience. He repeated this so often and so insistently that it merited the sharp criticism of present-day commentators, who found Augustine's perception of matters sexual to be indicative of neurosis if not psychosis. Present-day readers will probably find his analysis of "sexuality" uncommon reading:

Here this fellow [Julian] turns from those who are joined in marriage to those who are born from marriage. It is on account of these that we struggle on this question in such long debates against the new heretics. Driven by the secret inspiration of God, he makes a statement in which by his own admission he resolves this whole problem. He wanted to stir up greater hatred for us, because we say that even from a lawful marriage little ones are born under the power of sin. He says, "You claim that those people who were never born could have been good, but you declare these people who fill the world, these for whom Christ has died, to be the work of the devil, children of a disease, and guilty from their origin. I have, therefore, proved," he continues, "that you do nothing else but deny that God is the creator of these human beings who exist." Even though all are born under the power of sin and perish unless they are reborn, I say that God alone is the creator of all human beings. What was implanted in them by the persuasion of the devil as a result of which they are born under the power of sin is a defect, not the created nature by which they are human beings. If shameful passion, however, moved our members only when we willed it, there would be no disease. If the licit and morally good intercourse of a married couple did not cause them embarrassment so that they avoided being seen and sought privacy, there would be no disease. If the apostle did not forbid husbands to possess their wives in this disease, there would be no disease. After all, the Greek: *en pathei epithumias* (1 Thes. 4:5) has been translated by some into Latin as: *in the disease of desire or of concupiscence*, but by others as: *in the passion of concupiscence*, and in still other manuscripts still other forms may be found. But in the Latin language, especially in ecclesiastical usage, "passion" is not ordinarily used in a pejorative sense.

But regardless of what this fellow thinks about the shameful concupiscence of the flesh, pay attention to what he said about the little ones. Our struggle is on their behalf so that people will believe that they need a savior and they will not die without salvation. (*Marriage and Desire* 2.33.55–56)

In the midst of an avalanche of words, and with an awareness that his words may be distorted by others, Augustine reminded his listeners that his seemingly harsh remarks surrounding procreation were really about theology and not about sexual practice: "Our struggle is on behalf of 'the little ones' so that people will believe that they need a savior and they will not die without salvation."

Julian and Augustine avoided talking to one another throughout the last decade of Augustine's life, with occasional pauses that sometimes led Augustine to think—mistakenly—that his opponent had finally put down the pen. Julian continued to pepper his writings with insult, making clear that he had tried to read Augustine's early works with great care so that he could use "Augustine against Augustine." He attacks—again and again—Augustine's teaching on original sin, portraying it as a Manichaean idea.

In 426/427 CE Augustine returned to his desk and painstakingly reviewed all his writings, from the time of his conversion in 386 CE to the last work he had written. He called this review of his works, *Retractationes*, a Latin word which might best be translated as "re-considerations" or "re-treatments." Augustine looked back and "re-reconsidered" all the works he had written, placing them in chronological order, giving time and purpose, opening and closing lines, all the while correcting himself when necessary, "I was wrong to say . . . ." "I was working with a faulty text . . . ." "I should not have used that word but this word" and the like.

True to the originality that seemed to mark so much of his writings, this work was without precedent. It enables present day readers and scholars to put his enormous corpus of works in chronological order and, in that way, to trace his development. A familiar theme that can be found throughout his life is clearly stated in the preface: "Whoever will read this work ought not to imitate me in error but, rather, in making progress for the better" (*retr.* I. prol.). Augustine does insist that his thinking has been anything but static, and he readily acknowledges that, along the way, he made mistakes.

The last book mentioned in the *Retractationes* is called *Rebuke and Grace*. It is one of a series of four works that Augustine wrote on grace. It was preceded by *Grace and Free Choice*, and followed by *Predestination of the Saints* and The *Gift of Perseverance*. Each of these works was in response to the Pelagian controversy, but their tone was very different from those against Julian because they were not polemical. Instead, they were efforts to respond to some monks in Africa and in Gaul who found some difficulty in accepting Augustine's teaching on grace, freedom, and predestination to their monastic practice. If salvation was only attained by the grace of predestination, why bother to do anything? If all are predestined, then, no matter what is not done, it will work out. If all are not predestined, no matter what is done, it will not work out.

Augustine was alarmed by such a reading of his writings on grace. He worked hard to show that he did not intend to take every incentive away. Rather, he defended freedom and grace in a both/and context, not as alternatives (either/or). But, since he was convinced that he had interpreted the teaching of St. Paul correctly, he defended the biblical meaning of predestination by God. At the end of *The Gift of Perseverance* he stated this matter in a positive way, seeking to convey his understanding of what the controversy was all about:

> But what more shall I say? I think that I have sufficiently, or rather more than sufficiently, taught that both to begin to believe in the Lord and to persevere in the Lord up to the end are gifts of God. But even these men on account of whom we are dealing with these issues grant that the other goods which pertain to a pious life by which we correctly worship God are gifts of God. Moreover, they cannot deny that God foreknew all his gifts and those to whom he was going to give them. Just as, then, we should preach the other gifts so that their preacher is heard with obedience, so we should preach predestination so that one who hears this with obedience may boast, not in a human being and, for this reason, not in himself, but in the Lord. For this too is God's commandment, and hearing this commandment with obedience, namely, That one who boasts should boast in the Lord (1 Cor. 1:31), just as hearing the others, is a gift of God. I do not hesitate to say that one who does not have this gift has to no purpose whatever other gifts he has. We pray that the Pelagians may have this gift, but that these brothers of ours may have it more fully. Let us, then, not be quick in our arguments and lazy in our prayers. Let us pray, my beloved brothers, let us pray that the God of grace may give, even to our enemies, but especially to our brothers and those who love us, that they may understand and confess that, after that great and indescribable fall by which all fell in the one, no one is set free except by the grace of God and that grace is not a repayment as something owed in accord with the merits of those who receive it, but is given as genuine grace with no preceding merits. (*The Gift of Perseverance* 66)

The next-to-last paragraph provides Augustine's succinct statement of what he sees as at the foundation of the controversy, a concern that pointed directly to Christ:

> But there is no more illustrious example of predestination than Jesus himself. I discussed this already in the first book, and I have chosen to emphasize it at the end of this book. There is, I repeat, no more illustrious example of predestination than the mediator himself. Let any believer who wants to understand it well pay attention to him, and let him find himself in him. (*The Gift of Perseverance* 67)

Finally, he ends on what might be considered a surprising note.

> Let those who read this thank God if they understand it, but let those who do not understand it pray that he may be their interior teacher, from whose face there comes knowledge and understanding. Let those who think that I am mistaken carefully consider again and again what has been said lest they may perhaps themselves be mistaken. But since I not only receive more instruction, but also derive further correction from those who read my works, I acknowledge that the Lord is kind toward me, and I especially expect to receive this instruction and *correction* (emphasis mine) through the teachers of the Church, if what I write comes into their hands and they deign to come to know it. (*The Gift of Perseverance* 68)

These are words he could never say to Julian because of the hostility of the debate. Augustine's final illness made it impossible for him to provide a conclusion for his final work against Julian. So this citation can be considered Augustine's final words on the subject. His request that he might receive *instruction* and *correction* was a beautiful challenge to his readers. Posterity has struggled with that challenge ever since.

11

Augustine, the Spiritual Leader—*A Dying City*

Carthage, Rome, Milan, Hippo Regius: Augustine's life was always associated with certain places—with cities that provided the setting for the major events in his life: he learned rhetoric in the city; he declaimed before the emperor in the city; he listened to Ambrose in the city—and was converted; he experienced his greatest "triumph," the Conference of 411 in the city; at the summary execution of his dear friend, Marcellinus (this cruel act of political expediency happened on September 13, 413 CE), he fled the city; and in the city of Hippo Regius, for nearly four decades, he wrote, preached, debated, and died.

The city in Augustine's time was both a civic and a religious reality; it was never simply "secular," since "God" or "the gods" were an integral part of its life. Not only does the city provide the backdrop for so much of what we know of Augustine, the very "idea" of the city plays a foundational role throughout his writings. A comment from his work on *The Trinity* explains the difference between "image and reality":

> When I want to express Carthage I search about in myself in order to express it and in myself I find the image of Carthage. But I got this through the body, that is through the senses of the body, because I have been present there in body and seen and perceived it and kept it in my memory, so that I could find a word about "the city" to say when I wanted to say "the city." Its image in my memory is its word, not this sound of two syllables made when "Carthage" is named, nor even the name thought of silently in a space of time, but that which I am aware of when I utter these two syllables with my voice or even before I utter them. So too when I wish to express Alexandria which I have never seen I have its image ready at hand within me. I have heard about it from lots of people, and believed it to be a great city as people have been able to describe it to me, and so I have fabricated its image as best I could in my mind, and this is its word for me when I wish to express it even before I utter these five syllables which are its name and known to practically everyone. But if I could produce this image from my mind and show it to the eyes of men who know Alexandria,

they would all say at once "That isn't it"; or if by any chance they said "That's it," I would be very astonished indeed; yet looking at it in my mind, that is at its image, like a picture of it, I still would not know that this was really Alexandria but I would believe it from those who held in their minds the picture of what they had seen. . . . (*Trin.* 8.6.9)

Present day scholars regret that Augustine did not "fill in the blanks" with some concrete description of Carthage—its streets, "sky line," and so on—but there is no doubt that when Augustine thought of "city" he had a real picture of a real Carthage in mind.

Augustine was trained "for the city"—the art of the city was rhetoric and Augustine's practice of it from youth to old age drew city crowds. Augustine the "author" had to depend upon "city services," paper and ink merchants as well as *notarii*—those trained to take dictation, in order for his thought to take written form and circulate around the empire. And when he preached, he drew upon examples from the city—Greek sailors at the wharf of this port city swearing:

You hear Greeks every day, and those of you who know Greek – when he says *Ne ton Theon*, you know *Ne ton Theon* is an oath: "by God." (*ser.* 180.5)

Bankers:

You're doing good, but he hasn't got it yet [money to pay back a loan]. You aren't a financier or banker, and you want the person you favored with a loan to seek out a banker, in order to pay you back? If the reason you aren't demanding interest is to spare him experiencing you as a financier, why do you want him, for your sake, to experience someone else as a financier? You're squeezing him, choking him, even if you are only demanding as much as you gave. Yet by choking him and making things hard for him, you haven't conferred any benefit on him at all, but rather have made things harder, more difficult for him than ever. (*ser.* 239.5)

Merchants:

What about you? Did you conduct your business honestly? Did you never cheat anyone in that business of yours, never swear a false oath in the course of that business? Did you never say, "By the one who carried me safely across the sea, I bought for so much" something you didn't buy for so much? (*ser.* 302.16)

Such examples of "city" are abundant, and they remind us that in so many ways Augustine was a "city preacher" and drew upon "city life" to supply them. The city was also a place of "ambiguity and contradiction" for Augustine. It is where he lost his way (Carthage), publicly lied (Milan), and where a "pagan past" still held on tenaciously, notably in Carthage where Augustine, surrounded by reminders of that past, often came to preach:

Let there be an end to the survivals of sacrilegious rites, an end to vain concerns and silly games. Let the things that are customarily done be done no more; they may not be done any longer in honor of the demons, but all the same they are still being done according to the custom of the demons. Yesterday, after evening prayers, the whole city was ablaze with stinking flames; the smoke of them covered the whole sky. If you are indifferent to the religion involved, at least think about the damage to the common good. We know, brothers and sisters, these things are done by children; but adults ought to have forbidden them. (*ser.* 293B.5)

And if the children were involved in "sacrilege" the adults had their own temptations, among which was the Theater. ". . . there would be few going to the theaters—if Christians didn't go there too" (*ser.* 88.17). He pleads with his listeners: "Christians, I beg you, stay out of the theaters." (*ser.* 301A.7) Cities were full of opportunities:

> . . . demons take pleasure, don't they, in idle songs, they take pleasure in the trifling chatter and manifold indecencies of the theatres, in the mad frenzy of the chariot races, in the cruelty of the amphitheater, in the unrelenting rivalries of those who take up quarrels and disputes, to the point of open hostilities, on behalf of pestilential persons, on behalf of a comedian, an actor, a clown, a charioteer, a hunter. When they do these things, it's as though they were offering incense to demons from their hearts. . . . (*ser. Dolbeau* 26.3)

When thinking of "the theater," "the games," one must not think of a present-day theater or games. The public spectacles often displayed terrible violence, blood, and even explicit sex; there was always a connection with the stories of the ancient gods and their exploits. If the "city" was Augustine's arena, he had no illusions about its dangers and temptations. The church may have replaced the templum, but little else had changed. That also explains why "the city" was not only used for homey examples in preaching and teaching, but could also be given a symbolic role, pointing to something that went far beyond mortar and stones. "Now where a king, a court, ministers, and common people are to be found, there is a state." (*exp. ps.* 9.8)

The final Latin term in this brief excerpt from one of his psalm expositions is the very same word Augustine used for "city"—*civitas*, here rendered by the translator as "state." "*Civitas*-the city" can thus designate much more for Augustine than a place called Carthage, Rome, Milan, Hippo Regius; it can be virtually synonymous with *res publica*, the "state" or "commonwealth," and even more frequently interchangeable with the Latin *populus*—the people: "One people is one city"—*populus una ciuitas est.* (*On Order* 2.18)

While the city as place does indeed play a major role in the story of Augustine, it is the idea of "the city" as a symbolic reality that emerged as a dominant theme throughout his writings. We get a brief hint of this in *On True Religion*, written in 389–390 CE shortly before his ordination. He wrote that work with the intent of winning back a friend he had convinced to become a Manichee. He made a parallel between "the ages of a man" and "the ages of the world":

> After the laborious toils of youth, however, a certain amount of peace is granted to the elders. From there old age, with health deteriorating and fading, more liable to diseases and enfeebled, leads on up to death. Such is the life of

> human beings living from the body and wrapped up in greed and longings fo-
> cused on time-bound things. With them we talk about the old man and the out-
> ward and the earthly man (see Rom. 6:6; Eph. 4:22-24; Col. 3.9), even if they
> achieve what the common crowd calls happiness in a well-established earthly
> city, whether under kings, or under emperors, or under a constitution, or under
> all of these together . . . But take this man whom we have described as the old
> or outward or earthly man . . . [and compare him with the] new man, the in-
> ward and the heavenly man, and he too has certain equivalent spiritual ages of
> his own, distinguished by progress, not by years. . . . (*On True Religion* 26.48)

Augustine links "the earthly city" with "the old man," just as "the new man"
is linked by implication with a heavenly city, indicating that, very early in his
Christian life, he began to think of "the city" in what one might call "theological" terms. It is very likely that in the midst of his increasingly intense dedication to biblical studies, especially the psalms, he began to realize that the notion
of "the city" can take on a deeply spiritual meaning that far exceeds notions of
place and buildings. The psalms often mention the "holy city"—Jerusalem, and
Augustine had already inherited a Christian interpretation of this most Jewish of
images:

> Sing to the Lord, who dwells in Zion. This invitation is addressed to those
> whom the Lord does not abandon as they seek him. He himself lives in Zion,
> which means "watching," and bears the image of the Church which now is, as
> Jerusalem bears the image of the Church which is yet to be, that is, of the city of
> the saints who enjoy the angelic life. This is because Jerusalem means "vision
> of peace." Watching goes before seeing, as this Church precedes that other
> Church which is promised, the immortal and eternal city. (*exp. ps.* 9.12)

This text is from the early days of Augustine's priesthood; he speaks of the
Church as the immortal and eternal city, and not in terms of his actual or present
experience of Church where he was a pilgrim, a sojourner.

Two Cities

On August 24, 410 CE, Alaric and his Goths entered the city of Rome and laid it
waste. For three days terror reigned—murder, rape, looting. The only places of
refuge respected were the churches of Peter and Paul—their confines stretched
to the limits by Christians and non-Christians alike who sought asylum there—
an asylum that Alaric, Arian Christian, respected. Some of Augustine's first
words that we hear about the tragic events can seem to be distant, almost cal-
lous:

> Are you astonished at the world going to pieces? You might as well be as-
> tonished that the world has grown old. The world's like a man; he's born, he
> grows up, he grows old. Old age is full of complaints: coughing, phlegm, bleary
> eyes, aches and pains, weariness, it's all there. So, a man has grown old; he's

full of complaints. The world has grown old; it's full of troubles and pressures." (*ser.* 81.8)

He is preaching, it would seem, to his own people in Hippo Regius— although there were probably others present: "Look what Christian times are producing. . . . Look at all the terrible things happening in Christian times, the world is being laid waste" (*ser.* 81.7).

Augustine vocalizes what, from some quarters, seems to be being whispered at street corners and shouted in the city's forum—and Augustine seems to sense it may be creeping into the hearts and minds of those gathered before him in church. The argument went like this: "Rome's traditional gods have been abandoned, and the city's destruction is the result." Over the past decade there had been a simmering resentment among supporters of "traditional Roman religion," a resentment prompted by the outlawing of sacrifices and the closing of temples. There are intimations of a "pagan counter-offensive" in a number of the recently discovered "new" sermons—the longest of them bears the title "Discourse of Augustine the Bishop against the Pagans," and probably went on for some 3 hours (*ser. Dolbeau* 26), its very length suggesting that "pagan" was not merely an academic question.

> That's why I have to say, brothers and sisters, don't do things for which the pagans can jeer at us; enter the church in such a way that you don't give pagans an excuse for not wanting to enter the church. The reason we come to church anyway, you see is for the sake of getting together as brothers and sisters; because the temple of prayer is your own heart. Clean up the place where you pray and you will be heard. . . . (*ser. Dolbeau* 26.11)

His allusion to "pagan jeers" hints at what will become, at the time of the Sack of Rome, a veritable crisis of confidence. Many wondered: "where was the God of the Christians when Rome needed him most?" Augustine's response would be twofold: preaching, first of all, followed by a more substantial, indeed, a more monumental response: his book, the *City of God*.

A number of Augustine's sermons cannot be precisely dated, although they can be placed within the emotional aftermath of the news of Rome's tragedy, that is, sometime during Fall/Winter of 410 CE and into the following year. They offer a kind of eyewitness replay of the dramatic events:

> ". . . many were led away as captives . . ."
> ". . . many were killed . . ."
> ". . . many were tortured with a variety of excruciating torments . . ."
> "Horrific stories have been told us; of destruction, of fires, of rapes, slaughter, people tortured . . ."
> "It is true, we have heard many things, we have lamented them all, often shed tears, found little to console ourselves with. I don't brush it all aside, I don't deny that we have heard many things, that many bad things were done in that city." (*ser.* 397.2)

These comments come from what was perhaps Augustine's first preaching on Rome's Sack, a sermon that eventually became known under the title *"On the destruction of the city of Rome—De excidio urbis Romanae."* Augustine, like everyone else, shed tears—but he did not allow "despair" to have the final word: ". . . you suppose, brothers and sisters, that what counts as a city is walls, and not citizens?" (7)

The point of his comment was that "the city" was not really a question of bricks and mortar—a city is its inhabitants. In another sermon that he preached in Carthage sometime between 412 and 415 CE, the notion of "city" taken on profound theological meaning:

> Consider now the names of these two cities, Babylon and Jerusalem. Babylon signifies "confusion," and Jerusalem "vision of peace." You need to study the city of confusion now, in order to understand the vision of peace; you must endure the one, and yearn for the other. How can these two cities be distinguished? We cannot separate them from one another, can we? No, they are intermingled, and they continue like that from the very beginning of the human race until the end of the world. Jerusalem began to exist with Abel, and Babylon with Cain . . . Two loves create the two cities: love of God creates Jerusalem; love of the world creates Babylon. All of us must therefore ask ourselves what we love, and we shall discover to which city we belong. (*exp. ps.* 64.2)

This notion of the "two cities," already present in the early Augustine but now goaded and fueled by the sack of Rome and its polemical aftermath, will take him far beyond that single historical event to a much wider historical-theological horizon, prompting the writing of his largest single "book" *The City of God (De civitate Dei)*. Costing him more than 15 years of labor and eventually amounting to about 300,000 words; it will become the most copied of Augustine's works (and perhaps of all Latin early Christian writings). It survived in nearly 400 manuscripts, the earliest of which can be dated to Roman Africa during Augustine's lifetime. Its twenty-two books take the reader from Rome's founding myth to a vision of the "heavenly city"—with many pauses along the way to deal with topics as diverse as accounts of famous Roman battles and reports of contemporary medical lore. What is also evident is that the issues Augustine was battling elsewhere, most especially in relation to the Pelagian controversy, are thoroughly integrated into the work (the term grace occurs more than 170 times).

Given the fact that the work was written over a period of many years and that he had to write it in small segments because of other pressing necessities, The City of God can at times appear to be unwieldy and digressive. In his Retractationes, he offers a brief description of its scope:

"Burning with zeal for the house of God" (ps. 68:10; Jn. 2:17) I decided to write a number of books on "the City of God" against their [the "pagans"] blasphemies and errors . . . The first five books refute those who link human progress with the cult of many gods that pagans are wont to worship, and consider it so necessary that its prohibition gives rise to terrible evils. The next five books argue against those that say that such evils always have and always will exist, sometimes great, sometimes small, simply varying according to time, place and persons. Accordingly, they argue that the cult of their gods and the sacrifices to them serves for the after life. The first ten books accordingly contain the arguments against these two empty opinions, contrary to the Christian religion . . . Regarding the twelve books that follow, the first four speak of the rise of the two cities, one "of God," the other, "of this world"; the next four their evolution and progress; the other four and final four, the due ends of both. Thus all the twenty-two, although dealing with both cities, take the title of the better, *The City of God*. (retr. 2.43)

It is clear that Augustine is engaged in both "deconstruction" and "reconstruction"—deconstructing a notion of city as "idol" (an everlasting "sacred" empire surviving on its own power and glory, like imperial Rome) and reconstructing a theological vision of the heavenly city (the community of the everlasting blessed with God). The heavenly city is seen as a beacon of hope to the eyes of faith.

His resources for the deconstruction of the city are drawn from Rome's own classical tradition: Vergil, Cicero, Varro, Terence et al. Augustine uses Rome's own greatest writers of history and poetry and eloquence to respond to pagan claims against Christianity. In the process he replays Rome's own history from a variety of perspectives—religious, philosophical, moral, civic. That is one of the reasons why, in the middle ages, it was read as a veritable encyclopedia of information on ancient Rome.

The vision of God's city that he seeks to construct is based on texts from virtually every book of the Bible; those texts are made to interface with Christian history right down to Augustine's own day. Rome's pursuit of gloria is juxtaposed with a Christian vision marked by a most un-Roman virtue, humilitas-humility, a term he uses abundantly in this work. He often repeats the argument that present Christian experience is not yet to live in the City of God because that will have to wait for "the end of time."

That is one of the great ironies of what "happened" to this work. Subsequent thinkers often turned to it to justify their attempts to create an actual Christian realm or state. In fact, there are a number of specific arguments in the work that, over the course of history, have virtually taken on a life of their own. Most prominent among these is the notion of a "just war." Augustine does develop some criteria that make waging war truly a last resort for resolving problems. But his concern was that all possible efforts be used to avoid war, not to legitimate war. So, it cannot be said that he was proposing a concrete "theory of war." For example, war is often defended in the context of Manichaean rejection of the God of the Old Testament, who commanded the Israelites to slay their enemies; peace is worth defending; even thieves want peace. But comments such as these are never placed within a coherent framework to offer a "theology of war." It would, in fact, be easier to construct a "theology of peace" from what he says in the City of God.

Thus, in the final paragraphs of the work, Augustine offers a meditation on the "eternal Sabbath" which is the fullness of life of the "heavenly city." He draws upon abundant biblical texts to lay out a vision of overflowing peace and happiness, ending with a summation of all human history based upon the six days of creation.

After this age, as if it were the seventh day (see Gen. 2: 2-3), God will rest when he makes to rest in him the seventh day, which we ourselves will be. . . . This seventh day will be our Sabbath, without sunset, the Day of the Lord, as if an everlasting eighth day, made sacred by Christ's resurrection, prefiguring eternal rest not only for the spirit but, indeed, also for the body. There we will rest and we will see, we will see and we will love, we will love and we will praise. Behold, what that end will be like without end. For what else is our end but to come to that kingdom without end? (City of God 22.30.5)

It ends on a vision of hope—a hope not based upon any present "earthly kingdom" nor even on the present face of the visible Christian church, but on his vision of the heavenly city.

As Augustine's *notarius* put down the pen with the final "amen" that concludes the work just two short sentences later, there was much on the horizon that ominously suggested anything but the Sabbath peace with which the work concludes. In fact, and unbeknownst to anyone involved, the Western empire was beginning to die. Gothic tribes had already overrun much of Spain; Africa would be their next target. Within Africa itself, there was increasing violence on the borders as unconquered tribes made evermore successful incursions across the frontier, sending tremors throughout the African provinces. The Count of Africa, Bonifatius, had in many ways abandoned these defenses to pursue his own political ambitions, and he was eventually declared "an enemy of the state" by the imperial court—even though the court found itself unable to alter the course of events. One of Augustine's last letters addresses the state of uncertainty and crisis that is overtaking Africa. He strongly exhorts his colleague-bishop, Honoratus, to hold firm:

> When, however, there is a common danger for all, that is, for bishops, clerics, and laity, those who need others should not be abandoned by those whom they need. . . . (*Letter* 228.2)

Augustine is writing in 429 CE in response to Honoratus' desperate questions: Would it not be appropriate to flee if the chance presents itself? If "everyone" can flee, Augustine answers, "yes, you too may flee." But if not?

When we come to the most extreme of these dangers and there is no opportunity of escaping, do we not consider how many people of both sexes and of every age usually rush to the church, some demanding baptism, others reconciliation, still others acts of penance, and all of them the administration and conferral of the sacraments? If ministers are lacking in that case, what a great ruin results for those who leave this world either without rebirth or without absolution! What great grief there is for their believing families who will not have them with them in the repose of eternal life! What great groaning there is from all, and what a great blasphemy from some because of the absence of ministries and ministers! See what the fear of temporal evils causes, and the great accumulation of eternal evils entailed by it. But if ministers are present, in accord with the strength that the Lord supplies, all are helped. Some are baptized; some are reconciled; none are deprived of sharing in the Lord's body; all are consoled, edified, and exhorted to pray to God who is able to turn aside everything they fear. Let them be ready for either alternative so that, if this chalice cannot pass from them, the will of him may be done who cannot will anything evil. (*Letter* 228.8)

"If ministers are lacking." Augustine affirms that it is unthinkable for a bishop to provide for his own physical welfare without first considering the spiritual welfare of the people. The entire letter is a statement on the precarious quality of Christian existence in the "earthly city." Its precariousness, however, does not call for a kind of "escapism," nor for abandoning the city and its inhabitants. The bishop and clerics should do all in their power to insure the physical safety of their flock.

There are, of course, some who think that bishops and clerics who do not flee in such dangers, but remain, mislead the people, since they do not flee when they see their pastors remaining. But it is easy to turn aside this response or bad impression by addressing the same people and saying, "Do not let the fact that we are not fleeing from this place mislead you. For we are remaining here not for our own sake but rather for your sake, in order that we might provide for you whatever ministry we know is necessary for your salvation in Christ. If, then, you choose to flee, you have also freed us from these bonds by which we are held back." I think that one should say this when it truly seems useful to move to safer places. (*Letter* 228.13)

He concludes the letter with a marked sense of realism and faith, aware that in times of crisis, decisions are never easy, and critics will be many:

> Because you consulted me, my most beloved brother, I wrote this response for you with the truth and certain charity that marked my thoughts, but I have not forbidden you to follow a better opinion if you find one (emphasis mine). We cannot find anything better to do amid these dangers, however, than to offer prayers to the Lord our God that he may have mercy on us. By the gift of God some prudent and wise men have merited both the will and the strength not to abandon the churches of God, and they were not deterred from the goal of their resolve despite the teeth of their critics. (*Letter* 228.14)

"Follow a better opinion if you find one": just as with his teaching on grace, he does not claim to have the final word. And, remaining true to everything he has written in this last decade of his life, he ends by entrusting all to the mercy of God.

Possidius, Augustine's first biographer, fellow-monk and bishop, dear friend and disciple, tells us of Augustine's final days. As the port city of Hippo Regius was besieged by Vandal forces in the Spring of 430 CE, many sought shelter within its walls, including Possidius and, we can imagine, many of Possidius' own flock from nearby Calama. Alypius, Augustine's dear friend and collaborator is not there—we know he is making rounds in the territory and he is never heard from again—it has been suggested that he fell victim to the Vandals. "In the third month of the siege," Possidius tells us, Augustine took ill—his final illness. Certainly, the siege-conditions did not bode well for anyone elderly and in a weakened condition. But Augustine had long reminded his people and his interlocutors that he was senex—a wise old man:

> In this life we are all subject to death, and the last day of this life is always uncertain for every human being. Yet in infancy one looks forward to childhood, and in childhood one looks forward to adolescence, and in adolescence one looks forward to young adulthood, and in young adulthood one looks forward to maturity, and in maturity one looks forward to old age. Whether it will come is uncertain, and yet one looks forward to it. Old age, however, does not have another age that it looks forward to. It is also uncertain how long one's old age will be; it is certain, nevertheless, that no age remains that will come after old age. Because God willed it, I came to this city at a vigorous time of my life, but I was young, though, and now I have grown old. (*Letter* 213.1)

Augustine is speaking to his own people in September of 426 CE as he proposed his successor, the priest Heraclius: "now I have grown old."

The fact is that, despite fragile health and life of monumental labor he far outlived most men and women of his day—but the end had finally come, and Augustine knew it. He asked for quiet and solitude, that penitential psalms be placed upon the walls of his sick-bed room so that they could be prayed, and he waited. On August 28, 430 CE, as the "city" around him was dying, Augustine breathed his last.

Hippo Regius fell some 14 months later. The people fled, so Possidius tells us, and the city was destroyed. Historians are not completely convinced. Archaeologists have found no indication of such total destruction, and Augustine's library remained intact and made its way to the continent. Theories abound, but all agree that its survival should be described as either "remarkable" if not "miraculous." Even if his library had been destroyed, it may have still been possible to write a book such as this one because Augustine's most important works were already in circulation. But that library did contain "all" of his works, including his letters and sermons, and the latter are especially revelatory of who Augustine was—even more than is found in the formal works. The formal works often suggest a man invincible and indefatigable, utterly confident, always in possession of the Truth—the caricature of the "classic western man"! But in his sermons and letters Augustine often reveals another side, one not quite so invincible, indefatigable, incapable of error—"don't let your hope rest on me" echoes as a common refrain:

> So, what if the people get involved with a bad bishop? The Lord, and bishop of bishops, has given you security, so that your hope should not rest in man. Look, I am speaking to you as a bishop in the name of the Lord; I do not know what kind of bishop I am; how much less do you know! Well, what I may

be at the present moment, I can, after a fashion, perceive; what I'm going to be some time or other, how can I know that? . . . And so may the Lord grant, with your prayers assisting us, that we may be, and may persevere to the end in being, what you wish us to be, all those of you who wish us well, and what he wishes us to be, the one who called us and appointed us; may he help us to be what he appointed us to be. But whatever we may be, don't let your hope rest on us. (*ser.* 340A.8–9)

qualis sim ego, nescio: quanto minus uos? (What I'm really like, I don't know; how much less do you!)

Epilogue

Immediately after Augustine's death, his close friend, fellow monk, and fellow bishop wrote the first biography of Augustine. In many ways it stands apart from typical Christian "lives of the saints" of the period, for it emphasizes, not "Augustine the miracle worker," so typical of other lives, but rather, to quote Possidius himself "what I saw of him and heard of him" ("Preface," Life of Augustine). Without a doubt, as the work makes apparent, Possidius sought to solidify Augustine's intellectual/theological legacy, and appended his Vita with an extensive listing of Augustine's writings. But what this first Vita sought to facilitate even more powerfully is an encounter with Augustine himself. In many way's Possidius' efforts guaranteed the impact of "Augustine the writer" —and indeed his works have continued to be read, argued, discussed and debated for the last 1600 years – and there is little sign that this tendency is in any way abating. But once again, Possidius tried to communicate something the writings could never do:

> I believe, however, that they profited even more who were able to hear him speaking in church and see him there present, especially if they were familiar with his manner of life among his fellow human beings. (*Life of Augustine*, ch. 31)

To hear him and see him and to be familiar with his manner of life among his fellow-human beings – Possidius' goal resonates with much that is underway in contemporary scholarship and transcends any particular discipline, to treat "great thinkers" not as "containers of ideas" but in context, as flesh and blood.

Given the unique impact of his personality on his writings, the particular questions that he engaged, and the ever-creative insight he brought to whatever he wrote about, "Augustinian thought" has profoundly impacted upon western culture and civilization. This is made evident by the host of thinkers, down through the ages, who became avid readers of Augustine: distant readers such as Boethius, Thomas Aquinas, Erasmus, Martin Luther, John Calvin—just to name a few; more modern readers such as Wittgenstein, Heidegger, Camus, and Derrida—once again, just to name a few. What is it about Augustine that attracts? This, too, is open to debate: his intensive scrutiny of "the self"? his singular portrayal of the divine/human intersection? his probings regarding "freedom"? his resolve in the face of controversies? his artistry as a writer? the freshness he brings to even old questions? his very combativeness? Perhaps the reasons could be extended indefinitely. But as important as these suggestions may be, they always seem to revert back, beyond "ideas," to the man behind (or within!) the writings. While no single figure could ever claim the title "creator of the western self," perhaps what Augustine has contributed to this process is precisely the way his "self" so distinctly emerges from the writings, the controversies, the questions. What he says and how he says it always seems to bear a distinctive imprint—Augustine! And perhaps that explains why the ancient dialogue he initiated some 1600 years ago shows little sign of drawing to a close. He was often wont to say to his people in the course of his preaching "simul quaeramus—let us search together": that searching conversation is still underway.

A Note on the Sources

The volume of literature on Augustine of Hippo is vast. Every aspect of his thought, writings, and impact has been and continues to be the subject of scholarly analysis, resulting in a bibliography of journal articles and books that is, to say the least, daunting. The following is simply a concise sample of works, some of them classics, worth consulting for further investigation.

For a comprehensive introduction to all aspects of the life, thought, writings, and influence of Augustine of Hippo, see: Augustine Through the Ages: An Encyclopedia. General Editor, Allan D. Fitzgerald, O.S.A., Foreword by Jaroslav Pelikan. Grand Rapids, MI: William B. Eerdmans Publishing Company, 1999.

A good historical overview of the entire period is found in: Mitchell, Stephen. A History of the Later Roman Empire AD 284–641. Oxford, UK/Malden, MA: Blackwell Publishing, 2007.

Most helpful for entering into Augustine's world is the work of French scholar Claude Lepelley who has published extensively on the world of Roman Africa. Unfortunately, most of his writings are in French however, see his "The Perception of Late Roman Africa, from Decolonization to the Re-Appraisal of Late Antiquity" in The Past Before Us: The Challenge of Historiographies of Late Antiquity, edited by Carole Straw and Richard Lim, Smith Studies in History Series 54, Bibliothèque de L'Antiquité Tardive 6, 25–32. Turnhout, Belgium: Brepols Publishers, 2004.

Peter Brown's work, both on Augustine and "Late Antiquity," has defined the field in so many ways. Among his many works, see especially his: Augustine of Hippo: A Biography (A new edition with an epilogue). Berkeley: University of California Press, 2000; also, Late Antiquity: A Guide to the Postclassical World. Editors, G.W. Bowersock, Peter Brown, Oleg Grabar. Cambridge: The Belknap Press of Harvard University, 1999.

The most recent comprehensive biography of Augustine, sensitive to his Roman, African, and religious world, and offering a wealth of information is Serge Lancel's Saint Augustine, translated by Antonia Nevill. London: SCM Press, 2002.

Most of Augustine's major works are available in English. See especially the ongoing series that, when completed, will make available all of his works in English for the first time, The Works of Saint Augustine: A Translation for the 21st Century. General Editor, Boniface Ramsey, Hyde Park, NY, New City Press, 1990.

A useful introduction to the Roman political world in Africa is found in Augustine: Political Writings, Edited by E.M. Atkins and R. J. Dodaro. Cambridge Texts in the History of Political Thought. Cambridge: Cambridge University Press, 2001.

For a brief introduction to what might be called Augustinianism, the various readings of Augustine that have occurred across the centuries, see by the present author Our Restless Heart: The Augustinian Tradition. Maryknoll, NY: Orbis Books, 2003.

Possidius, friend and fellow-bishop of Augustine, wrote the first Augustine biography sometime soon after Augustine's death. It is available in English, "Life of St. Augustine." In Early Christian Biographies, Translated by Roy J. Deferrari, et al. Edited by Roy J. Deferrari. Fathers of the Church, vol. 15, 69–124. Washington: Catholic University of America Press, 1952; and The Life of Saint Augustine by Possidius, Bishop of Calama. Introduction and Notes by Cardinal Michele Pellegrino. Edited by John E. Rotelle, O.S.A. Villanova, PA: Augustinian Press, 1988.

The following offer valuable insight into Augustine, his thought, and his world:

A History of Private Life: From Pagan Rome to Byzantium. Paul Veyne, Editor. Arthur Goldhammer, Translator. Cambridge, MA: The Belknap Press of Harvard University Press, 1987.

Augustine and His Critics. Essays in Honour of Gerald Bonner. Edited by Robert Dodaro and George Lawless. London: Routledge, 2000.

Bonner, Gerald. St. Augustine of Hippo: Life and Controversies. Norwich: The Canterbury Press, 1986.

Burnell, Peter. The Augustinian Person. Washington, DC: The Catholic University of America Press, 2005.

Hadot, Pierre. Philosophy as a Way of Life. Spiritual Exercises from Socrates to Foucault. Edited with an introduction by Arnold I. Davidson. Translated by Michael Chase. Oxford: Blackwell Publishing, 1995.

Harrison, Carol. Augustine: Christian Truth and Fractured Humanity. Oxford: Oxford University Press, 2000.

Lawless, George, osa. Augustine of Hippo and his Monastic Rule. Oxford: Clarendon Press, 1987.

MacCormack, Sabine. The Shadows of Poetry: Vergil in the Mind of Augustine. Berkeley: University of California Press, 1998.

Markus, Robert A. The End of Ancient Christianity. Cambridge: Cambridge University Press, 1990.

Marrou, Henri. St. Augustine and his Influence Through the Ages. Translated by Patrick Hepburne-Scott. Texts of St. Augustine translated by Edmund Hill. New York: Harper Brothers, 1957.

O'Daly, Gerard. Augustine's Philosophy of Mind. Berkeley: University of California Press, 1987.

Rist, John R. Augustine: Ancient Thought Baptized. Cambridge: Cambridge University Press, 1994.

Rouselle, Aline. Porneia: On Desire and the Body in Antiquity. Translated by Felicia Pheasant. Oxford: Basil Blackwell, 1988.

Stock, Brian. Augustine the Reader: Meditation, Self-Knowledge, and the Ethics of Interpretation. Cambridge, MA: The Belknap Press of Harvard University Press, 1996.

TeSelle, Eugene. Augustine the Theologian. New York: Herder and Herder, 1970.

Van der Meer, F. Augustine the Bishop: Religion and Society at the Dawn of the Middle Ages. Translated by Brian Battershaw and G. R. Lamb. New York: Harper Torchbooks, 1961.

Wetzel, James. Augustine and the Limits of Virtue. Cambridge: University Press, 1992.

Index